Capitalists, Caciques, and Revolution

Mark Wasserman

CAPITALISTS, CACIQUES, AND REVOLUTION

The Native Elite and Foreign Enterprise in Chihuahua, Mexico, 1854–1911

The University of North Carolina Press

Chapel Hill and London

© 1984 The University of North Carolina Press

Manufactured in the United States of America

Library of Congress Cataloging in Publication Data
Wasserman, Mark, 1946–
  Capitalists, caciques, and revolution.

  Bibliography: p.
  Includes index.
  1. Elite (Social sciences)—Mexico—Chihuahua
(State)—History. 2. Terrazas family. 3. Chihuahua
(Mexico: State)—Economic conditions. 4. Business
enterprises, Foreign—Mexico—Chihuahua (State)—
History. I. Title.
HN120.C46W37 1984 305.5'24'097216 83-12481
ISBN 0-8078-1580-2

To Marlie Parker Wasserman

Contents

Contents

Tables

Acknowledgments

Over the past ten years I have incurred many debts. John H. Coatsworth of the University of Chicago has read every version of the manuscript, and his pointed comments have done much to improve it. His ready ear, keen advice, and encouragement have made him a valued friend. Friedrich Katz inaugurated me into the mysteries of Chihuahua, and his vast knowledge and insight concerning Mexican history have been a guide and a standard for my work. Richard M. Estrada has acted as booster, critic, and guide since we met in El Paso years ago. He has generously shared with me his extraordinary archival discoveries in Chihuahua.

Colleagues at Northern Illinois University and Rutgers University have contributed considerably to the book. In our collaboration on another project, Benjamin Keen taught me much about writing. Paul Kleppner introduced me to the world of social science and history. Samuel L. Baily, Allen Howard, and Michael Adas read versions of the manuscript and taught me more than a little about clear thinking.

Other teachers and colleagues have helped and encouraged me: T. Bentley Duncan, Akira Iriye, John Hope Franklin, Jordan Schwarz, and William Beezley. Enrique Florescano provided me with a scholarly home for a year at the Instituto Nacional de Antropología e Historia, Departamento de Investigaciones Históricas. Robert Parker, David Perry, and Lewis Bateman were helpful editors.

I owe special thanks to the librarians and libraries that have helped me. Bud Newman, head of special collections at the University of Texas at El Paso, has proven time and again that southwestern hospitality is no myth. The staff of the Bancroft Library at the University of California, Berkeley, has aided me extensively. Dr. Alejandra Moreno Toscano, the Director of the Archivo General de la Nación, kindly permitted me access to restricted papers.

Ingeniero Miguel Márquez, a grandson of Luis Terrazas, kindly supplied me with a family tree of the Terrazas. Francisco R. Almada, Chihuahua's greatest historian, allowed me to work in his library. Harold Sims furnished me with an invaluable inventory of the Terrazas estates. Sr. Eduardo Creel graciously gave me a copy of his son's biography of Enrique Creel and permitted me to use priceless pictures of his grandfather.

At various stages the Department of History of the University of Chicago and the Tinker Foundation have contributed financial support to my research. *The Americas* and *Latin American Research Review* allowed me to use earlier versions of material published in these journals.

I thank my children Aaron and Danielle for their patience and love.

My greatest debt is to Marlie Parker Wasserman. Without her perceptive criticism, good sense, encouragement, and love there would have been no book.

Capitalists, Caciques, and Revolution

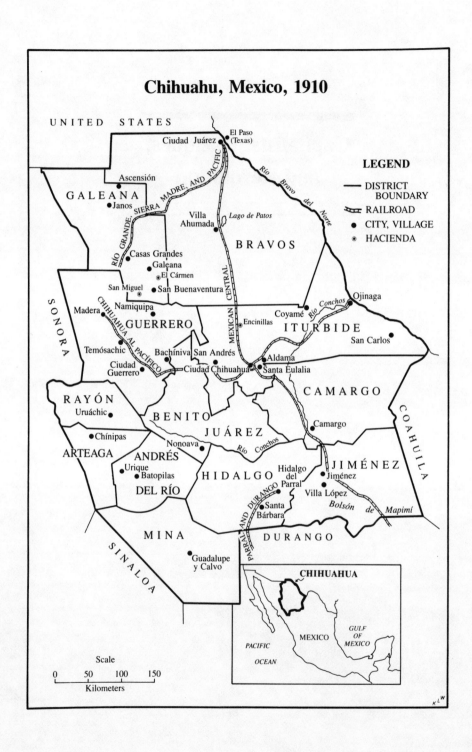

Chihuahu, Mexico, 1910

UNITED STATES

El Paso (Texas)

Ciudad Juárez

LEGEND

— DISTRICT BOUNDARY
⧉ RAILROAD
● CITY, VILLAGE
◉ HACIENDA

Ascensión

GALEANA
● Janos

Villa Ahumada
Lago de Patos

BRAVOS

Río Bravo del Norte

Casas Grandes
Galeana
◉ El Cármen
San Miguel
● San Buenaventura

Madera
Namiquipa
GUERRERO
Coyamé
Encinillas
Río Conchos
Ojinaga
ITURBIDE
San Carlos

SONORA

Temósachic
Bachíniva San Andrés

Ciudad Guerrero
Ciudad Chihuahua
Aldama
Santa Eulalia

CHIHUAHUA AL PACÍFICO

MEXICAN CENTRAL

SIERRA MADRE, AND PACIFIC
RÍO GRANDE

CAMARGO

COAHUILA

RAYÓN
Uruáchic

BENITO
JUÁREZ

Camargo

● Chínipas
Nonoava
Río Conchos

ARTEAGA
ANDRÉS
Urique ● Batopilas
DEL RÍO

HIDALGO
Hidalgo del Parral
Jiménez
JIMÉNEZ
Villa López

Bolsón de Mapimí

Santa Bárbara

PARRAL AND DURANGO

MINA
DURANGO

SINALOA

● Guadalupe y Calvo

Scale

0   50   100   150
Kilometers

CHIHUAHUA

PACIFIC OCEAN

MEXICO

GULF OF MEXICO

K L W

Introduction

The history of Mexico from independence (1821) to the Revolution (1910–20) is the history of its regions and localities.[1] For the first three decades after independence, there was in fact no nation at all.[2] With the elimination of royal central authority, regional and local leaders—known as *caudillos* or *caciques*—and families—known in some areas as *notables*—emerged to fragment political power.[3] During this age of chaos, regional leaders, especially in the isolated areas in the extreme north and south, ruled with virtual autonomy from the government in Mexico City. General Juan Alvarez, for example, presided over the state of Guerrero unchallenged by national authority for nearly half a century.[4] Remote Yucatán stretched its autonomy to the extent that it attempted to secede from Mexico.[5] Sonoran *notables* did not conclude it was in their best interest to be part of the nation until the 1870s.[6] Throughout Mexico, with the exception perhaps of the Mexico City–Veracruz region, there was little sense of nationhood, or *Mexicanidad*.

Isolation and regional autonomy persisted into the Liberal era, 1855–77, when presidents Benito Juárez and Sebastián Lerdo de Tejada began the process of national consolidation. They deposed recalcitrant *caciques* like Santiago Vidaurri of Nuevo León and Manuel Lozada of Nayarit, but left others such as Luis Terrazas in Chihuahua, Servando Canales in Tamaulipas, and Juan Alvarez and his son Diego in Guerrero in control of their respective regions with almost complete independence from Mexico City.[7]

Over the first twenty years of his thirty-four-year dictatorship—an era to which he was to give his name, the *Porfiriato*—Porfirio Díaz gradually, through the shrewd use of coercion and cooptation ("*pan o palo*," "bread or the club"), managed to bring even the peripheral regions under his hegemony. Nonetheless, the most instructive view of the process of national consolidation is from the states, not the center. Díaz had to adapt his methods to the peculiar circumstances in each state, and as a consequence, the extent of his control varied.[8]

The Revolution, the great watershed of Mexican history, was not a single movement, of course, but an upheaval with regional roots and characteristics. Of the areas where intense revolutionary activity took place during the early years of the Revolution (1910–13), at least four, Chihuahua, Morelos, Coahuila, and Sonora, spawned distinct uprisings.[9]

Although it may be a historical truism that the closer we examine the generalities of Mexican history, the less satisfactory they become, the fact is that regional studies have substantially altered previously held views on land tenure, economic opportunities, and the composition of elites. Only through investigation at the regional level can historians create a true picture of politics, economy, and society in Mexico.[10]

Most commonly, region in Mexican history refers to the geographic and political entity of the state. This conforms not only to historical necessity— archives and newspapers are generally confined to the political boundaries of the state—but to the self-perceptions of the residents. The inhabitants of Chihuahua regarded themselves as *chihuahuenses*, not northwesterners or Mexicans. On various occasions states were joined as political jurisdictions. Durango and Chihuahua together formed the province of Nueva Vizcaya during the colonial era, but the merger endured barely two years beyond independence. Santiago Vidaurri unilaterally joined Coahuila and Nuevo León in the 1860s. Geographic identification and rivalries were too strong for these combinations to persist.

Equating the state with the region by no means excludes larger comparisons. The politics, economies, and societies of all the northern states have common traits and histories that we can usefully compare with those states in the Center and South. Indeed one of the strengths of regional history is its easy adaptation to comparative studies.[11]

Capitalists, Caciques, and Revolution is a regional history, a study of the state of Chihuahua from the Liberal era to the onset of the Revolution. Chihuahua is of crucial importance for understanding the development of prerevolutionary Mexico.

Chihuahua was the home of the most powerful regional elite family in all Mexico during the nineteenth and early twentieth centuries, the Terrazas. This book is, first, a political history of the rise and fall of the Terrazas family from 1854 to 1911. Unlike any other regional political elite of the nineteenth century, the Terrazas maintained their power through the Reform era, the French Intervention, and the *Porfiriato*. Alone among the great regional bosses (*caciques*) of this period, General Luis Terrazas successfully resisted the Díaz dictatorship. Only in Chihuahua was one family so successful in forging the elite of a region into a single, homogeneous group.[12]

Introduction

This, then, is a study of a political elite, the object of which is to determine who had power, how they acquired, maintained, and lost it, and what effects the exercise of power by the elite had on the nonelite sectors of society. Since political power, at least in the case of prerevolutionary Mexico, cannot be separated from economic power, the study focuses on the relationship between politics and economics.[13]

I analyze nineteenth-century politics not as a jumble of coups and civil wars but as an era with a discernible pattern of struggles: the conflict between Chihuahua's elite and the centralizing authorities in Mexico City, especially presidents Juárez and Díaz; and the coincident, intertwined conflict between subregional elite families for control of the state. Mexican politics operated on (at least) three levels, national, state, and local. The key to unscrambling nineteenth-century history is to analyze the interactions between these levels. In fifty years of struggling in this milieu, the Terrazas emerged supreme. This study will explain why.

With its vast mineral resources, cheap land, and close proximity to the United States, Chihuahua received more nonrailroad foreign investment than any other region in Mexico before 1910. As a result, the state is a model for the study of a regional export economy. Thus, this is also an examination of three aspects of the development of this economy: the emergence of native elite entrepreneurship, the relations between foreign entrepreneurs and native elite, and the effects of massive foreign investment on nonelite sectors of the Chihuahuan economy and society.

Chihuahua produced the two greatest entrepreneurs of prerevolutionary Mexico, Luis Terrazas and Enrique C. Creel. Together with their family, they built a vast economic empire of land, cattle, banking, manufacturing, and mining that made them the equals of the great American tycoons of the same era. Creel was the "Mexican J. P. Morgan," dominating high finance and coordinating the interests of other financial and industrial giants. This study traces the development of the economic empire of the Terrazas-Creels and assesses its effect on Chihuahua. It is the first such investigation of Mexican entrepreneurship at the dawning of the industrial age. The record of the family's achievement causes us to reconsider many long-held views about Latin American elites and to reexamine the nature of native entrepreneurship in Latin America (and the Third World as a whole).

However extensive the economic domain of the Terrazas-Creel family, Chihuahua's prosperity ultimately depended on world market demand for its mineral exports. Foreign capital and technology, concentrated for the most part in the hands of a few large companies, provided the means to extract these minerals, and thereby played the key role in the state's economic development. The book, then, is also an economic history of Chihuahua that emphasizes the importance of foreign investment.

Capitalists, Caciques, and Revolution

At the heart of this economic history is the relationship between the native elite and foreign entrepreneurs.[14] This study explains the complex interaction of the regional (state) elite, the national regime, and foreign investors, and the relationship between political power and economic gain. Central to the analysis here is the notion that the effect of foreign investment on a hitherto underdeveloped area depends on the structure of the area's politics and society. Chihuahua was different from other regions in Mexico, like Sonora and Yucatán, that received large amounts of foreign investment or were highly dependent on world market conditions, because only in Chihuahua did one group control both political and economic power. Unlike most Latin American elites, the Terrazas were not subordinate to foreigners in the economic sphere.

The effect of massive foreign investment on Chihuahuan society in general is the next focus of the study.[15] The influx of foreign capital magnified already existing tendencies—the concentration of land and wealth and the formation of a highly mobile, relatively well-paid and well-treated working class—and caused profound social disruptions. It created a nascent (and soon-to-be-alienated) middle class and a despoiled, disgruntled peasantry. Most important, it put the region at the mercy of cyclical world economic conditions which subjected Chihuahua to periodic depressions that destabilized Chihuahuan society and engendered deep-seated social and political unrest.

Finally, *Capitalists, Caciques, and Revolution* is a study of the determinants of social upheaval. In Chihuahua a combination of an extraordinarily powerful political-economic elite and the profound dislocations created by the influx of foreign investment on the nonelite sectors of Chihuahuan society together produced the Revolution of 1910 in the state. In its initial stages, the uprising included peasants, workers, and members of the middle class. No *hacendado* (large landowner) fought for the Revolution in Chihuahua, as men like Maytorena, Carranza, and Madero did elsewhere. Nowhere else did the Revolution have as wide a nonelite base. The origins of these differences from the rest of Mexico lay in the Terrazas era.

In discussing the overall effects of foreign investment and export-oriented economic development and in seeking the causes of the Revolution of 1910 in Chihuahua, the study has applied and tested some aspects of the theories of economic dependence and revolutions. The means by which it accomplishes this is to break down the Mexican case into regions for comparative examination. The concluding chapter summarizes these (sometimes speculative) findings and discusses their more universal theoretical implications.

At this point it is important to note what this book is *not* as well as what it is. *Capitalists, Caciques, and Revolution* is not a biography of Luis Terrazas or his second-in-command, son-in-law Enrique C. Creel. I have chosen to concentrate on them less as individuals than as actors in a political or economic context. Nor is the book meant to be a history of working class or middle class or peasant life. It is concerned not so much with what it was like to be a miner, *vaquero* (cowboy), or small merchant in Chihuahua as with how the native elite–foreign enterprise system (as I have labeled the relationship between these two groups) affected them. In every instance I present considerable material to document the effects of the system on various classes, but delineation of their particular circumstances is not my primary objective. This is a study from the top down, a study of the effects of an elite on other classes.

1

A Harsh and Violent Land

On the eve of the Liberal era that dawned in Mexico with the overthrow of Emperor Antonio López de Santa Anna in 1855, Chihuahua lay in ruins. The worst circumstances of man and nature combined to leave the land in desolation. The harsh environment and a heritage of two and a half centuries of violence had left their mark.

A Land Apart

Chihuahua's salient geographic features at mid-nineteenth century were its arid climate and soil, isolation from the rest of Mexico, rich mineral resources, and proximity to the United States. These molded the region's economy and shaped the special attributes of Chihuahuan (and *norteño* [northern]) politics and society.[1]

Entering Chihuahua from the United States border, one confronts a vast desert spreading out to the southeast from the northwestern corner of the state. In the northwest, south of Ascensión, a complex of lakes and rivers turns the land lushly green. Today in the region between Nuevo Casas Grandes and San Buenaventura the fields are abundant with corn, wheat, and oats and the orchards with fruit. From the highway one can see the irrigation aqueducts snaking around the fields. From Nuevo Casas Grandes the agricultural zone continues into the Guerrero District, the state's breadbasket before 1910. To the west, from just north of Madera to Guadalupe y Calvo, is Mexico's most important commercial forest.

South of Ciudad Juárez the traveler crosses the sand dunes of Samalayuca that inflicted cruel suffering on the first explorers, colonial adventurers, and nineteenth-century merchants. South of Villa Ahumada the land becomes suitable for pasture. Many of the region's cattle graze on the semiarid grasslands of the central part of the state around the state capital, Ciudad Chihuahua. Fifty miles south of the capital, one reaches the state's second important agricultural region, in the drainage basin of the Río Conchos, centering around Delicias. From colonial times, the land watered by the Conchos, Río Florido, and Río del Parral, which intersect at Ciudad Camargo (Santa Rosalía), provided the staples that sustained the rich mining districts of Hidalgo del Parral and Santa Bárbara, located further south. The state's three great mining centers, Parral, Santa Bárbara, and San Francisco del Oro, form a triangle two hundred miles south of Ciudad Chihuahua, almost to the Durango border. Their great gray slag heaps are a grand, if eerie, tribute to centuries of production.

The eastern third of Chihuahua is sparsely populated desert. Its only city is Ojinaga, located at the confluence of the Río Bravo and the Río Conchos, two hundred miles southeast of Ciudad Juárez. In the far southeast corner of the state is the Bolsón de Mapimí, the desert refuge of the nomadic Indian tribes that raided northern Mexico during the nineteenth century.

The mountains of the Sierra Madre Occidental dominate the western part of the state, forming its backbone from north to south. Interspersed with deep isolated canyons (*barrancas*), these mountains for centuries were a nearly impassable barrier between Chihuahua and the Pacific coast.

Chihuahua's arid climate, vegetation, and isolation dictated extensive rather than intensive agriculture. Ranching fit an area where climate and inaccessibility discouraged settlement, and raising livestock required little manpower, only vast tracts of land. The grasslands were excellent pasture. The large landed estate, the *hacienda*, thus became the dominant economic and social institution of Chihuahua, and the North as a whole.[2]

Inhospitable surroundings and isolation profoundly affected the relations between employer and employee on the northern frontier. In the North, mine owners and proprietors of large estates, *hacendados*, had to attract labor with better pay and working conditions. The North did not have the large, sedentary Indian population available in central and southern Mexico, and the region suffered from the chronic shortage of labor. Those who came north, moreover, by the act of leaving their villages on the central plateau, were a breed apart. Divorced from traditional ties of land and village, they were, in relative terms, highly mobile and independent.[3]

These same environmental conditions gave the *hacienda* a unique role in the North. Often isolated from any government authority, the *hacendado* was the only law on his estates. Unlike on the more densely populated central plateau, there were few Indian villages to contain or contest the *hacienda's* spreading influence. The *hacienda* in the North thus acquired a more dominant position than elsewhere in Mexico. During the years of the Apache raids, the authority of the *hacendado* grew, for his estate became the sole refuge from terror for its residents.[4] Although on some estates *hacendados*, notably the Sánchez Navarro family of Coahuila, used force to hold their labor in virtual bondage, there were other *haciendas* where residents enjoyed a large measure of independence and still others where laborers, tenants, and sharecroppers toiled in far better circumstances than their contemporaries to the south.[5]

The relationship between white man and Indian in the North differed drastically from that on the central plateau. On the northern frontier the *conquistadores* encountered resolute, savage resistance from nomadic Indians. For three centuries, the settlers in the North, especially in Chihuahua, lived in constant fear and insecurity. The brutal conflict between Spaniard and Indian severely limited the mixing of the two races, *mestizaje*, and the interchange between the two cultures that were common in the South.

The region's isolation meant that settlers confronted the Indian terror and hardships with little help from central authorities (Spanish or Mexican). The people of the *haciendas*, mining camps, and villages learned to survive on their own. As one observer has noted, the northern "ethos" was one of hard work and "a determination to confront all kinds of dangers and difficulties in order to obtain the riches which . . . exist there."[6]

Not surprisingly, the *norteños* guarded their independence, regularly resisting the attempts of governments in Mexico City to impose centralized authority. The North became a bastion first of federalism and later of Liberalism, doctrines that opposed a strong central government. The Catholic church, a pillar of Conservatism, was weak in the North because the region lacked the sedentary Indian villages that were the base of its support on the central plateau.[7]

The characteristic spirit of northern independence, its isolation, and the dominant position of the *hacienda* led to another outstanding feature of the nineteenth century, *caciquismo*. Gaining their initial prominence as Indian fighters or as large landowners, regional leaders vigorously arose to uphold their autonomy from central authority. These *caciques*, like Santiago Vidaurri of Nuevo León and Ignacio Pesqueira of Sonora, dominated the first five decades after Mexican independence.[8]

Meanwhile, Chihuahua's rich mineral resources determined its economic development. From colonial times, the region's livelihood depended on its mines. The lure of great riches of gold and silver had enticed the *conquistadores* north during the sixteenth and seventeenth centuries. The prospect of high wages and better working conditions in the mines attracted labor, and farmers and ranchers came north to supply the mining camps. Until the

1880s, the great *haciendas* produced almost exclusively to supply the mining economy. The merchants who plied the great trade routes from the north and south found their markets in the mining camps. When mineral production declined, Chihuahua plunged into depression.[9]

Although distance and terrain made Chihuahua virtually inaccessible from Mexico City, it was not isolated to the same extent from the United States. The North of Mexico had a peculiar relationship with its northern neighbor. On the one hand, it was a victim: it suffered invasion, military defeats, loss of territory, and humiliation. As a result, *norteños* distrusted and resented Americans (especially in Sonora). On the other hand, the United States was the best market for the North's products and the source of the investment capital needed to extract its mineral riches. *Norteños* admired the enterprise and technology of Americans. Economic ties dated to independence. The legendary Santa Fe Trail (St. Louis to Santa Fe) and Camino Real (Santa Fe to Ciudad Chihuahua) were main arteries of commerce in the North throughout the first half of the nineteenth century.[10] Even after the bitter, disastrous war between the United States and Mexico (1846–48) these economic links persisted. Aside from the short-lived invasion and occupation of the state in 1847 and the loss of territory in the Gadsden Purchase (Treaty of Mesilla) in 1853, Chihuahua suffered the least of the northern states from the incursions and ambitions of the United States. It endured none of the filibusters that Americans inflicted on Sonora during the same period. Americans settled and conducted business in Chihuahua without sustained hostility throughout the second half of the nineteenth century.

The proximity of the border with the United States magnified the tendency toward higher wages and better working conditions. After 1900 an unending flow of Mexican workers went north across the border to earn double the wages offered in their homeland. As time went on and migration steadily increased, the boundary became less and less of an economic or cultural demarcation.[11]

Chihuahua (and much of the North) was literally and figuratively a land apart. Certainly, willingness to work hard, resilience, and fierce independence were found abundant elsewhere in Mexico. But in Chihuahua these characteristics were forged in an environment that uniquely combined violence with opportunity.

The Colonial Period

Endemic violence and political instability were the main features of Chihuahuan history during the colonial era and the first decades after independence.

Vicious conflict with nomadic Indians, foreign invasion, civil war, and political factionalism made even harsher the Chihuahuan economy and society already shaped by its cruel environment.

From the time the first white man set foot in Chihuahua in the sixteenth century, the prospect of great riches and chronic violence established the framework of Chihuahuan society. As elsewhere in the New World, the Spanish conquerors came to northern Mexico, which they named Nueva Vizcaya, in search of precious metals and converts. They were notably successful in finding gold and silver, but spectacularly unsuccessful in Christianizing the northern heathens, who fiercely resisted their incursions.[12]

Economy and society revolved around the mining industry. Farms and ranches sprang up to supply the mining camps, and merchants arrived to provide goods not available locally. Great mining centers arose in Santa Bárbara, Hidalgo del Parral, Santa Eulalia, and Cusihuiriachic. Because of its central location, Ciudad Chihuahua during the eighteenth century became the communications, transportation, and commercial hub of the region, while another group of smaller settlements grew up around the Jesuit and Franciscan missions.[13]

The native tribes stubbornly fought *conquistador* and friar alike. Indian rebellions racked seventeenth-century Chihuahua. The Tarahumara rose in bloody revolt four times between 1647 and 1697; each time they were crushed, but at terrible cost to the victors. The Indians revolted because the Spaniards stole their lands, herded them into settlements (*reducciones*), and enslaved them for arduous work in the mines. As it did for all the indigenous peoples of America, Spanish rule brought only misery and death for the Indians of the North.[14]

In the last quarter of the seventeenth century, the Spaniards encountered their most determined and dangerous foe, the Apaches. Their first rebellion exploded across northern Mexico in 1680, beginning two centuries of warfare that was to take a terrible toll in blood and property. The Indian raids abated during the first half of the eighteenth century, but in 1748 the Apaches resumed their forays. Headquartered in the Bolsón de Mapimí in southeastern Chihuahua and in the Gila River Valley in the northwest, the Apaches raided deep into Nueva Vizcaya. *Haciendas*, mines, and missions were abandoned. Travel was nearly impossible, for the danger was too great. Only at the end of the century, through the efforts of Teodoro de Croix and Brigadier Jacobo Ugarte y Loyola, did the Spaniards restore an unsteady peace by buying cooperation and fostering the age-old hatred between the Apaches and Comanches. The disruptions caused by the Hidalgo Revolt (1810), which diverted men and money from the frontier, undermined this peace, although it was two more decades before the Apaches returned again to their trails of plunder.[15]

Spanish policies to protect the region and exploit its riches established the major institutions of nineteenth-century Chihuahua, the *hacienda* and the *rancho*. Recognizing that the climate and soil made the North suitable for livestock raising and little else, the Spanish crown granted large tracts of land to favored settlers. The first great estates took form in Chihuahua during the eighteenth century. In response to intensified Indian attacks at the end of the seventeenth century, the crown established a string of garrisons across the northern frontier, known as *presidios*. Those who settled in the *presidios* received small land grants, *ranchos*, in return for service in the militia. These small holders, or *rancheros*, were to play a key role in the Indian wars and politics of nineteenth-century Chihuahua. The conflict between the *rancheros* and the *hacendados* who sought to expand their landholding at the expense of the *rancheros* was to be one of the sparks that ignited the Revolution of 1910.[16]

The Age of Chaos

The end of Spanish rule in 1821 left a power vacuum in Mexico, as it had elsewhere in Spain's New World empire. For nearly half a century no regime, government, or individual established a legitimate claim to succeed royal authority. The former colony disintegrated into a loose confederation of autonomous states. Chaos ensued.

Still, the first decade of independence brought relative prosperity and peace in Chihuahua. After two decades of depression, the mining industry, spurred by several new discoveries and bonanzas, boomed during the 1820s. The region's population doubled between 1803 and 1832.[17] Unfortunately, Chihuahuan politics followed the same pattern as politics in the rest of Mexico. No Chihuahuan governor completed his full term until Luis Terrazas accomplished this feat in his third term, 1869 to 1873.

Political disorder, poor transportation, and the resumption of Indian raids ended the state's economic recovery. In 1828, swept up in the nationwide fear of impending invasion by Spain, the state government expelled all Spaniards from Chihuahua. The outflow of capital and technical skills was ruinous to the local economy, and as a result, the mining industry faltered in the early 1830s.[18]

The Apache terror began again in 1832. Almost overnight the land was in ruins, cattle killed or stolen, *haciendas* and mines abandoned. In every year for the next two decades the raids grew more intense. The Apaches robbed, murdered, pillaged, burned, and brought indescribable misery. Enfeebled by constant turmoil, the national and state governments were unequal to the task of restoring peace.[19]

The main political struggles in Chihuahua mirrored those in the nation as a whole. The primary conflict was between the central government and the states. In ideological terms, this struggle evolved around the debate between centralism, which advocated a strong national authority in Mexico City, and federalism, which preferred a weak national government and strong, autonomous states. Eventually, the centralists became known as Conservatives and the federalists as Liberals. Although the socioeconomic foundations of the two factions are widely debated, generally the Conservatives won support among the clergy, army officers, and large landowners. They were most influential in the central plateau, where royal authority and the Catholic church had been most effective. The Conservatives represented in part the vestiges of the colonial ruling establishment fighting to preserve its position.

The Liberals were the political "outs." They came from the ranks of merchants, professionals, and landowners. Many of their leaders were *mestizos* (mixed Spanish and Indian blood). Geographically, the Liberals drew their main support from the periphery, where regional *caciques* fought to preserve their hegemony.[20]

In Chihuahua, as elsewhere in Mexico, the socioeconomic lines between Conservatives and Liberals were often blurred. It is difficult to differentiate between merchants and landowners; many members of the ruling class or elite were both. Merchants and *hacendados* did not necessarily have opposing political or economic goals. Furthermore, regional loyalties and opportunities for personal gain were often more important than political ideologies. Chihuahuans switched political allegiances easily (and sometimes treacherously).

Chihuahuans faced a crucial dilemma as the lines formed between Liberals and Conservatives. Historical circumstances (the weakness of the church and royal authority) and geography (isolation) inclined them toward Liberalism. But the state could not fight the Apaches alone. It had neither the funds nor the manpower to conduct an extensive, prolonged campaign against the Indians. Ideally, a strong central government could have provided the means to restore peace. Unfortunately for the Conservatives in Chihuahua, no central government showed any ability or inclination to put an end to the Indian depredations.

Intermittently during the late 1830s and 1840s Chihuahuans sought to solve their dilemma by offering a bounty for Apache scalps. Financed in part by state tax revenues and in part by private entrepreneurs, the bounty was supposed to take a heavy toll on the Apaches while maintaining the state's autonomy. Conservatives were among the firmest supporters and financial backers of the bounty. The scheme failed, however, because bounty hunters killed Mexicans, whose hair was indistinguishable from that of the Apaches and who were easier prey.[21]

The histories of the most prominent Conservative families in Chihuahua followed a common pattern. Descendants of soldiers, miners, and merchants who came to the region during the eighteenth century, they made their fortunes, acquired substantial landholdings, and became local political powers, particularly around Ciudad Chihuahua and the surrounding plain.

First and foremost among the Conservatives were the Zuloagas. Manuel José Zuloaga came to Nueva Vizcaya as a cadet in the company of his uncle Brigadier Jacobo Ugarte y Loyola in 1786. He settled in Chihuahua, married, and produced four sons, Luis (1803–64), José María (1804–68), Tomás (1805–68), and Félix (1813–98). Luis was a state legislator, magistrate of the state supreme court, state administrator of taxes, and a deputy in the federal congress. As governor of the state for six months in 1845, he engaged in an acrimonious dispute with the newly founded Chihuahuan Liberal party, which ultimately rebelled and deposed him. During the last dictatorship of Santa Anna in 1853, he acted first as a member of the ruling triumvirate and then as governor of the state.

The brothers were key leaders of the Conservative party both in Chihuahua and nationally. José María Zuloaga led the Conservatives in Chihuahua during the civil war between Conservatives and Liberals, the War of the Reform (1858–60). He was governor briefly in 1859. Earlier he was a well-known Indian fighter, state legislator, and *jefe político* (district political leader). Tomás, also a noted Indian fighter, was a lawyer who served as magistrate of the state supreme court and as a legislator. He too fought on the Conservative side in the War of the Reform in Chihuahua, and was deported from the state as a result. He returned to become imperial prefect of Chihuahua during Maximilian's empire (which was sponsored by the Conservatives). The youngest brother, Félix, initiated the Conservative rebellion in 1858 (the Plan de Tacubaya) in Mexico City that set off the War of the Reform. He was, under the Conservative banner, for a brief time president of Mexico.

Until discredited by their defeat in the War of the Reform and collaboration with the French (whose troops provided the underpinnings of the Maximilian regime), the Zuloagas exerted considerable influence in Chihuahuan politics. They originally maintained a strong political base at their home in Corralitos, where the mines provided the foundation of their fortune. After the French Intervention, the family played a more subdued, but equally crucial, role in state politics. The Zuloagas lent critical financial and political support to Liberal leader Luis Terrazas, who was related to them by marriage, against other Liberal factions in Chihuahua. In return Terrazas provided them with amnesty, political patronage, and access to church and public lands.

Capitalists, Caciques, and Revolution

Table 1–1
Executive Authority in Chihuahua, 1821–1911

Term	Governor/ Executive Authority	Substitute/Interim	National Regime
1821	Alejo García Conde[a]		1821. Plan de Iguala Emperor Agustín de Iturbide
1821– 1822	Mariano de Urrea[b]		
1822	Brig. Antonio Cordero[b]		
1822– 1823	Ignacio del Corral y Romero[b]		1823. Plan de Casa Mata Constitution of 1824 Federalist
1823	Juan Navarro del Rey[b] Luis de Iturribarria[b]		
1823– 1824	Mariano Horcasitas[c] Crl. José de Urquidi[c]		Guadalupe Victoria
1824	Simón de Ochoa[c] Crl. José de Urquidi[c]		
1824– 1825		Crl. José de Urquidi	
1825		T.C. José Antonio Arce	
1825– 1826		Crl. José de Urquidi	
1826– 1830	Crl. Simón Elías González[d]		
1826– 1827		T.C. José Antonio Arce	
1827	Lic. José Antonio Ruiz de Bustamente		
1827– 1828	Crl. Simón Elías González		
1828	Juan Manuel Rodríguez[e]		
1828		T.C. José Antonio Arce	
1828– 1830	T.C. José Antonio Arce		Vicente Guerrero José María Bocanegra Pedro Vélez, Luis Quintanar, Lucas Alamán
1830		José Andrés Luján	Anastasio Bustamente

Table 1 – 1 (continued)

Term	Governor/ Executive Authority	Substitute/Interim	National Regime
1830	T.C. José Antonio Arce		
1830– 1834	José Isidro Madero		Melchor Múzquiz (1832)
1833	Lic. José Rafael Revilla	Lic. José Rafael Revilla	Manuel Gómez Pedraza Antonio López de Santa Anna Valentín Gómez Farías
1833	José Isidro Madero		
1833		Lic. José Rafael Revilla	
1833– 1834		José María Sánchez Pareja	
1834	José Isidro Madero		
1834– 1838	Crl. Simón Elías González		
1834– 1835	Crl. José Joaquín Calvo		Miguel Barragán
1835	Crl. José Joaquín Calvo	José María de Echevarria	
1835– 1837	Crl. José Joaquín Calvo[f]		José Justo Carro Centralist Constitution of 1836: *Siete Leyes*
1837– 1838	Crl. Simón Elías González		Santa Anna
1838	Crl. Simón Elías González	Berardo Revilla Mariano Horcasitas	
1838– 1839		Berardo Revilla	Nicolás Bravo 1839–46
1839	Crl. Simón Elías González Crl. Simón Elías González Crl. Simón Elías González	José María de Irigoyen José María Irigoyen de la O José María Irigoyen de la O José María de Irigoyen	
1839– 1840		José María Irigoyen de la O	
1840		Pedro Olivares	

Table I – I (continued)

Term	Governor/ Executive Authority	Substitute/Interim	National Regime
1840–1842	Gen. Francisco García Conde		
1842–1845	Brig. José María Monterde	Crl. Mariano Martínez de Lejarza (1842, 1843)	José Joaquín Herrera (1844, 1845)
1845		Luis Zuloaga Joaquín Bustamente Pedro Olivares	
1845–1846	Crl. Angel Trías, Sr.		
1846		Crl. Mauricio Ugarte Crl. Cayetano Justiniani José María de Irigoyen Crl. Angel Trías, Sr.	Mariano Paredes Arrillaga Mariano Salas
1847		Crl. Angel Trías, Sr. Lic. Laureano Muñoz José María Sánchez Pareja Lic. Laureano Muñoz	Pedro María Anaya
1848	Crl. Angel Trías, Sr.		
1848–1849		Lic. Laureano Muñoz	
1849–1850	Brig. Angel Trías, Sr.		
1850–1852		Lic. Juan Nepomuceno de Urquidi	Mariano Arista
1852	José Cordero	Brig. Angel Trías, Sr.	Plan de Jalisco Santa Anna
1853	Triumvirate: Trías, Luis Zuloaga, and Dr. Juan Vivar y Balderrama	Luis Zuloaga	
1853–1855	Brig. Angel Trías, Sr.		
1855		Brig. Angel Trías, Sr.	Plan de Ayutla The Reform
1855–1856		Lic. Juan Nepomuceno de Urquidi	Juan Alvarez Ignacio Comonfort
1856		Lic. Jesús María Palacios	

Table 1 – 1 (continued)

Term	Governor/ Executive Authority	Substitute/Interim	National Regime
1856– 1857		Berardo Revilla	Benito Juárez, Liberal (1855–72)
1857		José María Juarietta	
1857– 1859	Lic. Antonio Ochoa		
1859	José María Zuloaga^c		Plan de Tacubaya,
1860		Lic. José E. Muñoz Luis Terrazas Lic. Juan N. Bárcenas^c	Conservative War of the Reform
1861– 1864	Luis Terrazas		
1864	Crl. Jesús José Casavantes		French Intervention Juárez, State of Seige
1864– 1865	Brig. Angel Trías, Sr.		
1865	Brig. Francisco Ortiz de Zarate Brig. Manuel Ojinaga Brig. Agustín Villagra		
1865	Gen. Agustín Enrique de Brincourt Tomás Zuloaga Lic. Tomás Irigoyen Julio Carranco Jesús Fontana		Empire of Maximillian
1865– 1866	Joaquín H. Domínguez Lic. Inocente Rubio		
1865– 1867	Brig. Luis Terrazas		
1867– 1869	Brig. Luis Terrazas		Juárez Restoration
1869– 1873	Luis Terrazas	Lic. Manuel Gómez y Luna (1872)	
1873		Juan Bautista Escudero	
1873– 1876	Lic. Antonio Ochoa	Manuel de Herrera (1876)	

Table 1 – 1 (continued)

Term	Governor/ Executive Authority	Substitute/Interim	National Regime
1876– 1877		Dr. Mariano Samaniego	
1877	Gen. Juan B. Caamano Gen. Pedro Hinojosa	José Eligio Muñoz	Plan de Tuxtepec
1877– 1879	Brig. Angel Trías, Jr.		Porfirio Díaz
1879– 1880	Luis Terrazas (Plan de Guerrero)		
1880		Lic. Gabriel Aguirre	
1880– 1884	Luis Terrazas	Dr. Mariano Samaniego (1881, 1882, 1883)	
1884		Ramón Cuellar Celso González	
1884– 1888	Gen. Carlos Pacheco	Brig. Carlos Fuero (1884–85) Félix Francisco Maceyra (1885–87) Lauro Carrillo (1887, 1888) Celso González (1887–88)	
1888– 1892	Lauro Carrillo	Manuel de Herrera (1888) Crl. Mauro Candano (1889) Lic. Rafael Pimentel (1890, 1891, 1892) Lic. Alejandro Guerra y Porras (1891)	
1892– 1904	Crl. Miguel Ahumada	Lic. Joaquín Cortazar (1894–1903, various times)	
1903– 1904	Luis Terrazas		
1904– 1907		Enrique C. Creel	
1907– 1911	Enrique C. Creel	Lic. Joaquín Cortazar José María Sánchez (1906–10, various times)	

Table 1–1 (continued)

Term	Governor/ Executive Authority	Substitute/Interim	National Regime
1910– 1911	Alberto Terrazas	Alberto Terrazas Miguel Ahumada	
1911		Abraham González	The Revolution

Sources: Francisco R. Almada, *Gobernantes de Chihuahua*; Michael C. Meyer and William L. Sherman, *The Course of Mexican History*.
a. Head of the four Internal Provinces.
b. Province of Nueva Vizcaya.
c. Province of Chihuahua.
d. Simón Elías González was the first constitutional governor of the state of Chihuahua. The state legislature named him to a four-year term, 1826–1830.
e. Rodríguez died before he took office.
f. Calvo was both governor and military commander under the centralist regime.

Crl. = Coronel T.C. = Teniente Coronel Brig. = General de Brigada Lic. = Licenciado

At the same time that the Zuloagas shifted their political strategy, the family, under the leadership of Carlos Zuloaga, moved its base of operations from Corralitos to the region around Cusihuiriachic. There during the 1880s they acquired major landholdings. They later added other properties in Satevó, south of Ciudad Chihuahua.[22]

Other important Conservative families also became tied by kinship and politics to the Terrazas and formed the basis of the latter's support in the factional wars among Liberals after 1860 in Chihuahua. These Conservative families and allied military leaders controlled the Chihuahuan state government until the early 1840s. (See Table 1-1 for a list of governors.) They were less concerned with national politics than with fighting the Apaches and protecting their property.

As can be readily seen from their alliance with the Liberal Terrazas after 1867, the old Conservative families were, above all, pragmatists. Ostensibly defenders of the church, they took expropriated church lands when the opportunity arose. They ruled Chihuahua for the first two decades after independence because they had solid local political bases, they formed wide familial ties with other elite families, they had won a degree of respect as public servants in the last decades of colonial rule, and they were in the forefront of the war against the Apaches. It was no coincidence that the Zuloagas, the leading Conservative family, were the best-known Indian fighters of the era.

LIBERALS

Although the Liberal awakening in Mexico resulted in great part from the self-examinations precipitated by the nation's humiliating defeat in the war with the United States, 1846–48 (and loss of half its territory), the Liberals in Chihuahua tasted power initially in 1845, when they overthrew the regime of governor General José María Monterde, who had crystallized opposition when he attempted to centralize state government.[23] A group of prominent merchants, professionals, and *hacendados*, including Angel Trías, Sr., Juan de Urquidi, José Cordero, Laureano Muñoz, and José Félix Maceyra, founded the Liberal party in Chihuahua in 1843. These capable, wealthy men sought political influence commensurate with their economic success. For two decades the Conservatives had failed to establish order and prosperity. It was time for a change. Conservatives had sought to protect what they had. The Liberals sought this too, but they wanted more: they strove to develop the land to its full potential.

The Liberals were sharply divided according to subregional and personal loyalties. The five principal leaders of the early Liberals, General Angel Trías, Juan Nepomuceno de Urquidi, José Cordero, Antonio Ochoa, and José Eligio Muñoz, each represented major segments of the party. Trías and Cordero were merchants from Ciudad Chihuahua who had acquired considerable landholdings around the capital—Trías to the north and Cordero to the southeast—where they established political bases. Ochoa and Urquidi came from mining regions, Guadalupe y Calvo and Hidalgo del Parral, respectively, where citizens bristled against control from Ciudad Chihuahua. Muñoz was representative of Liberal professionals and bureaucrats from Ciudad Chihuahua. These Liberal rivalries were to form the framework of Chihuahuan politics for the last half of the nineteenth century.

General Angel Trías, Sr. (1807–67), emerged as the first strong Liberal leader. He was, unquestionably, the dominant political figure in Chihuahua during the 1840s and 1850s. Trías was able and wealthy, a genuine, popular military hero, and a shrewd political opportunist who unfailingly caught the prevailing political winds. He abandoned the Conservatives in 1843 to lead the Liberal revolt in Chihuahua, then rejoined the Conservatives in 1852 when Santa Anna returned to power for the last time, and then rejoined the Liberals when they overthrew Santa Anna in the Plan de Ayutla revolt in 1855. He was a patriot who fought against the American invasion in 1846 and against the French Intervention.

Trías served as governor of Chihuahua several times, twice by election, in 1847 and 1851. His first term was interrupted by the American invasion and the second by his own adherence to the last coup of Santa Anna in 1852. At the request of Liberal President Benito Juárez, he became governor for a year during 1864–65, while Chihuahua was under martial law.

General Trías was a successful businessman as well as politician. Educated in Europe, he took over his grandfather's mercantile business in Chihuahua during the 1820s and built a considerable fortune, which he augmented by raising cattle on two large *haciendas* north of Ciudad Chihuahua. At one point his estate was worth over a half million pesos. He lost much of it, however, in the disruptions of the Indian and civil wars and the war with the United States. In 1847 he outfitted at his own expense an army of Chihuahuans to fight the Americans.[24]

Despite his considerable popularity and his impeccable reputation as a soldier and patriot, Trías never united the Liberals in Chihuahua, who fragmented into warring factions based on subregional and personal loyalties. Politics in the state evolved as a multicornered struggle between rival Liberal factions and the Conservatives, in which alliances and allegiances shifted treacherously. Trías himself converted to the Conservative side in 1852, when he was unable to gain the upper hand in the internecine warfare among the Liberals.

The stakes in this struggle were local. National issues were, until the late 1850s, secondary, taken up only when they were to the advantage of one or more of the contesting groups. Subregional factions sought to capture the state government for its potentially crucial resources: control of the distribution of public (and later church) lands and control of the militia. There were also a small amount of tax revenue and public jobs. The most crucial of these resources was control of the militia. The governor, who was at times also the military commander, determined where the militia would fight and what it would protect. This could mean virtual life-and-death power.

Juan Nepomuceno de Urquidi (1813–80) was scion of a distinguished landowning family in the Valle de Allende, east of Hidalgo del Parral. The Urquidis were local government officials, judges, and state legislators. José Ignacio de Urquidi was the state's first governor. Juan served as interim governor for two comparatively long periods, 1850 to 1852 and 1855 to 1856. In 1865 his younger brother Francisco (1821–81) ran unsuccessfully for governor in a three-way race with Angel Trías and Luis Terrazas. It was Juan de Urquidi who appointed Luis Terrazas to his first important political office in 1852. With the brothers' deaths in the early 1880s, the Urquidi family lost its political influence.[25]

José Cordero (1798–1867) was a founder of the Chihuahuan Liberal party. A merchant, miner, and *hacendado*, he was reputed at one time to be the richest man in the state. He was elected governor in 1852, but was deposed in the Conservative uprising (nationally, the Plan de Jalisco) that restored Santa

Anna as dictator of Mexico. Cordero was an unpopular governor even among Liberals, and his political career was later destroyed when questions were raised about his loyalty during the French Intervention.[26]

A third key challenger for the mantle of Liberal leadership was Antonio Ochoa (1811–83). Like the Urquidi brothers, Ochoa had a strong subregional political base in a mining district. He was a prosperous mine owner in Guadalupe y Calvo, Mina District, in southwestern Chihuahua. A lawyer, Antonio was a state legislator and deputy to the national congress in the late 1850s. He was elected governor in 1857, but the War of the Reform interrupted and he completed little more than two years of his four-year term. As *jefe político*, he led the resistance to the French in Mina. In 1873, Ochoa won a new four-year term as governor, defeating the *terracista* (followers of Luis Terrazas) candidate Dr. Mariano Samaniego in a very close election. He drew his main support from districts outside Ciudad Chihuahua, especially in the western part of the state. After less than three years in office, he was ousted by the rebel partisans of Porfirio Díaz (who revolted under the banner of the Plan de Tuxtepec) in 1876. Caught between the *porfiristas* and *terracistas*, both of whom he opposed, Ochoa never regained his previous stature.[27]

A fourth important Liberal leader was José Eligio Muñoz (1819–91). He and his four brothers held numerous political posts in Chihuahua from the 1840s to the 1880s. His brother Laureano was a founder of the Liberal party in the state and four-time governor during the 1840s. José Eligio was also interim governor for short periods in 1860 and 1877. He was an irrepressible and acerbic opponent of Luis Terrazas, whose election as governor in 1861 had dashed his own ambitions. Muñoz never mounted a substantial challenge for Liberal leadership, because he lacked a strong subregional political base or personal following. Moreover, as we shall see in chapter 2, his family abandoned him in favor of the Terrazas.[28]

Thus the founding fathers of Liberalism in Chihuahua saw their party fragmented by personal ambition and subregional rivalries. The major leaders quarreled among themselves, sometimes becoming implacable enemies. Ciudad Chihuahua, Hidalgo del Parral, the western mining districts, and (after 1860) the Guerrero Valley (see chapter 2) became centers of geographic rivalry between Liberal factions. Meanwhile, the Conservatives maintained considerable strength in the area around the state capital until the late 1860s. They took advantage of the cleavages among Liberals to remain key contenders for power until the defeat of Maximilian in 1867.

Because the contesting political groups and major economic and political centers were evenly balanced, no strongman emerged, as happened in other states in the first half of the nineteenth century. It would take the overwhelming economic power of the Terrazas and the growing economic and political hegemony of Ciudad Chihuahua and Ciudad Juárez to facilitate the establishment of the Terrazas *cacicazgo* during the latter half of the century.

Devastation and a New Challenge

Chihuahua sank to its nadir of economic depression and turmoil in the years 1848 to 1852. In 1848 Mexico signed the Treaty of Guadalupe Hidalgo, ending the war with the United States at the devastating cost of half its territory. The next four years witnessed the worst Indian raids since the coming of the white man. The Apaches, Comanches, and other tribes laid waste to the region. During the same years, a terrible drought struck, and an epidemic of cholera added to the widespread misery and killed several prominent political figures. Much of Chihuahua was abandoned.

The devastation at mid-century virtually wiped the slate clean. The state's mines were filled with water and caved in; its pasture land was empty. Those *haciendas* not abandoned by their owners were fortified with thick walls. The once-flourishing commerce of the northern trade routes was ruined. State government barely functioned. Factionalism tore apart its politics. Chihuahuans lived under siege in constant fear.

Chihuahua, of course, was not the only state whose politics were fragmented geographically or otherwise. Rivalries between the political and economic interests of Alamos, Hermosillo, and Guaymas (to name only the three major divisions) racked Sonoran politics throughout the nineteenth century. Similarly, in Sinaloa the competition between Culiacán, Mazatlán, and Rosario afflicted state politics.[29] Only in Chihuahua was one geographic center, Ciudad Chihuahua, and one family, the Terrazas, eventually able to dominate. In these other regions, coalitions and compromise were the necessary modes of political behavior.

During the mid 1850s and 1860s, amid the further chaos of the War of the Reform and the French Intervention, a new generation of Liberals arose to challenge the old leaders and to win final victory against Conservatives. Neither the old guard Liberals, like Trías or Ochoa, nor the Conservatives, especially the Zuloagas, gave up the fight easily. But the new Liberals were determined to rule the land and capture the great wealth of its mines and grasslands. It fell finally to the Terrazas to overcome the subregional divisions of Chihuahuan politics and mold agreements with the long-warring factions.

2

The Rise of the Terrazas

The history of Chihuahuan politics from 1854 to 1902 is a chronicle of the rise of Luis Terrazas. Coming of age during the Liberal revolt of 1854 and the War of the Reform (1858–60), he was the only regional *cacique* who retained his political base through the French Intervention, the purges of the Juárez restoration, and the Díaz dictatorship. No other *cacique* in prerevolutionary Mexico matched either the length of his career or the extent to which he controlled his domain. Luis Terrazas and his family overcame the opposition of Conservatives and rival Liberal factions through adept political maneuver, the astute choice of allies, a measure of good luck, and the shrewd use of their economic resources.

His rise took place against a backdrop of continued endemic violence, political turmoil, and economic depression. The first two decades of his career coincided with the bitter civil wars between Liberals and Conservatives that began with the Plan de Ayutla in 1854 and continued with the War of the Reform, and the French Intervention (the empire of Maximilian). The next twenty years brought the two insurrections of Porfirio Díaz, the unsuccessful Plan de Noria in 1872, and the victorious Plan de Tuxtepec in 1876. Each of these rebellions and wars engendered a related upheaval in Chihuahua.[1] After 1860 intense competition between Liberal factions in the state disrupted Chihuahuan politics, crippled the administration of state government, and wrought havoc on the state's economy.[2]

At the same time, the Indian wars continued unabated. During the 1860s and 1870s the Apaches terrorized northern and western Chihuahua. As late as 1879 a band of renegade Apaches captured Casas Grandes and held it for ransom. Without funds to raise an army to recapture the town, the governor gave in to their demands. The following year, however, state troops led by Colonel Joaquín Terrazas (a cousin of Luis) cornered and defeated the Apache chief Victorio at Tres Castillos. This ended the major Indian threat, although the

Apaches continued sporadic raids until the 1890s. Banditry in the southern part of the state and in the mining regions added to the turmoil and further hindered economic development.[3]

Warfare and banditry destroyed the already poor system of transportation and communication. At times the whole western sector of the state was virtually cut off. Throughout the period, the lack of currency and the proliferation of counterfeit money inhibited commerce. Crop failure and the resulting food shortages added to the misery.[4]

In the late 1870s, as it had been thirty years before, Chihuahua was in ruins. The crops of 1877 and 1879 failed. In some districts people starved. Commerce and mining were at a standstill.[5] From this devastation the Terrazas rose to create their political and economic empire.

Luis Terrazas and His Family

Luis Terrazas was born in Ciudad Chihuahua in 1829, the son of Juan José Terrazas, a local merchant and member of the city council (*ayuntamiento*), and Petra Fuentes. For a time he studied to be a priest, but his father's premature death in 1849 caused him to give up an ecclesiastical career. Now the head of a family with five other children, young Luis took over management of his father's estate, which consisted of a small grocery store, a soap factory, a slaughterhouse, a small herd of cattle, and a considerable number of urban properties, together worth perhaps 18,000 pesos. From this modest beginning he was to become the world's largest landowner and cattleman. In 1852 he married Carolina Cuilty Bustamante, the daughter of a wealthy *hacendado*.[6] They had fourteen children and seventy-one grandchildren (see family tree, appendix).

At the heart of the family were Luis, his four surviving sons, and eight sons-in-law. Three of the sons, Juan (1852–1925), Luis, Jr. (?–1918), and Alberto (1869–1925), were prominent businessmen and politicians, while a fourth, Federico, maintained a low profile as manager of the family's cattle enterprise. Juan was a state legislator, a deputy in the national Congress, and senator from Campeche. He was also for many years president of the chamber of commerce of Ciudad Chihuahua and headed the Club Electoral Porfirista in Chihuahua during the 1904 presidential reelection campaign. Luis, Jr., was a state legislator and a deputy in the national Congress. Alberto was governor of Chihuahua from December 1910 to January 1911.[7]

Of the eight sons-in-law, Enrique C. Creel (1854–1931) was the most important. He was the clan's second-in-command, assuming day-to-day supervision of its activities when the general retired in 1903. Creel was an internationally respected banker and an astute businessman, and a member of the

LUIS TERRAZAS, 1912
Courtesy of the Aultman Collection, El Paso Public Library

E N R I Q U E C. C R E E L , C I R C A 1 9 0 8
Courtesy of Sr. Eduardo Creel

científico circle led by José Y. Limantour, Díaz's minister of finance. Creel was governor of Chihuahua from 1904 to 1910.

Creel was the son of a former United States consul in Chihuahua, Reuben W. Creel, and Paz Cuilty de Creel, the sister of Luis Terrazas's wife. Enrique married the general's daughter Angela in 1880. He showed an early acumen for business, running a small store for his father at age fourteen. Enrique Creel's marriage brought him an excellent opportunity to show his abilities. Within a few years, he took over the management of all the Terrazas's non-agricultural enterprises. He had already begun in politics as a member of the *ayuntamiento* of Ciudad Chihuahua in 1877. He was a state legislator for four terms and sat in the national Congress for four terms before embarking on his career as governor and diplomat. He served as Díaz's ambassador to the United States and secretary of foreign relations.[8]

Son-in-law Federico Sisniega held a key position as manager of the Chihuahua branch of the Banco Nacional, Mexico's largest bank, allowing him to complete the family's control of the state's financial institutions and providing it with vital contacts in Mexico City. Sisniega, a millionaire, was one of the leading textile and clothing manufacturers in the country.[9]

Another of the general's sons-in-law, Dr. Miguel Márquez (1853–1913), was czar of the state's health and educational facilities, serving as director of its primary school system, the Instituto Científico y Literario, and the most important local hospital. He was also a state legislator for six terms.[10]

Other sons-in-law and relatives brought other key political and economic ties. Son-in-law Rafael Horcasitas, for many years a magistrate of the state supreme court, linked the Terrazas to an old Chihuahuan family with substantial landholdings and political influence in Santa Eulalia and Aldama.[11] Another son-in-law, Dr. Jesús Muñoz, came from a prominent family of professionals and bureaucrats from Ciudad Chihuahua that once opposed Luis Terrazas.[12]

Luis Terrazas's ties to the Zuloagas originated in his marriage to Carolina Cuilty Bustamente. Her brothers, Enrique and Alejandro Cuilty, were important landowners and entrepreneurs in Iturbide district, thus adding to the political and economic alliances formed by Luis Terrazas in Ciudad Chihuahua and the surrounding countryside.[13]

Kinship also provided links to the Lujáns, *hacendados* and political bosses in Jiménez (and La Laguna region in Durango), and the Falomirs,[14] who had extensive properties and political influence in Aldama, Iturbide, and Jiménez districts.[15]

Marriage brought other key political and economic connections to the Terrazas. The general's brother-in-law Carlos Moye, a German-American immigrant and landowner and merchant in Ciudad Chihuahua, helped finance the general's early textile ventures.[16] Enrique Creel's son-in-law Joaquín Cortazar, Jr., established ties to his politically influential family in the state capital.[17]

The Rise of Luis Terrazas

Governor Juan de Urquidi appointed Luis Terrazas to his first public post in the office of the state administrator of taxes, in 1851. Three years later, he won election to the *ayuntamiento* of Ciudad Chihuahua. When the Liberal Plan de Ayutla revolt broke out in 1854, he initially sided with the Conservative Santa Anna, but after the Liberals ousted the dictator, Terrazas quickly joined the victorious party. He again won election to the *ayuntamiento* in 1859, and also as an alternate (*suplente*) to the state legislature.

At the end of 1859, Luis, barely thirty years old, received his first political break when Governor Angel Trías, Sr., appointed him *jefe político* of Iturbide District. The following year Trías named him to the *junta de guerra* (war council) against the Apaches and Comanches.

On 21 September 1860, the state legislature named him governor, although according to the state's constitution he was too young for the office. He was subsequently elected to a full four-year term. Amid the War of the Reform, with the state's most prestigious soldier and statesman, Angel Trías, Sr., in the South fighting and the Chihuahuan Liberals badly split into fragments loyal to former governors Trías, Ochoa, Cordero, and Urquidi, Luis Terrazas was a compromise choice as governor. Because he had received important appointments from two key Liberal leaders, Trías and Urquidi, Luis was acceptable to the rival groups. Moreover, Terrazas had crucial family ties to the state's Conservatives, who still retained considerable influence. But if the Liberals expected Terrazas to be a stand-in, they were mistaken.

The next four decades of Terrazas's career and, in fact, of the history of Chihuahuan politics can be seen as a series of challenges to his power from local rivals acting alone and in conjunction with national regimes that sought to extend their control to the state. Luis Terrazas and his family met these challenges and won out in the long struggle for several reasons. First, Luis Terrazas formed a close financial and political alliance with the state's Conservatives. Second, as governor from 1860 to 1884, he brilliantly mastered the lessons of economics in politics, using the resources of the state government and his own financial empire to co-opt real and potential foes and reward allies. Third, better than any other regional elite the Terrazas took advantage of the opportunities afforded by the development of an export economy in Chihuahua. As a result, the Terrazas overcame the subregional divisions of state politics.

Luis Terrazas had extensive kinship links to the state's Conservatives. After the War of the Reform and collaboration with the French had discredited these families, they provided silent political and financial support for Luis Terrazas, enabling him to gain the upper hand in the state's delicate balance of Liberal factions. The Conservatives gave Terrazas a stronghold in the central area of the state around Ciudad Chihuahua, where they still controlled local politics.

The Terrazas used their control over the state government and their great financial resources and widespread business interests to purchase the cooperation of their potential rivals and most adamant opponents. Some were made partners in family enterprises, some were permitted to acquire valuable contracts, concessions, and favors, while others married into the family, received hard-to-get loans, or got access to public lands. By 1910 most of the leading families in Chihuahua were related by blood, marriage, or money to the Terrazas.

Two cases particularly illustrate the way the Terrazas co-opted their rivals, and show clearly why the Terrazas controlled Chihuahua by century's end. Felipe Arellano, a prominent merchant, miner, and *jefe político* of Arteaga District in southwestern Chihuahua, was a *porfirista* during both Díaz rebellions, acting as governor for a short period in 1872. He had three sons, Salvador, an engineer, Felipe, a lawyer, and Lorenzo. Continuing his family's traditional opposition to the Terrazas, Lorenzo supported the *querreristas* against them during the factional battles of the 1880s. He was state treasurer under *porfirista* governor Miguel Ahumada during the 1890s. By 1902, however, the Arellanos were business associates of the Terrazas. Lorenzo managed the Terrazas-owned insurance company, "La Equidad." He and Felipe were on the board of directors of the Terrazas-controlled Caja de Ahorros de la República Mexicana, a savings bank.[18]

The Muñoz family included five brothers, José Eligio, Jesús, Laureano, Manuel, and Juan. José Eligio was a bitter opponent of Luis Terrazas through the 1860s and 1870s. Although the Terrazas never managed to co-opt José Eligio, they isolated him from the rest of his family, winning over his brothers through intermarriage and appointments to prestigious political offices. Dr. Jesús Muñoz, with his brother José Eligio, opposed Luis Terrazas in 1860. Later, however, he married the general's daughter Adela, and he loyally stood by his father-in-law against Porfirio Díaz in 1872 and 1876. Terrazas won over another brother, Laureano, by appointing him president of the Supremo Tribunal de Justicia of Chihuahua in 1865. The fourth brother, Juan, a long-time clerk in the state's Administración de Rentas (tax administration), was appointed head of the department in 1868. And the last brother, Manuel, originally a *porfirista*, helped arrange peace in the aftermath of Terrazas's revolt against Díaz's agent in Chihuahua, Governor Angel Trías, Jr., in 1879.[19]

Juárez and Terrazas

From the beginning of his first term as governor, Terrazas encountered serious opposition. Some state legislators objected to his taking office on the constitutional grounds that he was too young to be governor. Led by José Eligio Muñoz, this group looked to the central government of President Benito Juárez to depose Terrazas. This established a pattern in Chihuahuan politics whereby Liberal challengers to the Terrazas sought the support of the national government. Successive national regimes saw these circumstances as opportunities to extend centralized control over Chihuahua.

Luis Terrazas was already at odds with the Juárez government over his refusal to release federal revenues from customs collections at Paso del Norte and to supply the state's quota of troops to the federal army.[20] Juárez desperately needed these funds and soldiers. Cut off from the major customs port, Veracruz, and in control of only scattered parts of the nation, his government had severely limited financial resources. Furthermore, the loyalty of several regional *caciques*, initially Liberals and Republicans, was questionable. Santiago Vidaurri of Nuevo León and Coahuila betrayed Juárez to join the French and Maximilian, and the president feared Terrazas was about to do the same.[21]

Faced with a deteriorating military situation and Vidaurri's treachery, Juárez decreed martial law in Chihuahua and replaced Terrazas as governor with well-known Indian fighter Jesús José Casavantes. The Chihuahuan legislature, however, refused to support these actions and threatened armed resistance. In the midst of the furor, Casavantes resigned and returned to his home in Guerrero District. Juárez then appointed Angel Trías as governor.

Trías was governor and military commander of Chihuahua for thirteen months (June 1864 to July 1865), but his position steadily deteriorated. Terrazas continued to control the state legislature. The young *cacique* also enjoyed popular support, for Chihuahuans bristled at the loss of local autonomy brought about by martial law. Juárez was an outsider, and Chihuahuans distrusted outsiders. Consequently, Luis Terrazas won a new four-year term in elections held in April 1865. When several members of the Terrazas extended family collaborated with the French after the French army occupied the capital in 1864 and Terrazas himself received an appointment from Emperor Maximilian as imperial prefect of Chihuahua in October 1865, it became clear that Juárez, then making his last stand on the border, would have to reassess his attitude toward Terrazas.[22] The two men reconciled in October 1865. Terrazas subsequently led the Republican forces that drove the French from Chihuahua in the spring of 1866.

Restored as governor, General Terrazas, as he had in the aftermath of the War of the Reform, moved to reconcile the warring groups. He was especially lenient with French collaborators in the Guerrero District, where he sought to counterbalance the influence of the Casavantes family.[23]

During his first and second terms, Luis Terrazas shrewdly employed the resources at his disposal to solidify his political position. Thirteen of the twenty-six members of the state legislature that met from 1863 to 1865 received church or public lands through grants by the state government. (Three other legislators were family members.) In the next legislature, 1865 to 1867, fifteen deputies obtained these grants. Little wonder then that they supported Luis Terrazas against Juárez, who sought initially to invalidate these awards. Moreover, the governor did not discriminate between Liberals and Conservatives, for prominent adherents to each party acquired properties. Terrazas thus added to the support already gained through his earlier policy of reconciliation and his family connections.[24]

Juárez had attempted initially to depose Luis Terrazas by using political rivals in Chihuahua to counteract his power. Jesús José Casavantes, however, at best enjoyed limited subregional support. The old Indian fighter was ill-suited for the political intrigue required of the governorship. It would be the next generation of the Casavantes family that would broaden its political base and successfully challenge the Terrazas. The old warhorse Trías, easily Terrazas's match in popularity and political acumen, was tired, sick, and to some extent out of touch with his constituency. While Luis Terrazas had steadfastly remained in Chihuahua, Trías spent many years outside the state campaigning for Liberalism and Republicanism. His support eroded as a result.

Equally important, neither the Casavantes nor Trías could match the economic resources of the Terrazas family. Casavantes was a modest landowner, and Trías had lost his fortune outfitting troops to fight the invading North Americans in 1847. Angel Trías, Sr., died in 1867 of tuberculosis.

Juárez restored constitutional government to the state in December 1867. Terrazas then completed the remaining two years of his term and won a third term in 1869. Despite his reelection, the general's hold over the state was by no means absolute. The legislature split badly in 1870 and 1871 over Juárez's reelection; at one point, rival factions threatened to plunge the state into civil war. Severe fiscal problems and ongoing Apache raids contributed to the political uncertainty.[25] Terrazas continued to solidify his standing among Conservatives when in 1871 the legislature decreed amnesty for all those Chihuahuans who had collaborated with the French.

Porfirio Díaz and Luis Terrazas

The most serious challenge to Terrazas came from General Porfirio Díaz, military hero of the struggle against the French and Maximilian. After losing the presidential election, Díaz proclaimed the Plan de la Noria in 1871. Terrazas remained loyal to Juárez. During the summer of 1872 *porfirista* troops invaded Chihuahua and defeated General Terrazas. The general, however, bribed the *porfirista* commander to withdraw shortly thereafter.[26] And then in October 1872 Juárez died and the cause of the rebellion died with him.

Meanwhile, Porfirio Díaz had traveled north to Chihuahua. Terrazas helped negotiate amnesty for the rebel with new president Sebastián Lerdo de Tejada. He personally escorted Díaz to the Chihuahuan border. Díaz never forgot the humiliation.[27]

Thus, after a dozen years as governor, Luis Terrazas was still not master of the unruly, treacherous politics of Chihuahua. Despite his solid ties to the national government under Lerdo, the split among state Liberals over Juárez's reelection and his military defeat at the hands of the *porfiristas* in 1872 had weakened his authority.

Ochoa and Trías

All this made it possible, during the early 1870s, for two popular leaders to challenge the Terrazas' hold on local politics. Lic. Antonio Ochoa, a former governor, who was very popular in western Chihuahua, reemerged as a political power, and Angel Trías, Jr., sought to claim his father's position as Liberal leader.

After the uproar over Juárez's reelection and the near victory of the Díaz revolt, Luis Terrazas was in no position to run for a fourth term in 1873, and as a result lost control of the governor's office. In an election decided by 105 votes, Antonio Ochoa defeated *terracista* Dr. Mariano Samaniego, the political boss of Paso del Norte.

For the next three years, Chihuahua was in turmoil. Then in 1876, protesting President Lerdo's reelection, Porfirio Díaz again rose in rebellion (the Plan de Tuxtepec). In Chihuahua, Angel Trías, Jr., took command of the *tuxtepecano* rebellion. An army led by Luis Terrazas and his cousin Joaquín Terrazas defeated the *porfiristas* at the battle of Avalos in August 1876. Caught in the crossfire between *terracistas* and *porfiristas*, Governor Ochoa soon resigned in favor of Samaniego. His departure marked the last gasp of the western mining regions as equal competitors in Chihuahuan politics. Thereafter, they exerted political influence only through association with other factions. After the 1870s, subregional political bosses in the mining districts cooperated with statewide factions in return for a high degree of local autonomy. These bosses shrank from competition at the state level, selling their cooperation to the highest bidders, who, as we shall see, were the Terrazas.

Although the *porfiristas* lost in Chihuahua, they won everywhere else. In

January 1877, Díaz dispatched his forces north to take control of Chihuahua. Angel Trías, Jr., became governor in August 1877. Terrazas quietly withdrew.

Despite the advantages of his esteemed family name, a fine military record, and the support of the Díaz regime, Trías could not dislodge the Terrazas, who in a brief revolt with the key support of the Casavantes family in western Chihuahua overthrew him in 1879 (the Plan de Guerrero). Several weaknesses brought about young Trías's downfall. He did not have the financial resources to match the Terrazas, for his father's substantial fortune was lost, nor did he possess the Terrazas' extensive family ties. Because Trías had spent his early years outside Chihuahua in pursuit of his military career, he had not formed an extensive network of local political alliances. He was, in fact, not even dominant in his strongest political base, Ciudad Chihuahua, where the Terrazas and their Conservative allies were especially influential. Intensified Indian raids and a severe economic depression in Chihuahua brought on by the disruptions of civil war and harvest failures in 1877 and 1879 added to his political misfortunes.[28]

At the same time, Trías's policies and actions undermined his support. He alienated wide sectors of the elite when he raised taxes, imposed forced loans, and proclaimed the end of the *tienda de raya* (company store).[29] He violated the conventions of Chihuahuan politics when he eliminated all opposition in the state legislature and jailed his predecessor Ochoa. Even his personal behavior was suspect, for he was allegedly a drunkard. Most important, he could not obtain sufficient backing from Porfirio Díaz, who was busy cementing his grip on central and southern Mexico and could not spare troops to send to Chihuahua.[30]

With the renewal of widespread Indian depredations, Trías, his treasury empty, imposed an extraordinary tax to finance the war against the Apaches. Using this as a pretext, rebels issued the Plan de Guerrero in late August 1879 and quickly defeated him.

In November the legislature reconvened and appointed Luis Terrazas governor. A large federal force arrived a few weeks later, but the Terrazas were in control and the federal commander accepted the *fait accompli*. In March 1880, Terrazas resigned, succeeded by his close ally Gabriel Aguirre, in order to legitimize his election later in 1880 to a full term and avoid any protests against his "reelection."[31]

The *Guerreristas*

Terrazas was governor until 1884, when he prudently retired to look after his manifold business interests. By this time, Díaz and his successor as president, Manuel González (1880–84), had consolidated their control over most of

Mexico, in the process deposing several recalcitrant regional *caciques*.[32] Given his role in the humiliation of Díaz in 1872 and his refusal to join either *porfirista* rebellion, Luis Terrazas·was high on the list for removal. At the same time, the completion of the Mexican Central railroad in 1884, connecting Ciudad Chihuahua to Mexico City, had removed the military and communications obstacles that had stymied previous attempts to subordinate Chihuahua to central authority.

Díaz set about to establish his rule in Chihuahua within a framework that had succeeded elsewhere. He chose a loyal subordinate, usually a general, to serve as governor. Then the dictator and his agent sought out allies among the rival Liberal factions in the particular state. In this manner General Bernardo Reyes took control of Nuevo León and Julio Cervantes took control of Coahuila during the 1880s.[33] Díaz sent General Carlos Pacheco to Chihuahua in 1884 to administer the transition from Terrazas' rule and to make arrangements with local allies. Pacheco, a native Chihuahuan, found such allies in the Guerrero group, led by the Casavantes family. For the next seven years, the *guerreristas*, in conjunction with *porfirista* agents, ran the state government. Pacheco, who as minister of development (*fomento*) in the national cabinet spent most of his time in Mexico City, served as the crucial link between the Guerrero group and the Díaz regime.[34]

Modest landowners in the Guerrero Valley, 150 miles west of Ciudad Chihuahua, the Casavantes family had fought Indians, Conservatives, and French at the side of Luis Terrazas. For a short time, President Juárez had split the allies, when he appointed Jesús José Casavantes governor of Chihuahua in 1864, but they had reunited in opposition to Angel Trías, Jr., whom they jointly overthrew in 1879.

The renewed association did not last long, however. Luis Terrazas was unwilling to share power with the *guerreristas*, and the new generation of Casavantes, led by Celso González and Manuel de Herrera (each related to the Casavantes by marriage), sought to expand the family's influence beyond the Guerrero District.

To challenge the entrenched Terrazas for control of Chihuahua, the *guerrerenses* broadened their political base by acquiring allies in other subregions. They found ready allies in the western mining districts in Lauro Carrillo, who had mining interests in Guerrero, Andrés del Río, and Rayón districts, and Jesús E. Valenzuela, a leading literary light of the *Porfiriato* and a long-time favorite of dictator Díaz, whose family had large landholdings and substantial political influence in the western districts.[35] In addition, they brought into their circle Juan María Salazar, a wealthy merchant and landowner. Salazar gave the *guerreristas* political influence in the stronghold of the Zuloagas, Cusihuiriachic, and a foothold in the Parral region, as well as a considerable infusion of capital. He became a partner in the mercantile firm

González, Herrera, and Salazar.[36] They all found an important ally in Ciudad Chihuahua, Félix Francisco Maceyra, a former business partner of Luis Terrazas. Maceyra, whose father was a founder of the Liberal party in Chihuahua, provided a key link to the Liberal tradition and commercial and social circles in the capital.[37]

The *guerreristas* sought to extend and strengthen their political power by broadening their economic base. González, Herrera, and Salazar shifted their center of operations from Ciudad Guerrero to Ciudad Chihuahua, branching out into banking and urban transit. They founded the original Banco Minero Chihuahuense in 1880 and later were principals in the Banco de Chihuahua. The firm also received the first concession to build an urban transit line in Ciudad Chihuahua in 1883.[38] Most important, the *guerreristas* acquired large tracts of *terrenos baldíos* with the aim of establishing footholds in areas where they were politically weak: southeastern, southern, and eastern Chihuahua. As partners in various surveying companies (*compañías deslindadoras*) the *guerreristas* obtained title to approximately five million acres.[39]

Despite these efforts, the *guerrerista* coalition had glaring regional weaknesses. The Terrazas had an enormous headstart in subregional politics. For more than two decades, Luis Terrazas had carefully cultivated the great Conservative families of central Chihuahua. As we have seen, marriage ties added politically powerful families in Iturbide, Camargo, and Jiménez to the *terracista* circle. The *guerreristas* were unable to make inroads into these areas.

Furthermore, the *guerreristas* had no allies in fast-growing Paso del Norte. There the Terrazas had the ironclad backing of the local *caciques*, the Samaniego-Ochoa family. Dr. Mariano Samaniego was the city's leading politician throughout the second half of the nineteenth century. An early and indefatigable *terracista*, Samaniego fought by the side of Luis Terrazas against both *porfirista* revolts during the 1870s and had been the *terracista* candidate for governor in 1872. Samaniego and his son-in-law, millionaire Inocente Ochoa, were founding partners with Luis Terrazas in the Banco Minero of Chihuahua.[40] As Paso del Norte grew in population and economic influence, the political stranglehold of the Samaniego-Terrazas alliance took on even more significance.[41]

The *guerreristas* were weak in Hidalgo del Parral, the state's third largest city and leading mining center. There the Terrazas obtained the cooperation of two of the most politically influential families, the Botellos and the Porras. José María Botello, Jr., one of Parral's leading mine owners, as *jefe político* and state legislator was a key ally of the Terrazas in Hidalgo District (which included Parral),[42] and Anastasio Porras and his sons served the same function in Hidalgo and, later, Jiménez districts.[43]

The Terrazas even undermined the *guerreristas'* support in the western mining regions, where they had initially picked up considerable backing. In

Rayón the Terrazas reached accord with the political bosses of Uruáchic, the Rascóns. This numerous family controlled virtually all mining activity in their district and monopolized local political office. The Rascóns were long-time allies of the Terrazas, having fought with them against the *porfiristas* in 1876. In return for their cooperation at the state level, the Rascóns gained autonomy in local affairs.[44]

The Becerra family dominated Urique, Andrés del Río, in much the same way the Rascóns controlled Uruáchic. Brothers Buenaventura and José María Becerra had presided over the area's mining industry and politics since the mid-nineteenth century, and their political power overflowed into Chínipas in Arteaga District. During the 1870s, they had briefly shown statewide ambitions, when José María ran for governor against Angel Trías, Jr., but thereafter they retired to Urique, where they grew rich. The Becerras collaborated with the Terrazas on the same terms as had the Rascóns.[45]

During the 1880s, the Terrazas acquired as allies three of the leading local political bosses in Guerrero, Urbano Zea, who was *jefe político* of the district from 1894 to 1910, Joaquín Chávez, the chief of *rurales* in the western part of the state, and Luis Comadurán, the boss of Bachíniva.[46]

By the early 1890s, the *guerreristas'* once solid base in the Guerrero District had begun to crumble. Living and working in Ciudad Chihuahua, while having the advantage of putting the group at the center of political and economic activity, had the disadvantage of eroding political support at home. The leaders of the *guerreristas*, primarily González and Herrera, lost touch with their constituents. There had always been a strong *terracista* element in the district, and the neglect of the Guerrero group allowed it to make further inroads.

As their political support diminished, the *guerreristas* suffered a long series of economic setbacks that critically undermined their ability to compete with the Terrazas, who during the same period built an economic empire of enormous proportions. The *guerreristas* failed to capitalize on the great cattle boom of 1883 to 1889. Although members of the faction acquired millions of acres of land during the 1880s, virtually none of it was in cattle-raising areas. The Terrazas accumulated large profits from cattle exports, which they used to expand and diversify their economic interests. They were thus able not only to withstand the depressions that hit Chihuahua during the 1880s and 1890s and ruined the *guerreristas* but also to underwrite extensive political opposition to the Guerrero-Díaz alliance.[47]

Perhaps more serious, the Guerrero group was unable to sustain its own bank. González, Herrera, and Salazar began the Banco Minero Chihuahuense in 1878. Later Lauro Carrillo and Celso González were principals in the Banco de Chihuahua. But neither bank was successful. The Terrazas took over the Banco Minero in 1882 and transformed it into a family profit center, generating a million pesos between 1883 and 1896. The Banco Minero absorbed the Banco de Chihuahua in 1896, after the depression had sharply reduced its assets.[48]

Without their own credit resources, the *guerreristas'* commercial ventures could not survive the depression of the 1890s. Celso González borrowed $200,000 from Enrique C. Creel. He had not repaid the loan upon his death in 1897, and as a result, Creel, in foreclosure proceedings, acquired all the land González had obtained during the 1880s, which had been collateral for the loan.[49] The *guerreristas* were unable to use their control of the state government to expand or protect their economic holdings as the Terrazas had done. They simply could not keep pace with the Terrazas.

The Guerrero group was, moreover, unable to tap the only other source of capital, foreign entrepreneurs. Unlike the Terrazas, members of the Guerrero faction viewed foreigners primarily as competitors. Their commercial and mining operations competed directly with foreign ventures. The transfer of the González, Herrera, and Salazar merchant house to Ciudad Chihuahua in the early 1880s, for example, coincided with the founding of several foreign commercial firms in the capital. The *guerreristas* were hampered in their dealings with foreigners by the fact that none of their members were lawyers.[50] As a result, they did not easily assume the role of intermediaries. Nor did they have a counterpart to Enrique C. Creel, who was a highly successful go-between for the Terrazas in their business arrangements with foreigners.

After two years of watchful waiting from 1884 to 1886, the Terrazas began a two-pronged assault on the *guerreristas* and Porfirio Díaz. The first part of the attack came in the form of increased pressure on the *guerreristas*. The second involved the efforts of Enrique C. Creel to effect a reconciliation between his father-in-law and Porfirio Díaz.

The Terrazas clandestinely encouraged a series of uprisings in western Chihuahua in Cusihuiriachic, Guerrero, and Tomochi. In 1887 they provoked a bitter split in the state legislature. Luis Terrazas and ally Carlos Zuloaga also financed a revolt by Catarino E. Garza in Tamaulipas in 1891.[51] The split in the legislature in 1887 illustrates the Terrazas' dual strategy. While the family provoked a confrontation in Chihuahua, protesting the imminent reelection of Pacheco as governor, Enrique Creel manuevered in Mexico City. The crisis discredited Pacheco, who was unable to resolve it, and, finally, Díaz picked a compromise governor, Lauro Carrillo, acceptable to the Terrazas.[52]

In the gubernatorial campaign in 1891 and 1892 the Terrazas intensified their pressure against the *guerreristas*. Amid the violence and disorder of the election, a series of petty abuses and blunders by local authorities in the Guerrero District led to a religious uprising in Tomochi that ended with the slaughter of all its residents. There is strong suspicion that the Terrazas promised support to the insurgents. Whatever the role of the Terrazas, the disaster severely undermined the standing of the *guerreristas* with Porfirio Díaz.[53]

Meanwhile, events on the national scene worked against the Guerrero group. Pacheco fell from favor with Díaz in 1891, which deprived the faction of its only link to the dictator. The Terrazas, at the same time, strengthened their ties to the regime, as Enrique Creel became a member of the *científico* group, which exercised growing influence in the councils of the dictatorship. The Terrazas were very careful not to jeopardize Creel's position, for even as they prepared to oppose Carrillo's bid for reelection in 1892, they openly supported the reelection of Porfirio Díaz, and Luis Terrazas himself headed the state's *porfirista* political club.[54]

The catastrophe at Tomochi and the disorderly gubernatorial election convinced Díaz that Carrillo could no longer effectively govern Chihuahua. For the second time in four years, then, Díaz had to find a suitable compromise candidate. He chose Coronel Miguel Ahumada, who had been chief of the *resguardo fiscal* in Chihuahua. Ahumada proved an excellent choice. Not only did he restore peace but he also stabilized state government finances, began a substantial program of public works, and streamlined the state government. Ahumada, like Manuel Alarcón, the governor of Morelos from 1894 to 1908, was a popular and respected governor who kept order among the state's squabbling political factions. Although he did not regard the Terrazas with special favor, and, in fact, opposed their restoration in 1902, the governor maintained a working relationship with the family.[55]

Reconciliation

Creel continued to labor diligently for a complete reconciliation. He became a close ally of José Y. Limantour, Díaz's minister of finance and leader of the *científicos*. Perhaps as a result of pressure from Limantour or because of dissatisfaction with recent efforts by Ahumada to consolidate his control in Chihuahua at the expense of military zone commander Juan H. Hernández, Díaz decided to restore Luis Terrazas to political authority in the state in 1903.[56] In return, the Terrazas were, reportedly, to guarantee a specified annual number of recruits for the federal army.[57] Díaz went ahead with the restoration of the Terrazas despite the warnings of Ahumada, who insisted that the family was unpopular in Chihuahua.[58]

The Terrazas had by the mid-1890s fought the powerful Díaz dictatorship to a standstill. The repercussions of their restoration in 1903 were to reverberate throughout Chihuahuan politics for a decade. In their victory lay the seeds of the great Revolution.

The Terrazas' political rise had no parallel in prerevolutionary Mexico. Juárez and Díaz both had determinedly eliminated the major regional *caciques* and *notable* families from political power in the states. None of the *caciques* and families that had exercised power before Díaz's second term began in 1884, such as Diego Alvarez in Guerrero (state), Ignacio Pesqueira in Sonora, and the Maderos of Coahuila, ever again gained political authority under Díaz.[59] As in the case of the Maderos, the old leadership was permitted to grow rich through government concessions, subsidies, and tax breaks, but never allowed to regain power.[60] Only the Terrazas rose again. Those governors who served for long periods, such as Alarcón, Reyes, and Ahumada, were trusted agents of the dictator, usually brought in from the outside with no local political base. If a governor appeared to acquire too substantial a regional following, Díaz transferred him. The dictator shrewdly played off local factions against each other, never letting one group get the upper hand. In Sonora, where politics were badly fragmented geographically, three men, including Ramón Corral, Díaz's vice-president from 1904 to 1911, shared power.[61]

The Terrazas were able to recover from the political disaster of the 1880s primarily because they dominated their region's economy as no single family anywhere else in Mexico. Alone among the great *caciques* of the nineteenth century, Luis Terrazas had the resources to fight the Porfirian juggernaut and win. Ironically, it would be the very omnipotence of the Terrazas in Chihuahua that led to their fall. Alone at the top, the Terrazas acted as a magnet for the discontent in Chihuahuan society.

3

The Economic Empire of
the Terrazas

The Terrazas built an economic empire unequaled in prerevolutionary Mexico
or nineteenth-century Latin America. In their ambition and success, they
rivaled even the great "robber barons" of the same era in the United States.
Remarkably, the Terrazas constructed their realm of land, livestock, banks,
commerce, transport, and industry amid the rubble and turmoil of war-torn
Chihuahua, while simultaneously defending themselves from a series of grave
political challenges, at a time when Latin America entered the world economy
and other Mexican and Latin American elites succumbed to the dominance of
foreign capitalists.[1] It was the Terrazas' economic dominance and their ability
to take advantage of the cattle and mining booms that underwrote their political survival.[2]

Mounting historical evidence indicates that the common image of the Latin
American elite as nonentrepreneurial, neofeudal landowners addicted to conspicuous consumption needs reevaluation.[3] The Terrazas and their contemporaries, the Maderos of Coahuila, the Molinas of Yucatán, the Garzas and
other families of Monterrey, Nuevo León, were shrewd, innovative, modern
businessmen, unafraid to invest their own money and unintimidated by ad-
vanced technology.[4] What distinguished them from their North American
counterparts was that they operated in an environment hazardous for entrepreneurial activity, for at least the first sixty years after independence.[5] The pre-
requisites of economic development—stable government, public order, cheap
transportation, capital, and markets—were lacking until the mid-1880s.[6]

The breakdown of political authority after independence left the economy
in shambles. Government invested no funds or attention on transportation and
communications. Laws and policies changed suddenly, and enforcement was
erratic. Public finances and the judicial process remained painfully outdated

and corrupt. The end of the tithe in 1831 and the attack on church landholdings by Liberal governments during the Reform era (1855–67) virtually destroyed the financial strength of the Catholic church, which had in colonial
times been the major source of credit for the elite.[7] The lack of coherent government policies and efficient financial administration and the chronic shortage of investment capital delayed the railway age in Mexico until the 1880s.[8]

The Terrazas turned these calamitous circumstances to their advantage and
then, when the Díaz dictatorship established a stable government and public
order, they expanded, diversified, and gained vast wealth. The family based
its success on its ability to use its hard-won political influence to abet and
protect its economic holdings and on its capability to obtain scarce capital
resources initially through kinship ties and connections with foreign entrepreneurs and later through control of a far-reaching banking enterprise.

Politics, Credit, and Economics

During his long tenure as governor of Chihuahua (1860–73, 1879–84, and
1903–7), Luis Terrazas used his political influence to secure extensive landholdings at low cost. In particular, he secured for himself and his family a
preferred position in acquiring expropriated church properties (the Reform
Laws forced the church to dispose of its enormous landholdings) and *terrenos
baldíos*. He used his office and its control of local police and military forces to
protect his properties from Indian raids (although with only limited success
until the 1880s) and to intimidate villagers and small landholders whose lands
his surveying companies stole (see chapter 7). By 1884 he owned over 3.5
million acres of the state's most fertile and best-watered land. As a result,
when the Mexican Central railroad, which ran between Mexico City and Paso
del Norte, opened up a market in the United States for north Mexican cattle,
the Terrazas were well situated to benefit from the ensuing boom. From 1883
to 1889, the Terrazas earned between $US 500,000 and 1 million from cattle
exports across the border.[9] While their competitors were battered by the depressions of the mid-1880s and early 1890s, the Terrazas prospered and initiated new ventures.

Luis Terrazas received financial backing from foreign capitalists and relatives. His first partner was Henrique Müller, a German immigrant, with
whom he rented and then purchased the huge Hacienda Encinillas, north of
Ciudad Chihuahua. Another German immigrant, brother-in-law Carlos Moye,
backed the general's first textile business, and the Zuloagas were partners in
early banking and textile enterprises.[10]

In this early stage, then, the Terrazas followed a traditional pattern. From
modest beginnings, Luis Terrazas rose to political power and employed his

position to acquire substantial landholdings, which provided the basis of his fortune. He also branched out into light manufacturing for local market with ventures in textiles and flour milling. The latter was an outgrowth of his agricultural pursuits, for the general grew wheat on his estates.

It soon became clear, especially in light of the unlimited opportunities that the construction of the Mexican Central promised, that the informal network that supplied capital resources for the Terrazas' first ventures would not suffice. Under the guidance of Enrique C. Creel, the family moved into banking. The Banco Minero de Chihuahua became a profit center for the family and a ready source of capital for its manifold enterprises.

In banking, as in land acquisitions, control of the state government proved crucial. As governor, Luis Terrazas fought off a concerted effort by the González administration to revoke the Banco Minero's charter. Later, when the Terrazas recaptured the governorship in 1903, their banks received the preponderance of government business, in the form of loans and deposits.[11]

From the base of banking, Creel instigated a broad-ranged diversification that led the Terrazas from their family-run regional base into national ventures and the world of the modern corporation. During the 1890s, the Terrazas took the profits from cattle and banking (there was a cattle boom from 1896 to 1904) and set up transportation and industrial enterprises. Creel made several attempts to establish North American–style trusts both in Chihuahua and nationally.[12]

The family's business interests continued to benefit from its political influence, receiving substantial tax exemptions and subsidies.[13] Control of the courts after 1903 added to the Terrazas' competitive advantage.[14] Control of the state government meant that the Terrazas could protect their ventures from competition, especially from foreigners. Any economic venture of any consequence in Chihuahua had to have the approval of the Terrazas. If a prospective enterprise competed with a family business, it received no tax breaks or subsidies and was assured of legal difficulties both from the courts and local authorities. If the projected enterprise was acceptable to the family's interests, then the investors had to pay for its cooperation. Sometimes the Terrazas received stock or commissions; other times they sold concessions or mines at above market value. Everyone paid.[15]

The privileged position of the clan's enterprises in relations with the state government not only provided a considerable competitive advantage but also gave them a crucial hedge against the exigencies of Chihuahua's boom-and-bust economy. While banks all over Mexico failed during the depression of 1907, the Banco Minero, fortified by the income from interest payments from loans to the state government and state deposits, remained profitable.[16]

The very size and diversity of the family's enterprise, like that of modern-day conglomerates, further protected them from the cyclical nature of the export economy. When cattle sales slumped because the United States Mc-Kinley tariff (1890) ended exports across the border, the Terrazas relied on the Banco Minero or on new textile ventures. Other regional elites were not as fortunate. The depression of 1907 nearly bankrupted the Madero family, whose cotton-growing and mining interests suffered from plummeting prices on the world market.[17]

Thus, the family enterprise combined both traditional and modern enterprises, changing over time in response to the changing political and economic circumstances. The Terrazas continued to acquire land right up until 1910. They continued to act as intermediaries (*compradores* or collaborators) for foreign capitalists. Even in the traditional sphere of their economic interests, the Terrazas innovated. They brought in modern irrigation and breeding techniques to their *haciendas*. Their involvement in foreign businesses grew more sophisticated; they were less likely to sell potentially productive resources outright and more apt to retain stock interest in any prospective venture that included use of their properties.

Moreover, as the number of family members multiplied, the amount of capital available for investment increased, and as the interregional and national contacts of the family, especially Enrique Creel, proliferated, the Terrazas were less likely to leave economic development, even in heavy industry, to foreigners. After the depression of 1907, the family greatly expanded its mining interests. Although some of this activity was speculative, they invested large sums in equipment and development of their mines.[18] While the Terrazas were not going to challenge the American giants like the American Smelting and Refining Company (ASARCO) that controlled Chihuahuan mining, they no longer left the industry entirely to them. Family members also were major shareholders in large industrial ventures in La Laguna and Monterrey, where there were strong native elite industrial groups who were less affected by competition from foreigners.[19]

Hence the key to the Terrazas' success, and perhaps to their downfall at the hands of the Revolution as well, was their control over both the state government (or at least strong influence over it) and the region's credit resources. That the family achieved great wealth in the state where foreign investment in nonrailroad enterprises was the highest in Mexico was no coincidence, for the Terrazas were the most adept of any regional elite in dealing with foreigners and using the opportunities presented by foreign investment to their best advantage.

Government in nineteenth-century Mexico (and Latin America) played a much more important role in the economy than it did in the United States, where regulation was virtually nonexistent in the Gilded Age. In Mexico, as a heritage from Spanish colonial rule, government customarily monitored (usually inefficiently) the most minute aspects of business. After independence, government at all levels was run erratically by transient regimes. In these circumstances it became imperative for economic entrepreneurs to ensure some degree of stability for business. The most efficient method to accomplish this was to take control of the government. Since businessmen operated for the most part on the local or regional level, these governments were the primary targets. The object was to fix the rules in your favor. The Terrazas, whose empire building illustrates well the close relationship between political endeavor and economics, were more successful at this endeavor than any other group in prerevolutionary Mexico.

But the tightness of their control eventually worked against the Terrazas. Their omnipresence in both politics and the economy shut off the possibilities for middle sectors to advance, especially during the depression of 1907. When Chihuahuans had cause to protest unfair economic or political actions by the family, there was no one to hear their protests. They had no recourse within the Terrazas system.

The Terrazas empire permeated all aspects of Chihuahuan economy and society. The family was the largest employer in the state. Nearly five times as many people worked for the Terrazas as worked for ASARCO, the second largest employer. At least 8,500 people lived and worked on the Terrazas *haciendas* (and there may have been a good deal more); the family also employed approximately 40 percent of the state's nonmining industrial work force. Altogether, more than 13,000 Chihuahuans depended on the Terrazas for their livelihood.[20] As a result, the family's operations set the standard for employer-employee relations throughout the state.

The Terrazas' flour-milling and meat-packing companies controlled a large percentage of the sales of these staples in Chihuahua. While they did not monopolize either industry, the Terrazas, with 70 percent of the state's flour sales and half of its cattle, had much to say about the prices of these commodities.[21] In Chihuahua, where wheat tortillas were as popular as those made of maize and where meat consumption was high, the Terrazas had considerable impact on the day-to-day life of the state's citizens.

The family played a predominant role in the state's transportation system and public utilities. It owned the transit systems in the three major cities, Ciudad Chihuahua, Ciudad Juárez, and Hidalgo del Parral, and supplied electricity and telephone service to the capital.[22] The family's factories supplied most of the work clothes for the state's peons and miners. Even life's small pleasures fell under the family's sway. The Terrazas had a virtual monopoly on the production of beet sugar in Chihuahua and operated the state's only brewery.

All this, added to the Terrazas' control of state government after 1903, had an enormous effect on the daily lives of Chihuahuans. When anything went wrong, the Terrazas could be blamed. Their omnipotence acted as a lightning rod for discontent.

A Kingdom of Land and Cattle

Among them, Luis Terrazas, his sons Alberto and Juan Terrazas, and son-in-law Enrique C. Creel owned more than ten million acres in Chihuahua. When we add the property of the extended family, including the Falomirs, Lujáns, Zuloagas, and others, the total exceeds fifteen million acres. On Luis Terrazas' land alone grazed more than 400,000 cattle, 100,000 sheep, and 25,000 horses. On the whole, their land was the most fertile and best watered in Chihuahua, much of it excellent pasture with thousands of acres suitable for non-irrigated and irrigated cultivation. In addition, these holdings included five hundred thousand acres of prime timberland. Almost all the land was easily accessible to railroad transportation, which enabled the family to sell its livestock and produce in the markets of Ciudad Chihuahua, Mexico City, and the United States.[23]

The family's agricultural property was concentrated in five blocks: (1) the municipalities of Casas Grandes, Galeana, and San Buenaventura in Galeana District in northwestern Chihuahua; (2) a massive tract which spread from the outskirts of Ciudad Chihuahua north to Villa Ahumada in Bravos District, east to Aldama in Iturbide District, and west to the holdings in Galeana; (3) the municipalities of Jiménez and Villa Coronado in the Allende Valley of Jiménez District in the southeastern part of the state; (4) the municipalities of Meoqui and Julimes in Camargo District, southeast of Ciudad Chihuahua; and (5) a large tract in the municipality of Ojinaga in Iturbide District, in extreme eastern Chihuahua.[24]

Outside Chihuahua, the Terrazas held several lots in Kansas, used for fattening cattle; Alberto Terrazas speculated in land in Quintana Roo; and Creel owned two large properties, the Hacienda de Peregrina, a sugar plantation in Veracruz, and the Hacienda de San Nicolás de la Torre in Querétaro.[25]

Of the extended family, the Zuloagas were the largest landowners. Their properties consisted of 1,154,000 acres due west of Ciudad Chihuahua and a 450,000-acre tract in Satevó. With smaller holdings, the Zuloaga latifundia totaled 1.75 million acres. They ranked second as cattlemen only to the Terrazas.[26]

The Falomirs owned approximately 270,000 acres southeast and east of the capital, as well as considerable urban property in Ciudad Chihuahua, Aldama, and Cusihuiriachic.[27] The Lujáns held 600,000 acres in Camargo and

Economic Empire of the Terrazas

Table 3–1
The *Haciendas* of Luis Terrazas

Name and Location	Date Acquired	Estimated Size (acres)	No. of Residents	Acres Cultivated
Aguanueva—Chihuahua, Iturbide	1867	270,294	334	2,000[a]
Rancho de Avalos y Anexos—Chihuahua, Iturbide	1865	17,712	27	
La Cañada—Chihuahua, Iturbide	1870	11,115	364	
La Carbonera—Casas Grandes, Galeana				
El Carmen—San Buenaventura, Galeana	1892	877,502	837	5,000
Encinillas—Chihuahua, Iturbide	1868	1,302,000	1,109	2,500[a]
Gallego—Villa Ahumada, Bravos			270	
Las Hormigas—Aldama, Iturbide		851,843	360	
Hinojeno—Aldama, Iturbide				
Hinojos				
La Luga—Chihuahua, Iturbide				
La Nariz—San Buenaventura, Galeana				
Quinta Carolina—Chihuahua, Iturbide	1886	49,400	243	500
Sacramento—Chihuahua, Iturbide			163	
San Diego—Casas Grandes, Galeana	188?	122,306	108	2,500
San Dionisio—Allende, Jiménez				
San Felipe—Jiménez				
San Felipe—Iturbide	1884	35,424		
San Isidro/San Ignacio—Villa Coronado, Jiménez	1907	477,400	469	
San Isidro—San Buenaventura, Galeana				
San Lorenzo—San Buenaventura, Galeana	1872	246,464	624	3,000
San Luis—San Buenaventura, Galeana	1898	826,968	266	4,000[a]
San Miguel de Bavícora—San Buenaventura, Galeana	1874	867,271	336	2,500[a]
San Pedro—Janos, Galena	1893	69,678	9	
Santa María—San Buenaventura, Galeana				
Las Sauces—Chihuahua, Iturbide				
El Sauz—Chihuahua, Iturbide			296	
Tabaloapa—Chihuahua, Iturbide			394	
Tapiecitas—Casas Grandes, Galeana	1898	191,212		
El Torreón—Chihuahua, Iturbide	1898	173,600	178	
Virginia—Camargo				

a. Irrigated land.

Hidalgo districts and much land in La Laguna in Durango, where they were leading cotton growers.[28]

It is indicative of the resourcefulness and entrepreneurship of Luis Terrazas and his family that they used diverse methods to acquire their immense landholdings. They used their political influence, their insider's position in banking, and outright coercion to amass their properties. General Terrazas purchased a dozen of his *haciendas* in private transactions with members of the Chihuahuan elite, usually for very low prices during times of Indian raids or economic depression, when the land was virtually worthless.[29] He obtained his largest *hacienda*, Encinillas, in stages over four decades. The general and partner Henrique Müller originally leased the property from Pablo Martínez del Río. They were able to purchase it from the federal government in 1866 after the Juárez administration expropriated it in retaliation for Martínez del Río's collaboration with Maximilian. Terrazas bought Müller's share from his heirs in 1905.[30]

The family acquired several large holdings through foreclosure proceedings. The most spectacular won them the Hacienda de Orientales and 1.125 million acres in four other districts that belonged to Celso González, the longtime political foe of the Terrazas.[31]

Extensive acquisitions of public land augmented the clan's private purchases and foreclosures. As partners in several surveying companies, Luis Terrazas, Juan Terrazas, and Enrique Creel procured 2.4 million acres during the 1880s. What set the Terrazas apart from others who acquired *terrenos baldíos* and *terrenos nacionales* during this period was not the extent of their acquisitions (although they were enormous) but the fact that they kept these lands. The family was not interested in the lands for speculation; they sought to make the land productive, employing their own capital and management. Other individuals and companies obtained the land and quickly resold it.[32]

The expansion of the Terrazas landholdings, as was typical for the North during the 1880s, was often at the expense of small holders and *pueblos*. Surveying companies were notorious for usurping village common lands. Between 1884 and 1886, Luis Terrazas expanded his Hacienda de San Miguel de Bavícora by invading 52,000 acres of the *ejido* (village common lands) of Cruces in the Guerrero District.[33] The Hacienda El Carmen was enlarged in the same manner at the expense of *ejidos* in Galeana.[34] In 1909, Enrique Creel, then governor of Chihuahua, tried to appropriate the lands of the *ejido* of San Carlos in Ojinaga, Iturbide District, but was met with heated protests from residents.[35] The Terrazas' expropriation of village lands in Carichic, Nonoava, and Sisoguichi in southeastern-central Chihuahua during the 1880s earned them long-standing bitterness in that area against the family,[36] and the tactics of the clan's surveying company in Balleza in 1884 caused widespread agitation among the region's Tarahumara Indians.[37]

The Terrazas landholdings were not limited to the countryside. Luis Terrazas and Enrique Creel were the largest owners of urban property (*fincas urbanas*) in Chihuahua. Each owned over a hundred lots which together produced over $M 100,000 per year in rents in 1913.[38] Ciudad Chihuahua was almost surrounded by the properties of the family, which inevitably benefited as the city expanded to meet the needs of a booming economy and population.[39]

Proceeds from the sale of cattle in the United States were the foundation of the Terrazas economic empire. Two major booms in cattle exports, from 1883 to 1889 and from 1895 to 1898, provided the basis for the family's political survival and economic diversification. The bonanza of profits from cattle exports during the 1880s, which may have reached $US 1 million, enabled the Terrazas to withstand the challenge of Porfirio Díaz and his Chihuahuan allies. While their rivals foundered in the depressions of the mid-1880s and early 1890s, the Terrazas used cattle profits to finance their offensive against the dictatorship. Luis Terrazas used another portion of these funds to buy more land. Profits from the second boom (the first ended with the passage of the McKinley tariff's high duties on imported livestock) enabled the family to merge two competing banks into the Banco Minero and start three new banks in the state. They also embarked on a diversification program. The flush of new capital encouraged Creel to try to put together North American–style trusts in Chihuahua in meat packing and flour milling. The Terrazas expanded their interests nationally at this time as well.

Labor Conditions on the Terrazas *Haciendas*

Conditions on the Terrazas *haciendas* varied according to the time period; the status of the worker—whether he was a resident, tenant, sharecropper, or temporary worker; the accessibility of the *hacienda* to the railroad and its proximity to the United States border; and the prevailing customs of the particular area (although the Terrazas, as the largest agricultural employers, often established these customs). Hard evidence on actual conditions on the Terrazas *haciendas* is fragmentary, and this remains a topic of lively debate.[40]

As they did throughout the North, wages and working conditions on the Terrazas *haciendas* improved over time in response to the area's chronic labor shortage. Although wages in the North were always better than in central or southern Mexico, substantial increases did not come until after 1900, when the demand for labor in the United States Southwest and the booming local mining industry created a severe labor shortage.[41]

A Texas businessman traveling through Chihuahua in the 1870s observed that on a *hacienda* owned by a Terrazas kin the resident *peones* "belonged" to the *hacendado*.[42] During the 1880s, *peones* on the Hacienda del Carmen were so deeply in debt as to be virtual slaves. Uncooperative workers were drafted into the army.[43]

Generally, workers on the Terrazas *haciendas* were paid and treated better than those in the center of the country. Cowboys (*vaqueros*) were the privileged group on the family's estates. Legend has it that even when General Terrazas was in his eighties, he rode with his *vaqueros* daily and actively participated in roundups.[44] *Vaqueros'* wages doubled from 1902 to 1913 because they were in high demand across the border.[45] Some *vaqueros* were permitted to graze their own cattle on *hacienda* land to supplement their incomes. They also had good prospects for upward mobility. If a *vaquero* became a foreman (*caporal*), his wages rose to thirty pesos a month.[46]

Some *vaqueros* may actually have been better off before the Revolution than afterward. In 1919 one wrote Venustiano Carranza, the president of Mexico, that rents for pasturage on the *haciendas* expropriated from the Terrazas by the revolutionary government had doubled.[47] It is indicative of their privileged position that, for the most part, *vaqueros* did not join the Revolution until 1913, when there was no other work.[48]

In Chihuahua, *haciendas* in less accessible areas and districts furthest from the United States paid the least. Wages tended to be high in Galeana and Iturbide districts, where the Terrazas had extensive landholdings.[49] The worst conditions on the Terrazas *latifundia* were on the Hacienda de San Miguel de Bavícora, at the southernmost tip of the Galeana District and overlapping into Namiquipa in Guerrero. Geographical and historical circumstances combined to produce bitter antagonism between the Terrazas and the people of the area.

During the 1880s, Luis Terrazas, who had purchased San Miguel in 1874, expanded the *hacienda* by taking land from the common lands of Cruces, a section of Namiquipa. Because the area was inaccessible and there was a shortage of labor, it is likely that the general was not able to import *peones* from elsewhere, as was sometimes the practice in such cases of expropriation.[50] Instead the *hacienda* continued to employ local workers. Bitterness festered, and the hostility between *patrón* and *pueblo* was intensified by the fierce independence of the people of the region.

The *hacendado* used coercion to maintain his interests. Since Galeana was controlled tightly by the Terrazas, they had considerable force at their disposal. The pay scale on the *hacienda* was comparable to others in the state, but various social obligations, of which marriage was the most important, sunk the peons into debt large enough to constitute a form of peonage.[51] Nelle Hatch maintains that her father was able to purchase the freedom of several *peones* from San Miguel.[52] It is also alleged that foremen on the *hacienda* exercised wedding-night rights with peons' brides.[53] As evidence of the harsh conditions, several *vaqueros* and other resident workers on San Miguel joined the Revolution in 1910.[54]

Whatever the wages on the Terrazas *haciendas*, they lagged behind those in other sectors of the economy. In 1911 forty laborers on the Hacienda Quinta Carolina complained that the fifty centavos (one hundred centavos equal one peso) they earned a day was but a third of what workers in the lumber camp at

Madera in western Chihuahua earned.[55] Higher wages were also paid on the railroad construction crews and in the mines.

The line between sharecropping or tenantry and debt peonage in Chihuahua was unclear. All the Terrazas *haciendas* in Galeana had *tiendas de raya*.[56] The stores customarily made advances in pay for *peones* to buy staples, and the *hacienda* illegally paid the workers in scrip redeemable only at the store.[57] Though not everyone was satisfied—the tenants on one Terrazas *hacienda* in Santa Eulalia complained that their rents were too high—sharecropping arrangements on the Terrazas estates were more favorable than in central or southern Mexico.[58]

Evidently, Luis Terrazas adapted his methods to the specific circumstances of each *hacienda*. When he had to offer competitive wages and benefits, he did. When he felt force was needed, he used it. The general typified the paternalistic *hacendado*, whose word was law throughout his domain and who looked upon his peons as children in need of occasional discipline.[59]

Few Terrazas peons joined the Revolution in 1910, which may indicate the relatively good conditions on their *haciendas*. One *caporal*, Nicolas Fernández, became one of Pancho Villa's most famous lieutenants. Had he administered a harsh regimen, he would never have found acceptance as a revolutionary leader. (Villa indeed would have shot him.)[60]

Banking

After 1900, the Terrazas virtually monopolized banking in Chihuahua. The family owned the state's largest bank, the Banco Minero de Chihuahua, and two smaller banks and managed the Ciudad Chihuahua branch of the Banco Nacional de México, the nation's largest financial institution. Their banking interests extended to Mexico City, La Laguna, Monterrey, Guanajuato, Sonora, and the United States. In 1910 the total assets of the banks in which they had substantial interest exceeded $M 200 million, approximately 20 percent of Mexico's total bank assets.

The Banco Minero, Mexico's fourth largest bank and second largest outside Mexico City, was the base of the family's banking empire.[61] Five partners, Luis Terrazas, Enrique Creel, Pedro Zuloaga, Inocente Ochoa, and Mariano Samaniego, founded the bank in 1882.[62] The Banco Minero grew steadily over the next two decades, absorbing three other state banks, the Banco de Hidalgo del Parral (1885), the Banco Mexicano (1895), and the Banco Comercial de Chihuahua (1900).[63]

Under Creel's management, the Banco Minero increased its capital prudently and grew extremely profitable. In twenty-eight years the bank's assets rose from $M 152,000 to $M 23.2 million. From 1883 to 1905 it distributed

$M 5,567,270 in profits to its shareholders. Bank profits remained high even in 1907 and 1908 amid a severe depression (see Table 3-2).[64]

Enrique C. Creel, his brother Juan, Joaquín Cortazar, and other family members founded the second large Terrazas bank in the state, the Banco Comercial Refaccionario, in 1903. With $M 2.5 million in assets, it ranked among the largest and fastest-growing banks of this type in the country in 1910.[65] Creel also set up the Caja de Ahorros de la República Mexicana in 1903. This bank was considerably smaller than the other two Terrazas banks in Chihuahua, but it was very profitable and, like the Banco Comercial, was a training ground for younger members of the clan. The Terrazas established the state's Monte de Piedad in 1895 "to end the enormous usury charges now gotten by pawnbrokers in the city [Chihuahua]."[66] Luis Terrazas' son-in-law Federico Sisniega managed the Chihuahua branch of the Banco Nacional from 1885 to 1909, completing the family's control over the state's major credit institutions.[67]

Banking linked the Terrazas with other regional elites, particularly in La Laguna and Monterrey and the inner circle in Mexico City. Juan Terrazas was a stockholder and director of the Banco de la Laguna Refaccionario and the Investment Discount Company of Torreón, both of which were operated by Laguna industrialists led by the Madero family. The Banco de la Laguna was one of the nation's largest banks, with assets of $M 13 million in 1911.[68] And Enrique Creel was president of the Banco Mercantil of Cananea, which provided the Terrazas connections with the Sonoran elite. He also served on the board of the Banco Mercantil de Monterrey.[69]

Creel was the family's link to Mexico City financial circles. He established two banks in the capital, the Banco Central Mexicano and the Banco Hipotecario de Crédito Territorial Mexicano, S.A. Founded with heavy investment from the French community in Mexico City and several large foreign banking houses, the Banco Central was the country's second largest bank in 1910, with $M 90 million in assets.[70] The Banco Hipotecario had $M 38 million in assets in 1910.[71]

As they had in acquiring their large landholdings, the Terrazas used their political power to protect and expand their banking interests. Through the naked use of his political power, Luis Terrazas retained his first two banking concessions, the Banco Mexicano in 1878 and the Banco Minero in 1882, despite the federal bank reform of 1883. While governor in 1883 and 1884, the general prevented the application of the new national commercial code, which transferred jurisdiction over banking from the states to the national government, in effect canceling the charters of the Terrazas banks. Díaz permitted the Terrazas to keep the banks most probably in an attempt to buy peace in Chihuahua.[72]

Political influence also assured that none of the Terrazas banks was taxed

Table 3–2

The Banco Minero de Chihuahua

Year	Capital	Assets	Outstanding Loans	Net Profits
1883	$ 100,000	152,389	$ 20,336	
1887	250,000	1,351,450		
1888	450,000	1,608,398		$930,821
1889	500,000	—		distributed
1890	600,000	1,749,932		profits
1891				1883–96
1892	700,000	1,565,562		
1893				
1894				
1895	1,500,000[a]	2,857,876		
1896		4,323,603	1,696,758	
1897	1,500,000	4,591,186[c]	1,419,379[c]	
1898	1,500,000	6,229,800	2,797,904	
1899	1,500,000	6,975,895	3,198,373	
1900	4,000,000[b]	7,073,286	2,244,611	
1901	4,000,000	10,023,437	2,727,177	
1902	4,000,000	11,747,703	3,954,376	
1903	5,000,000	14,672,553	5,123,038	
1904	5,000,000	15,216,455	5,424,893	
1905	5,000,000	15,237,176	5,337,521	707,235
1906	5,000,000	18,708,529	7,902,620	719,900
1907	5,000,000	19,362,063	8,062,707	550,000
1908	5,000,000	18,524,599	5,700,421	620,000
1909	5,000,000	18,434,433	8,516,258	375,000+
1910	5,000,000	25,038,342	8,803,948	
1911	5,000,000	23,181,172	4,673,883	

Sources: Banco Minero de Chihuahua, Consejo de Administración, *Informes* del Consejo de Administración y Comisario a la Asamblea General de Acionistas de 28 de marzo de 1908, p. 13; U.S., Department of Commerce and Labor, Bureau of Manufactures, *Commercial Relations of the United States with Foreign Countries during the Year 1904*, pp. 502–3; Mexico, Secretaría de Estado y del Despacho de Hacienda y Crédito Público, *Boletín de Estadísticas Fiscal*, no. 336 (1910–11): 248–49, 264–65; *Mexican Financier*, 18 January 1896, p. 415, 15 November 1890, p. 189, and 16 February 1889, p. 494; *El Clarín del Norte*, 16 June 1906, p. 5; *Bankers' Magazine* 80 (1910): 793, 309, and 84 (January 1912): 83; *Mexican Herald*, 5 January 1909, p. 9; *Revista de Chihuahua*, January 1896, pp. 378–79; Walter U. Falla, "A Study of Economic Development Banking in Mexico during the Victorian Age, 1857–1910," p. 374; Frank A. Waring, "A History of Mexican Banking" (Ph.D. dissertation, University of California, 1932), p. 54.
a. Year of merger with the Banco Mexicano with capital of $750,000.
b. Merger with the Banco Commercial de Chihuahua with capital of $600,000.
c. From 1897 to 1911, the statistics for assets and outstanding loans are for the fiscal year ending 30 June.

Table 3-3
The Debt of the State of Chihuahua to Terrazas Banks

Bank	Year	Amount (pesos)
Banco Minero de Chihuahua	1903[a]	15,800.72
	1908[b]	118,424.94
	1909[c]	497,628.51
	1910[d]	497,628.51
	1911[e]	567,584.95
	1912[e]	613,967.17
Banco Nacional de México	1903[a]	104,738.93
	1908[b]	300,000.00
	1909[c]	26,133.00
	1910[d]	26,133.00
	1911[e]	96,406.30
	1912[e]	101,875.00
Banco Central Mexicano	1908[b]	210,000.00
Banco de la Laguna	1908[b]	100,000.00

Sources: (a.) *El Correo de Chihuahua*, 3 June 1903, p. 2. (b.) Chihuahua, Tesorería General, *Presupuestos de Egresos para el Ejercicio Fiscal de 1907 a 1908* (Chihuahua, 1907), and Chihuahua, Secretaría de Gobierno, Sección Estadística, *Anuario Estadística del Estado de Chihuahua, 1908*. (c.) Chihuahua, *Anuario, 1909*, p. 205. (d.) *El Periódico Oficial del Estado de Chihuahua*, 17 July 1910, p. 10. (e.) Francisco R. Almada, *Vida, Proceso, y Muerte de Abraham González*, pp. 195-96.

by the state government. When Luis Terrazas became governor in 1903, he shifted all state business to the Banco Minero. Most important, from early on, the Terrazas obtained the lion's share of the lucrative business of loaning money to the state. During the 1890s, family banks held more than half the state's debt. When Terrazas and Creel, as governors from 1903 to 1910, undertook a massive program of public works, financed by heavy public borrowing, the family's banks lent Chihuahua more than one million pesos (see Table 3-3).[73] Interest income from these loans enabled the Terrazas banks to withstand the depression of 1907 to 1909.

Just as the Terrazas used their political power to strengthen their control over banking, so they used their control over banking to further their own business and political interests. The clan's banks financed several family enterprises. The largest loan to a family business was made by the Banco Minero to the Compañía Eléctrica y Ferrocarriles de Chihuahua for $M 600,000 in 1911.[74] Family members also received extensive unsecured personal credit (which was illegal).

Loans were also used to gain the cooperation of subregional political bosses. Several *jefes políticos* were deeply indebted to Terrazas banks. (More often than not the banks had to write off these loans.) Credit was a reward for long-time political henchmen as well. During the 1890s, the Banco Minero bailed many *hacendados* out of severe economic straits, which may have in part accounted for the Terrazas' ability to stage their political comeback.[75] As we have seen, the family even lent money to its political opponents.

In these characteristics, the Terrazas banks differed little from other banks in Mexico, which were notorious for granting loans to insiders and hiring (often incompetent) family for management. The Banco de Campeche, for example, lent 75 percent of its assets to its president.[76] Unlike the big banks in Mexico City, including those organized by Creel, the Terrazas' state banks were native owned and operated. Like the banking groups in La Laguna and Monterrey, the Terrazas welcomed foreigners as investors, but the family held majority control.[77] Typically for underdeveloped nations, a substantial portion of the Terrazas banks' venture capital was lent to foreign firms in the export sector. During the 1880s and 1890s, the Banco Minero loaned large sums to big foreign mining companies, like the Batopilas Mining Company, to which it lent $M 225,000 from 1892 to 1894.[78] One newspaper attributed to the bank the increase in silver production in Chihuahua.[79] Another Terrazas bank, the Guaranty Trust of El Paso, Texas, was a major creditor of William C. Greene's enormous lumber enterprise, the Sierra Madre Land and Lumber Company.[80]

While solidifying the family's political power and furthering its business interests, the Terrazas' virtual monopoly on credit in Chihuahua had the long-term effect of alienating the expanding middle sectors of Chihuahuan society. Control of credit was bitterly resented by small businessmen and ranchers, especially during the depression of 1907, when capital was scarce and many of these enterprises failed from lack of funds. Finally, the furor over the Banco Minero robbery in 1908 brought to a head Chihuahuans' resentment of the family's banking policies.

On 1 March 1908, the bank discovered a shortfall of $M 300,000. Officers of the bank claimed that it had been robbed. In searching for the culprits, the local and state governments, operating much of the time under the personal supervision of Governor Creel, openly abused the rights of a string of suspects (to an extent offensive even in Chihuahua). Several men and women were unjustly imprisoned for months and separated from their children, who became destitute. Rumors surfaced that there had been no robbery at all and that the affair had been made up to cover the embezzlement of one of the bank officers, Juan A. Creel. For many months the robbery dominated the head-lines of the state's newspapers. The muckraking *El Correo de Chihuahua* sold out every issue. The Terrazas' *El Norte* insistently defended the family's actions. When *El Correo* began to raise money for the indigent families of imprisoned suspects, donations poured in from all over the state. The money came in small sums, usually less than a peso. Mutualist societies with predominantly working- and middle-class memberships took an active and visible role in fund-raising, and petitions signed by hundreds of Chihuahuans eventually forced the government to provide the accused with defense counsel. The original suspects were freed, but others took their places in equally trumped-up circumstances. Months after the robbery was discovered, *El Correo* declared that liberty and justice in Chihuahua were a fiasco.[81] Clearly, the affair had aroused the Chihuahuan people. Years of bitterness against the system of privilege surfaced in a storm of protest. In this instance, the culprits were obvious: the mighty Terrazas.

Food Processing

The Terrazas were Chihuahua's largest meat packers, flour millers, beer brewers, and sugar beet refiners. Meat packing was an outgrowth of their cattle interests. Luis Terrazas had begun his career as a butcher in Ciudad Chihuahua in the 1850s. During the cattle boom of the 1890s, the family invested heavily in new facilities and formed the Compañía Empacadora "La Internacional," which they tried to develop into a "trust." In 1902 the company expanded nationally, obtaining a contract to run the stockyard complex in Mexico City. During the depression of 1907 to 1909, the family had to sell off much of their meat-packing operation, but its company remained the largest in Chihuahua.[82] Despite the setbacks caused by the depression, the Terrazas maintained a vertically integrated enterprise with ranches, stockyards, meat packing, cattle brokering, and feed lots.[83]

Luis Terrazas and his brother-in-law Carlos Moye established the state's first flour mill in 1874. In 1900, Enrique Creel and Federico Sisniega organized the Compañía Hariñera de Chihuahua, the Chihuahuan flour trust. The firm's three mills supplied almost all the flour for the market in Ciudad Chihuahua, and 70 percent of the supply for Chihuahua as a whole.[84] The family also owned the state's only brewery, the Compañía Cervecería de Chihuahua.[85]

Manufactures

The Terrazas' earliest and most extensive manufacturing interests were in textiles and cheap clothing. By 1910 the family was supplying most of the cheap work clothes and textiles in the state. The general and several partners founded the Fábrica de Hilados y Tejidos de Llana (textiles and wool yarn) "La Concordia" in 1890. In two decades the company's capital rose tenfold and the number of workers 250 percent. In 1898 the firm built a branch factory in Ciudad Camargo (Santa Rosalía) to produce cotton fabric. In their heyday the factories employed over three hundred workers and represented a capitalization of one million pesos.[86] Sisniega founded two other textile operations, the Compañía Industrial y Agrícola de "Bellavista" in 1873 and the Fábrica de Ropa (clothes) "La Paz" in 1892, both of which later set up subsidiaries in Mexico City.[87] Sisniega was a major stockholder in a large mill in Guadalajara; Enrique Creel purchased an enormous textile complex in Durango in 1909.[88]

Table 3–4
The Enterprises of the Terrazas Family

Family Member(s)	Date Founded	Capital (Pesos)	Description and Comments
Cía. Empacadora "La Internacional"	E. C. Creel	1898		Meat packing
Cía. de Rastros de la Cuidad de México				Subsidiary of La Internacional; sold to Mexican National Packing Co. in 1908; Meat packing
Cía. de Rastros de Torreón y Parral				Stockyards
Cía. Hariñera de Chihuahua		1900		Sales of $700,000; three mills: Ciudad Camargo, Jiménez, Ciudad Chihuahua; Flour milling
Molinero de Villa Ahumada				Sales of $18,000 per year; Flour milling
Fábrica de Galletas "La Estrella"		1904		Sold in 1910; crackers
Cía. Cervecería de Chihuahua		1896		Sales of $80,000 in 1909; brewery

Table 3–4 (continued)

	Family Member(s)	Date Founded	Capital (Pesos)	Description and Comments
"La Industrial"	Luis Terrazas	1871		Purchased from Carlos Moye; Textiles
Fábrica de Hilados y Tejidos de Llana "La Concordia"		1890	500,000	Textiles
Fábrica del Río Florido		1898	500,000	Subsidiary of La Concordia in Santa Rosalía (Cd. Camargo); clothing
Cía. Industrial y Agrícola de "Bellavista"	Federico Sisniega	1873		Clothing, textiles
Fábrica de Ropa "La Paz," S.A.	Federico Sisniega	1892	500,000	Subsidiary in Mexico City in 1900; clothing
Covadonga	Federico Sisniega			Guadalajara; textiles
La Amistad	E. C. Creel			Cotton mills; Gómez Palacio, Dur.
Cía. Industrial Mexicana	E. C. Creel	1897		Metal foundry
Chihuahua Mill and Lumber Company	Juan A. Creel			Sold to W. C. Greene
National Mill and Lumber Co.	Juan A. Creel			Sold to W. C. Greene
Chihuahua Powder Co.	Juan A. Creel, V.P.			Blasting powder; with Anderson and Scobell
Copper Sulphate and Iron Factory	Juan A. Creel	1903		$100,000 invested
Broom Factory	Juan A. Creel	1906		
Ladrillero "Hercules"	Juan A. Creel	1900		Inactive; bricks
Fábrica de Zarapes "La Unión"	Luis Terrazas			
Fábrica de Zapatos "Tequias"	Manuel L. Luján		50,000	

Economic Empire of the Terrazas

Table 3–4 (continued)

	Family Member(s)	Date Founded	Capital (Pesos)	Description and Comments
La Industrial Fronteriza	Guillermo Muñoz			Sold to García Acosta for $50,000, 1904; pasta
Ice Factory	E. C. Creel, Juan Terrazas, F. Sisniega	1900	50,000	
Vidriera Monterrey, S.A.	Juan Terrazas	1908	1,200,000	With Juan Brittingham; initially failure; glass, bottles
Fábrica Cementos Hidalgo	Juan Terrazas		750,000	With Brittingham; San Nicolás Hidalgo, N.L.
Cía. Industrial Jabonera de la Laguna, S.A.	Juan Terrazas	1903		Madero family and other Laguna industrialists, four factories—one in Chihuahua; Soap
Fábrica de Azúcar de Betabel	Luis Terrazas, Jr.	1898		Beet sugar
Guayule	Guillermo Muñoz, Salvador Madero	1904	50,000	Hacienda de Hormigas
Rail Factory	E. C. Creel, Joaquín Cortazar	1902		
Starch Factory	Francisco Molinar, Manuel Prieto	1904		
Cía. de Constructora de Fincas de Gómez Palacio	Francisco C. Terrazas			Low-cost housing
"Tivolí"	Juan A. Creel	1910		Restaurants, cantinas
Race Track	Alberto Terrazas	1909	400,000	Ciudad Juárez; with Jack Follansbee, mgr. of Hearst Estate
Sociedad Constructora Chihuahuense, S.A.	R. F. Luján			With R. L. O'Neill and Otto Kuck; houses sold on installment plan

Table 3–4 (continued)

	Family Member(s)	Date Founded	Capital (Pesos)	Description and Comments
Fuel wood	Juan A. Creel	1903		San Andrés
Sociedad Colectiva Mercantil	Guillermo F. Terrazas, Luis F. Robinson			Fodder, feed, other merchandise
Commission House	Jesús L. Terrazas	1907		
Merchant House	Juan Terrazas	1882		Branches: ASARCO Smelter at Avalos, Cd. Chihuahua, Santa Eulalia
"La Universal" Cía. Mutualista de Negocios y Comisiones	Luis Terrazas, Jr.			
Dry Goods Store	Julio Laguette			
Imports, Commission Agent	Guillermo C. Moye			
Cía. Telefónica de Chihuahua	E. C. Creel	1884		
Chihuahua al Pacífico (Ferrocarril)	E. C. Creel	1898		Leased to KCM&O RR; 1903
Ferrocarril Mineral de Chihuahua	E. C. Creel	1898		Merged with Planta Eléctrica of the Cía. Industrial Mexicana 1907
Cía. Tranvías de Chihuahua				Merged with Planta Eléctrica above 1907
Cía. Eléctrica y de Ferrocarriles de Chihuahua		1908		Formed by merger of two above and Planta Eléctrica 1907
Cía. Tranvías de Ciudad Juárez	E. C. Creel			Urban transit
Cía. Tranvías de Hidalgo de Parral	E. C. Creel, Juan Creel, and Manuel L. Luján			Urban transit

Table 3–4 (continued)

	Family Member(s)	Date Founded	Capital (Pesos)	Description and Comments
Cía. de Navegación y Mejoras del Valle y Río Balsas	Luis Terrazas, Jr.	1910		Michoacán
Cía. de Seguros "La Mexicana"		1887		
Cía. de Seguros "La Equidad"			200,000	Life insurance
Cía. Anónima "La Protectora"	J. A. Creel, E. C. Creel, etc.		200,000	Fire insurance

Clan members also engaged in a wide variety of other manufacturing enterprises. The most important was the Compañía Industrial Mexicana. One of the largest native-owned metal foundries in Mexico, it specialized in custom-made equipment for the mining industry, competing successfully for many contracts with both native and foreign mining companies.[89]

Juan Creel invested in a series of small manufacturing enterprises with mixed results. At various times after 1900, he owned shares in two lumber companies, a copper sulfate factory, a broom factory, and a brick factory. He was also vice-president of the Chihuahua Powder Company, which produced blasting powder.[90] Other younger members of the family, such as Luis Terrazas, Jr., Guillermo Muñoz, and Salvador Madero, formed companies to exploit guayule, manufacture zarapes, and produce shoes; still other family members owned a cement factory, a rail factory, an ice plant, a mineral water plant, a gas factory, and a starch factory.[91]

Along with their joint banking ventures, the Terrazas and the Monterrey group were partners in industrial enterprises. Juan Terrazas was a major shareholder in the Fábrica de Cementos Hidalgo, a cement company in Nuevo León, and the Fábrica de Vidrios (glass) de Monterrey, which initially made beer bottles for the Monterrey brewery.[92] With La Laguna entrepreneurs, Juan Terrazas was a principal in the Compañía Industrial Jabonera de la Laguna, a soap manufacturer with plants throughout the North.[93]

Transportation and Utilities

The urban transit lines of the state's three largest cities, as well as its major feeder and connector railroad lines, were either owned or partly managed by the Terrazas. Enrique Creel set up the Chihuahua al Pacífico to construct an east-west railroad network across the state and the Ferrocarril Mineral de Chihuahua to connect the major mining center at Santa Eulalia to the main line of the Mexican Central. The Chihuahua al Pacífico merged with the Kansas City, Mexico, and Orient Railway (KCM&O) in 1900. Creel became vice-president of the KCM&O. Creel was also vice-president of another east-west line, the Mexican Northwestern Railway, and a highly paid board member of the Mexican Central.[94]

The family also had transport interests outside Chihuahua. Creel was a consultant to the Ferrocarriles Sudorientales de Yucatán, and Luis Terrazas, Jr., was president of the Compañía de Navegación y Mejorar del Valle y Río Balsas, which was to build a railroad and furnish river transportation in Michoacán.[95]

Through their ownership of the Compañía Telefónica de Chihuahua and the Compañía Eléctrica y de Ferrocarriles de Chihuahua, the Terrazas supplied the essential utilities to the state capital. The family was also involved in two hydroelectric projects, which they sold before completion.[96]

Retail and Miscellaneous Enterprises

The clan was active in an array of retail, commercial, construction, financial, and entertainment businesses. Juan Terrazas ran a store in Ciudad Chihuahua for nearly three decades. He also operated the company store at the Avalos smelter owned by ASARCO.[97] Several other family members owned stores. The clan had two large construction projects in Gómez Palacio, Durango and Ciudad Chihuahua. The latter aimed to sell low-cost housing to workers on the installment plan.[98] And it had major interests in two life insurance companies, the Compañía de Seguros "La Mexicana" and the Compañía de Seguros "La Equidad," and owned a fire insurance firm, the Compañía Anónima "La Protectora."[99] Its most ostentatious projects were a racetrack in Ciudad Juárez and a restaurant-bar complex in Nombre de Díos, a suburb of Ciudad Chihuahua.[100]

Mining and Smelting

Between 1880 and 1910, the Terrazas invested in a large number of highly profitable mining ventures. Generally, they employed foreigners as managers or rented out their properties or sold them outright. Rarely did the family manage the day-to-day operations of its mining concerns. The case of the Río

Tinto mines at Terrazas Station just north of Ciudad Chihuahua is illustrative. Enrique Creel bought the mines in the 1890s, initially leasing them to an American firm for a large lump sum and a guaranteed annual royalty. This arrangement terminated in 1897 or 1898. Three years later, Creel added several new mines and organized the Compañía Río Tinto Mexicana, 25 percent owned by an American company. Creel sold the properties in 1907, but the buyer defaulted. The next year, he sold the properties to Corrigan, McKinney, and Company, a large United States firm. During the course of his ownership, Creel received almost $US 400,000 from three different sales.[101]

The Terrazas were so successful in selling mining property for large sums to foreign companies that one suspects the high purchase prices were a payoff for services rendered. Creel, for example, sold two mines to William C. Greene for $US 800,000, while as governor he granted Greene a huge concession for mines and timber in western Chihuahua.[102]

After the depression ended in 1909, the Terrazas sharply increased their investment in mines, partly because there were many bargains and partly because the family had to expand its economic activities to sustain its ever-growing number of dependents.

The family was quick to become involved in the potentially lucrative oil industry. Alberto Terrazas was vice-president of the International Oil and Gas Company, an American firm set up to explore in southern and eastern Chihuahua. Enrique Creel explored for petroleum on the Hacienda de Orientales. He was a major shareholder in the Compañía Petrolera del Pacífico and president of the Aguila Oil Company, one of the nation's biggest oil companies.[103] They also invested in smelting as speculation, taking in large profits by selling concessions to foreign firms.[104]

Industrial Working Conditions

As they did their agricultural work force, the Terrazas generally paid their industrial employees better than the prevailing rate in Mexico as a whole and on par with what was customary in Chihuahua. There is, nonetheless, evidence that conditions were poor and workers mistreated in Terrazas factories, where discontent burst forth in 1911 after the victory of the Madero revolution. In July 1911 employees of the transit line in Ciudad Chihuahua struck for higher wages and demanded the resignation of manager Martín Falomir.[105] Workers at three family-owned textile factories also struck in July, demanding a shorter work day and better wages and at one factory seeking to oust the manager.[106]

Wages in Terrazas textile factories rose between 1893 and 1907 by from 33 to 133 percent. But during the depression the factories reduced wages sharply.[107]

Capitalists, Caciques, and Revolution

Table 3-5
The Mining Ventures of the Terrazas

Mine or Company	Location	Family Member(s)	Information
Abundancia mine			1911 option to Fr. synd.
Alvarado Consolidated Mg. Co.	Parral	J. A. Creel	1908 La Palmilla
La Alianza	Iturbide	Alberto Terrazas	1910
Los Angeles	Aldama	Manuel L. Luján	
Buen Pastor mine		Alberto Terrazas	
Calamine Mg. Co.	Los Lamentos	Luis Terrazas	
Cía. Carbonífera del Norte de Chihuahua	Iturbide	E. Creel, F. Sisniega Manuel Prieto	Capital, $24,000
Cía. Carbonífera de Monterrey		Enrique Creel	1902, cap. $2 million
Cía. Minera Carolina de Naica		R. F. and M. L. Luján	
Cerro Colorado		M. Luján	Amer. co. operated
Cinco Amigos Mg. Co.	Los Lamentos	Luis Terrazas, Jr.	1907, cap. $25,000
La Concepción	Sta. Eulalia	Luis Terrazas	sold 1903, $40,000 pesos
Cía. Corregidora y Anexas	Cusih.	Carlos Cuilty	1903
Cuperiachic	Guerrero	J. Cortazar	
Dos Cabezas mine	N. Casas G.	Juan Terrazas	J. T. purch., $70,000
Cía. Min. Evangelina y Anexas, S.A.	B. Juárez	Abraham Luján	
Florencia mine	Sta. Eulalia	Enrique Creel	1908 sold to foreign
Cía. Min. Gibraltar y Anexas de Naica		J. A. Creel	
Gibraltar	Naica	J. A. Creel	Big strike 1910, lead
Guadalupe mine	Parral	A. and L. Terrazas, Jr.	Sold to U.S. co., $300,000
Hacienda de Santa Rosa	Morelos	E. C. Creel	
Julieta mine		Luján	
Cía. Min. Los Lamentos	Montezuma	L. T., F. Molinar	
Cía. Beneficiadora del Magistral, S.A.	Magistral	J. A. Creel, Eduardo C. Cuilty, J. Cortazar	Liquidated 1907
La Mascota	Aldama	Luis Terrazas, Jr.	zinc
Las Mercedes			sold to Chih. Mg. Co., $100,000
Mexican Mines Corp.	Sierra Almoloya	Alberto Terrazas	N.Y., $3.5 million cap.
Cía. Min. de Naica	Naica	E. C. C., J. Cortazar	E.C.C. interest 1904
Propagadora	Nombre de Dios	Luis R. Creel	1909
Cía. Min. El Refugio		J. A. Creel	

Table 3–5 (continued)

Mine or Company	Location	Family Member(s)	Information
Río Tinto Mexicano		E. C. Creel	Copper
San Andrés mine	Sta. Eulalia	E. C. Creel	
San Carlos de Ojinaga		E. C. C., A. Terrazas	Iron, manganese
San Pedro mine		Alberto Terrazas	1910
Soledad mine			
San Salvador Mg. Co.	Terrazas	Alberto Terrazas	sold for $100,000
Santa Bárbara mine	Guazapares	J. Cortazar	sold to Rio Plata Co.
Santa Eduviges		E. C. Creel	sold to W. C. Greene
Santa María mine	Aldama	Luis Terrazas	
Cía. Min. Santa Rita	Chorreras	Alberto Terrazas	
Santa Juliana	Ocampo		sold to W. C. Greene
Cía. Ben. de	Ocampo		sold to Amer. co. 1908
Sahuayacan			
Cía. Sensitiva de Naica		R. F. & M. L. Luján	1904, cap. $40,800
Centro de Tarahumara		L. Terrazas, Jr.	lead, silver
Tres Amigos Mg. Co.,		Luis Terrazas	
S.A.			
Las Tres Mercedes	Sta. Eulalia	E. C. Creel	1895, sold 1904
Cía. Min. La Virgen,	Aldama	L. T. Jr., M. Falomir	1910
S.A.			
Yoquivo gold mine		E. C. Creel	
Cía. Min. Emilio Zola		Abraham Luján, Z. &	Reorg. of Naica cos.
y Anexas		M. L. Luján	
Cía. Min. de Zolar,	Naica	M. L. Luján	
S.A.			

As in the more famous mills in the state of Puebla, the Terrazas significantly reduced the number of employees at their textile mills, especially the older mills, as they introduced new machinery.[108] At the Compañía Industrial Mexicana the depression and modernization cut into the labor force too, although the company was one of the few in Mexico that trained Mexicans in technical skills to replace foreigners.[109]

The Terrazas ran their factories in the same paternalistic manner they ran their *haciendas*. When ninety laborers at one of their textile factories asked for higher pay in the 1880s, they closed the factory. At Bellavista, where the workers were evidently more cooperative, Federico Sisniega built homes for his employees, subsidized the local school, and donated improvements to the local park.[110] In 1902, *El Correo*, later critical of the Terrazas, praised working conditions at another factory (La Paz).[111]

A Comparative View

The Terrazas' control over the local economy and the range and diversity of their enterprise had no parallels in prerevolutionary Mexico. Their closest rival was probably the Molina-Montes clan of Yucatán, which controlled the henequén trade of the peninsula in conjunction with the International Harvester Company. The family patriarch, Olegario Molina, like Luis Terrazas (and later Enrique Creel), exerted enormous political and economic power as governor of Yucatán from 1902 to 1911 and minister of development in the national cabinet. Molina too used his office to further his economic interests, especially to acquire substantial landholdings. He too had a son-in-law of considerable ability, the Spaniard Avelino Montes, who acted as second-in-command. The Molinas too branched out from their original base, a merchant house, into banks and railroads. The Molinas' two banks, the Banco Yucateco and the Banco Mercantil de Yucatán, together were bigger than the Banco Minero. But they suffered drastically from the depression of 1907, while the Banco Minero prospered. The Molina landholdings, while large, did not approach those of the Terrazas. Although the Molina-Montes were undoubtedly the most powerful family in Yucatán, and in some respects clearly rivaled the Terrazas, they could not match the vast scope of the Terrazas empire or its impact on the everyday lives of residents of their region.[112]

The entrepreneurial elite of Monterrey paralleled Terrazas' independence from foreign capitalists and even surpassed their involvement in capital-intensive heavy industry with large investments in foundries, smelters, and factories. Foreigners, however, had not flooded into Monterrey as they had into Chihuahua after the completion of the main north-south railroads during the 1880s. Like that of the Molinas, much of the capital of the Monterrey elite originated in commerce. Like the Molinas, too, the Monterrey elite was tied closely to the export economy. Its opportunities depended on foreign investment in mining and smelting and transportation. Monterrey's giant smelters—one owned by the Guggenheims, one by natives, and one a mixed venture—relied on world market demand for minerals. The diversity of the Monterrey group's interests, however, protected it from the boom-and-bust cycles of the economy as was the case of the Terrazas. Because the Monterrey elite did not participate as overtly in politics as did the Terrazas and their power was more diffused, they survived the Revolution almost unscathed, while the Terrazas suffered heavy losses.[113]

In Sonora, where American investment in mining actually surpassed that in Chihuahua, because of geographic rivalries no one family gained the economic or political power of the Terrazas. The triumvirate that ruled Sonora—Izábal, Torres, and Corral—never established a similar dominance or homogeneity among the Sonoran elite. Unlike in Chihuahua, where the capital city of Ciudad Juárez dominated the rest of the state, in Sonora several urban centers were evenly matched, so that economic power was more fragmented and conflicts arose more readily. *Hacendados* and mine owners, for example, fought bitterly over labor policy.[114]

In Coahuila there were several highly successful entrepreneurial families; the best-known among them were the Maderos. These families, primarily from La Laguna region, had large textile, soap, and smelting operations. The Maderos, of course, owned the largest native-run smelter in Mexico during the *Porfiriato*. Although they owned or had a share in several banks, the Maderos' credit resources were not as extensive as those of the Terrazas. Moreover, the Maderos were vulnerable to any decline in world demand for cotton, guayule, or minerals, and the 1907 depression left them with a severe shortage of capital. After the mid-1880s, Díaz excluded the Maderos from Coahuilan political power, although they retained close ties to the Limantour family.[115]

There were many families with extensive landholdings and manufacturing interests based in Mexico City. In the Landa y Escandón clan, for example, one family member was president of the Aguila Oil Company, and the family owned extensive stockholdings in major mining companies and railroads. They were, however, a more traditional Latin American elite, for they acted primarily as intermediaries for foreigners. They were close associates of Lord Cowdray, the British tycoon with substantial investments in Mexico. Guillermo Landa y Escandón was governor of the Federal District, and the family was very influential in the capital. Typical of the Mexico City elite, the Escandóns traded on their family position and influence rather than entrepreneurial daring.[116]

The elite of the northern states, particularly the Terrazas family, the Laguna group, and Monterrey entrepreneurs, formed partnerships in banking, textiles, and manufacturing. In some cases, as with the Terrazas and Maderos, there was intermarriage. The northerners, furthermore, after the turn of the century, became actively involved in ventures with the Mexico City elite.

All the groups worked with foreigners, though the Monterrey and Sonoran elites somewhat less so. As we shall see in chapter 5, the relations between foreigners and the native elite varied considerably according to the particular time period and circumstances.

Thus various state elites could match the power of the Terrazas in particular categories, but only the Terrazas incorporated all the different characteristics of nineteenth-century Mexican entrepreneurship: local political control, national political influence, large landholdings, representation of foreign investors, light manufacturing, and venture capital in heavy industry. Not surprisingly, it was against the Terrazas that the Revolution erupted.

Scarcity of capital and technology dictated that in most instances the native elite in Latin America had by 1900 (or certainly by 1914) lost control of the region's major mineral exports and the processing aspects of the agricultural exports. The guano trade in Peru was an exception, because the government took over its extraction and trade.[117] In sugar-producing countries processing, but not refining, remained in the hands of natives. National elites were left to develop only light industry and services. Banking, too, was dominated by foreign capitalists until most Latin American governments established central banks. The classic cases were in Chile, where the British took over the nitrate industry and the Americans copper mining, and Argentina, where first the British and then the Americans came to control the meat-packing industry.[118]

In Chihuahua the economy was divided into dual spheres, foreign and native, until 1907, when the Terrazas moved tentatively into mining. The difference between Chihuahua and these other areas was that there were actually two export sectors, mining, controlled by foreigners, and cattle, controlled by the native elite. Except for minor incursions, each shied away from the other's "turf." The Terrazas dominated their own export sector, cattle. Unlike the Argentines, they ran a vertically integrated operation from breeding to meat packing.[119] Moreover, unlike other exporters, for example, Brazilian coffee growers (until the government rescued them through valorization in the twentieth century), they could withhold their exports from the market when demand and prices fell.[120] Their vast ranges could have supported even more livestock than they had. When cattle exports declined, the family's diversified enterprises took up the slack.

Despite the enormous economic power and impact of the Terrazas, they were responsible for neither dynamism nor the prosperity of the Chihuahuan economy after 1880. Rather, foreign investment in transportation and mining spurred the rapid expansion of the state's economy. As it had been for centuries, Chihuahua's economic fate was inextricably tied to mining. The Terrazas took advantage of the manifold opportunities provided by the influx of foreign capital and succeeded in fortifying their interests against the cycles of the mining-dependent economy, but ultimately it was foreigners who exercised control of the state's economic fate.

In the next two chapters, I shall trace the development of foreign enterprise in Chihuahua and elucidate the evolution of the elite-foreign enterprise system, which helped create the conditions that led to revolution. The remainder of the book will then analyze how the system affected the nonelite sectors of Chihuahuan society and how in combination with the profound dislocations brought about by the export economy fermented the Revolution of 1910.

4

Foreign Enterprise and Economic Development

Mexico's attachment to the world market during the last two decades of the nineteenth century profoundly affected the nation's economy and society. As in other Latin American countries, export-led economic development produced deep-seated political crises between 1900 and 1925. While in Argentina, Chile, and Brazil the sociopolitical structure, for the most part, survived the crisis intact, Mexico experienced a revolution and more than ten years of civil war. The Revolution erupted in those regions where the export economy had its most profound effect. And nowhere did the export economy destabilize society more than in Chihuahua, where the Mexican Revolution began in 1910.[1]

The export of minerals and, to a lesser extent, agricultural commodities fueled the economic development of the *Porfiriato*, especially in Chihuahua and the North, where the mining industry dominated.[2] Mineral exports from Chihuahua (and Mexico as a whole) were generally financed and controlled by foreign entrepreneurs. With a few exceptions, only foreigners had the required capital, technology, and managerial skills to run large-scale mining and smelting ventures. Since foreigners managed the major railroads and provided the markets for Mexican minerals, the lifeblood of Mexico's economy was almost entirely under foreign control.

The massive influx of foreign investment into Chihuahua after 1880 to develop the mining industry had far-reaching and, to some extent, contradictory economic and political effects. All sectors of society benefited from the economic boom brought by the expansion of mining. The elite received large sums from land and mine speculation, property sales, and their position as intermediaries. Supplying and servicing the growing economy created a rising middle class. Demand for scarce labor drove up wages and produced a relatively privileged group of workers.

Nonetheless, dependence on the cyclical boom and bust of world demand for minerals put Chihuahua (and Mexico) at the mercy of events beyond its control. Mexico endured three major depressions (1884 to 1886, 1890 to 1895, and 1907 to 1909) in thirty years, all from sharply reduced demand for its exports. Each struck harder than the one before it, for they followed periods of ever greater prosperity that benefited increasingly more people. The depressions of the 1880s and 1890s, although accompanied by political unrest, were not enough to touch off revolution. The depression of 1907, however, helped cause widespread political discontent and produce a major upheaval.

In the short run, expansion through foreign investment preserved the political power of the Terrazas and their henchmen, who used their financial gains to capture the allegiance of subregional elite families and pay for any needed coercion. In this way, foreign capital strengthened subregional and regional elites. In the long run, however, economic expansion undermined the system erected by the Terrazas and Porfirio Díaz. Their network of privilege and political monopoly frustrated and alienated the rising middle class. Small landowners and villagers grew disgruntled when foreigners and local elites stole their lands, the value of which rose sharply from the export boom. All classes, other than the Terrazas and their allies, were crushed by the depression of 1907.

The flow of foreign investment into mining destabilized Chihuahuan society.[3] It magnified all the characteristics of the region's earlier development—a relatively well-off working class; an independent, fiesty class of small landowners; and an exceptionally strong elite—and added to them and the long heritage of violence a rising, vocal middle class. The result of this volatile mix was a revolution.

The pattern of destabilization was repeated elsewhere in Mexico, particularly in the North, where foreign investment brought economic expansion. Of the eight states (including the Federal District) with the largest amount of foreign investment between 1902 and 1910, six—Chihuahua, Sonora, Coahuila, Oaxaca, Sinaloa, and Durango—had significant revolutionary activity in 1910 and 1911.[4] Together these six states received more than 60 percent of all nonrailroad foreign investment in Mexico. The Revolution was most virulent in the states where foreign investment had increased at a rapid rate from 1902 to 1910—Sonora, Chihuahua, and Durango—where the amount of investment approximately doubled during these years. In contrast, in Nuevo León, where foreign investment, though substantial, remained at the same level during this period, there was little revolutionary activity in 1910–11.[5]

States in which the economy depended on agricultural exports also underwent profound change that produced widespread discontent and ultimately revolution. The commercialization of agriculture in the sugar-producing areas of Morelos, Oaxaca, and Veracruz, as well as in the cotton region of Durango (La Laguna) and the cattle areas of Chihuahua, raised land values and brought a wave of expropriations from small landowners and villages. These regions all spawned revolution. The despoilment of Yaqui lands in Sonora, though slightly different, engendered similar discontent and rebellion.[6]

The states where economic change was the direct result of foreign investment gave birth to a relatively modest reform movement. The revolutionary movements in Chihuahua, Sonora, and Coahuila were led by the middle class (and sometimes *hacendados*) who sought a throwback to nineteenth-century liberalism. The Revolution was most radical in the agricultural regions victimized by the commercialization of agriculture for exports, such as western Chihuahua, La Laguna, and Morelos.[7]

The difference was that those who were discontented in the North benefited directly and, before 1907, substantially from export-led economic development. They wanted not to destroy the old system so much as to modify it to give them their fair share, both politically and economically. On the other hand, in the agricultural regions small holders and villagers were directly hurt by the export economy or the commercialization of agriculture, which had taken away their land and capacity to feed themselves. Not surprisingly, they sought to destroy the system.

Foreign Enterprise and the Chihuahuan Economy

The Terrazas' struggle for political survival coincided with the growing importance of foreign investment in Chihuahua's economy. A series of circumstances came together after 1880 to create a favorable environment for foreign investors. Internationally, the burgeoning economies of Western Europe and the United States furnished a potential market for Chihuahuan (and Mexican) products. New technological innovations not only provided the means to extract and transport needed commodities but also created new demands. The industrialized nations at the same time sought new markets for their products and new areas in which to invest increasing amounts of venture capital.[8] Undeveloped countries with rich natural resources, such as Mexico, were potentially lucrative markets and investment targets. As one American mining engineer observed, "It was Mexico that attracted Americans the most. Proximity, rich mines, cheap labor, and the potential for applying modern equipment and procedures brought both capital and technical know-how."[9]

Simultaneously, on the national level, the Díaz dictatorship brought "order and progress" to Mexico and a favorable milieu for foreign investors. Díaz and his advisers believed that foreign investment was the least costly method (in political and social terms) of economic development. As Díaz pacified the country, it grew attractive for investment. His sponsorship of major railroad projects ended the isolation of many regions rich in natural resources and enabled him to bring them under his control. In Chihuahua, the 1880s brought the first railroad link to Mexico City and the United States and an end to a century of violence. Its proximity to and tradition of economic ties with the United States, great mineral riches, generally amenable elite, new peace, and railroad transportation all made Chihuahua one of the most attractive areas for foreign investors.

Foreign businessmen and companies invested more money in nonrailroad enterprises in Chihuahua than in any other state (with the possible exception of Sonora) in Mexico during the *Porfiriato*. By 1902, American investors alone had sunk thirty million dollars into Chihuahua. At the peak of the economic boom in 1907, the total exceeded fifty million, and by 1910 American investment approached one hundred million dollars.[10] Foreign companies dominated the mining industry, owned more than ten million acres of land, and controlled the region's largest commercial firms. Big and small, foreign entrepreneurs were ubiquitous in all aspects of Chihuahuan economy and society.

The first American businessmen came to Chihuahua during the early 1820s. By 1825 trade prospects were so promising that the United States Congress authorized a consular office for Ciudad Chihuahua. American goods flowed into the region over the Santa Fe Trail (St. Louis to Santa Fe) and the Camino Real (Santa Fe to Ciudad Chihuahua). The value of this commerce grew from only a few thousand dollars in the 1820s to nearly a million dollars in 1846, when the Mexican-American War (1846–48) disrupted trade between the two countries.[11]

Indian raids, government instability, high tariffs, capricious taxation, lingering anti-American sentiment, and generally poor, sometimes desperate, economic conditions limited foreign business activity in the region for two decades after the war with the United States. Nonetheless, foreigners came to Chihuahua during the late 1840s, 1850s, and 1860s, and prospered and assimilated. Henrique Müller, born in Germany and a naturalized United States citizen, arrived in 1847. In partnership with Luis Terrazas, he would become one of the state's leading landowners.[12] The Moye brothers, Carl, Gustave, and William, became important merchants. Carl married a sister of Luis Terrazas' wife.[13]

Foreigners also immigrated into Sonora and Sinaloa on the northwest coast at the same time, drawn by the flourishing trade with California during the gold rush and with newly settled Arizona and by various colonization schemes to populate the region. They became the richest merchants in the Pacific ports and after a generation assimilated into the *notable* families.[14]

Foreign business interests revived during the 1870s. In 1872, Emilio Ketelsen established what was to become one of the largest hardware and clothing wholesale firms in Mexico.[15] American investment in Chihuahuan mining reached approximately two million dollars by 1873.[16]

Civil war, Indian raids, border disputes between Mexico and the United States, and the financial panic of 1873 in the United States stopped the inflow of American investment. Only a handful of American merchants remained to be harassed by local political factions demanding forced loans, and only one American mining company continued to operate.[17]

The defeat of the Apache chief Victorio in 1880, coupled with the completion of the Mexican Central railroad in 1884, made Chihuahua increasingly attractive to American investors. The railroad gave access to markets in the United States, where Chihuahuan products—cattle, silver, copper, lead, zinc, and, later, timber—were in growing demand. The state's mining industry presented foreigners with unprecedented opportunities. They were to fill the void that native entrepreneurs, who had neither the necessary capital nor the technology, had left.

At a time when labor unrest struck the southwestern part of the United States, investors were drawn to Chihuahua (and all of northern Mexico) by the relative cheapness and docility of Mexican labor. The Chihuahuan elite, especially the Terrazas family, created a favorable climate for foreign investment leading the state government to provide lucrative incentives for investors, including tax exemptions and subsidies.[18]

The uneven economic development of the 1880s reflected Chihuahua's dependence on foreign markets and investment. The decade brought the first of the great boom-and-bust cycles that were to plague the state during the *Porfiriato*.

The effect of peace was immediate: six mining companies sprang up in Santa Eulalia in 1881, only a year after Indian raids had forced abandonment of the camp.[19] Several new American merchant houses opened their doors in Ciudad Chihuahua. Alexander Shepherd expanded his operations in Batopilas, while other American companies started work in Cusihuiriachic and Hidalgo del Parral. George Hearst, then a United States senator, purchased the 900,000-acre Hacienda de Bavícora in western Chihuahua in 1882.[20] The completion of the Mexican Central in 1884 brought a further influx of investors in land, mines, and commerce. By mid-decade, the Corralitos Company and others had joined Hearst in buying huge tracts. *The Two Republics* reported that American and British entrepreneurs owned twelve million acres in Chihuahua in 1886. In that year a bad winter in the United States created a large demand for Chihuahuan cattle, setting off a boom in ranch land.[21] British entrepreneurs invested heavily in mining, setting up two large concerns, the Palmarejo Mexican Goldfields and San Francisco del Oro in 1885 and 1886.[22]

Despite the cattle boom and influx of foreign capital, Chihuahua suffered an economic depression from 1884 to 1887, the result of a downturn in the United States. Two years of drought and bad harvests worsened the crisis.[23] There was a short-lived recovery in 1888 and 1889, stimulated by the ongoing cattle boom and a new surge of investment in mining. Chihuahuan copper mines were particularly attractive because of the high demand for copper wiring to transmit electric power in the United States.[24]

But the first half of the 1890s brought economic disaster to Chihuahua. Financial panic in the United States slowed investment in Mexico and destroyed the market for minerals. Five years of drought and harvest failures created widespread misery. In addition, the provisions of the McKinley tariff of 1890 struck a heavy blow at the state's exports. It placed a high tax on animals imported into the United States, virtually ending cattle exports from Chihuahua across the border. It also levied prohibitive duties on imported, unsmelted ores. At the same time, demand for the state's major mineral export, silver, plummeted when the Congress repealed the Sherman Silver Purchase Act and the government of India closed its mints. Silver imports into the United States fell 50 percent. The decline of silver badly hurt the region's two leading mining camps, Parral and Batopilas.[25]

A revived mining sector led the way to recovery by the end of 1895. The McKinley tariff, so devastating initially, in the long run served Chihuahuan mining well. High duties on unprocessed ore spurred large-scale investment in Mexican smelting, which in turn caused an influx of investment in mining. The introduction of the cyanide process to treat low-grade ore drew more foreign investors.[26] Parral, the largest silver camp, was more prosperous in 1897 than at any time in the nineteenth century.[27] Meanwhile, the lowering of United States duties on livestock and a new market for cattle in Cuba created a new boom in Chihuahuan ranching that threatened to exhaust the supply of cattle on the ranges of northern Mexico, a boom that continued until 1904.[28]

The years from 1897 to 1907 were a time of unprecedented prosperity in Chihuahua. Spurred by the east-west expansion of the state's railroads, begun in 1897, foreign, particularly American, investment flowed into Chihuahua. American companies took over the state's mining industry. By 1903, the stream of capital had become a torrent. Every day, reported *El Correo de Chihuahua*, more and more people poured into Santa Eulalia, where Americans had purchased most of the mining property, leaving only two mines in the hands of natives.[29] In a series of spectacular sales, foreigners purchased the Dolores, San Francisco del Oro, and Lluvia del Oro mines for over a million dollars each.[30]

The railroads opened up hitherto inaccessible regions. The Chihuahua al

Pacífico and its successors (KCM&O and Mexican Northwestern) tapped northwestern Chihuahua. The Mexican Central built key extensions to Parral and Santa Bárbara. For several years Parral profited from exceptionally low freight rates that permitted its low-grade-ore-producing mines to flourish.[31]

New competition in the smelting industry also abetted the boom, particularly in Parral. In Torreón, Coahuila, the Madero family built a smelter (the Compañía Metalúrgica de Torreón) to rival the American Smelting and Refining Company's monopoly. After a rate war, they reached a pooling agreement with ASARCO which, to the detriment of the mining industry as a whole, raised smelting rates. Mining in Parral collapsed as a result.[32]

The federal government considerably increased the attraction of Mexican mining to foreign investors when in 1905 it adopted the gold standard, a move which apparently solved the endemic monetary problems caused by the decline of silver. The government also lowered duties on imported mining machinery and reduced the tax on mining property.[33] The restoration of the Terrazas to political power in Chihuahua in 1903 and the subsequent accession of Enrique Creel to the governorship further enhanced the environment for foreign investors in Chihuahua.

The years 1905 and 1906 were the most prosperous Mexico and Chihuahua had ever known. Mining flourished as foreign investment reached massive proportions. News of big mining deals filled the pages of the *Mexican Herald*, the *Mexican Investor*, the *Engineering and Mining Journal*, and *El Correo de Chihuahua*. Capital flowed over from mining into new railroad projects, manufacturing, ranching, and hydroelectric power. Millions of American dollars created an economic euphoria.[34]

But beneath the boom were disturbing signs of trouble. Bottlenecks in smelting and transportation began to appear as early as 1903. The Maderos' pooling agreement with ASARCO dealt a devastating blow. Even managers of the larger companies complained bitterly that higher smelting rates "meant loss rather than the previous small profit." The crisis worsened in 1905, when the new Mexican dynamite trust drove up the price of explosives.[35] Later that year freight rates began a steady rise. Then a shortage of railroad cars during the first months of 1907 halted ore shipments. Small operators, already suffering from high freight and smelting charges, were especially hard hit because they received none of the preferential treatment accorded the larger companies. Many mines and milling plants closed.[36]

The Depression of 1907

A new financial crisis engulfed the United States in 1907, and its repercussions were felt in Mexico by the end of the summer. Foreign investment stopped. Combined with the collapse of mineral prices on the world market, this closed down much of the already depressed Chihuahuan mining industry for the next two years. Ongoing transportation problems and escalating fuel costs exacerbated the crisis. High overhead and low prices devastated the industry.[37] By the end of 1907 even the largest companies in Parral had shut down. ASARCO stopped mining at its Santa Eulalia silver and lead mines and cut back production at the Tecolotes works in Santa Bárbara; in early 1908, William C. Greene's extensive operations in western Chihuahua went bankrupt.[38]

Conditions in the United States and neighboring regions were as bad. The giant Velardeña complex in Durango and Greene's camp in Cananea, Sonora, closed down, and thousands of Mexican migrants lost their jobs in the mines and farms of the Southwest.[39]

The impact of the depression was, however, uneven, for the larger foreign companies suffered little, if at all. Although many stopped mining new ore, they continued to ship ore profitably from reserves. Financially sound, the big corporations could afford to cut production and await the return of higher prices. In the meantime, they took advantage of the crisis to reduce overhead through layoffs and wage reductions, to institute capital improvements, and to acquire new properties cheaply. Small companies, though, were squeezed on the one hand by low ore prices (if they could sell ore at all) and on the other by the rising cost of smelting and transportation.[40]

At the end of 1908, the mining industry received yet another jolt when the national congress debated Article 144, a proposed constitutional amendment that prohibited foreign ownership of Mexico's subsoil resources. Foreign investors withheld funds until the measure was defeated. Americans in particular were sensitive to what they saw as a wave of anti-American sentiment following a violent strike at the Greene-Cananea Copper Company camp in Sonora in 1906. The English-language press in Mexico City interpreted the ensuing outbreak of strikes as a manifestation of antiforeign feeling. In 1906 and 1907 the Flores Magón brothers' aborted rebellion in Galeana District and a rash of labor strikes put foreigners on their guard in Chihuahua.[41]

The worst of the depression was past by mid-1909, although some districts never fully recovered. By the time the Madero revolution broke out in 1910, ore prices had generally returned to predepression levels and mineral output had risen. Several new ore processing facilities were under construction and the Ciudad Chihuahua and Terrazas Station smelters were expanding. The Pearson syndicate of Canada revived Greene's lumber and railroad interests in western Chihuahua.[42]

But continuing bottlenecks in smelting and transportation hampered the recovery. ASARCO maintained its near monopoly. Rate reductions anticipated

Table 4-1
Mineral Production of Chihuahua

Year	Estimates of Value (Pesos)	Alternative Estimates
1877–78	902,077.95	
1878–79	764,978.71	
1879–80	1,073,950.29	
1880–81	1,172,484.28	
1881–82	1,285,328.66	
1882–83	1,500,100.29	
1883–84	1,899,713.32	
1884–85	1,952,427.83	
1885–86	1,464,280.86	
1886–87	2,534,495.20	
1887–88	2,543,036.33	
1888–89	2,378,477.93	
1889–90	2,496,216.12	
1890–91	2,080,412.44	
1891–92	3,680,493.32	
1892–93	3,934,107.41	
1893–94	4,817,607.66	
1894–95	4,578,871.21	
1895–96	3,461,132.88	
1896–97	2,870,108.76	1,918,460
1897–98	5,640,826.00	6,431,083
1898–99	6,843,954.00	22,347,294
1899–1900	7,269,706.00	
1900–1901	12,274,946.00	
1902	13,641,195.00	
1903	12,903,010.00	
1904	10,378,816.00	
1905	15,832,049.73	
1906	16,906,917.36	16,906,917
1907	23,854,309.02	23,979,809
1908	23,008,547.00	21,990,164
1909	—	20,576,849

Sources: *Mexican Mining Journal* 2(1910): 33; Chihuahua, *Anuarios Estadísticos, 1905–1909*; Mexico, Ministerio de Fomento, Dirección General de Estadística, *Anuario Estadístico de la República Mexicana, 1897, 1904*; Chihuahua, Gobernador, *Memoria, 1900*.

from the construction of its Ciudad Chihuahua smelter never materialized because the company treated ores only from its own mines. Railroad cars continued to be scarce.[43] And in 1909 the Payne Tariff, which placed a high tax on zinc imports into the United States, forced two major companies to close.[44]

Even more than previous depressions during the 1880s and 1890s, the crisis of 1907 pointed out the structural weaknesses of the Chihuahuan (and Mexican) economy. Because it depended on exports, it was vulnerable to oscillations in world financial and market conditions, as well as the whims of United States government policy. The Chihuahuan economy was especially at the mercy of cycles in the United States economy, its largest market. Investment in the state ebbed and flowed with financial conditions in the United States. Moreover, the depressions had grown progressively more harsh as foreign investment increased. The depression of 1907 served ultimately as the catalyst for revolutionary discontent.

Foreign Investment by Sector

Foreigners, especially Americans, penetrated every aspect of the Chihuahuan economy. Giant American and British companies dominated the state's mining industry. Other large firms owned vast tracts of land and timber. Four thousand foreigners (in 1910 Chihuahua had more foreign residents than any other state, although they were proportionally more numerous in Sonora) lived and worked in Chihuahua. Some, mostly merchants, flourished and assimilated into Chihuahuan society, with several even marrying into the local elite. Others who operated small ranches and mines or were skilled or supervisory employees of the large companies lived apart from the Mexican community and made no effort to assimilate. In addition, there was a floating population of speculators, promoters, itinerant peddlers, and skilled workers, whose numbers fluctuated.[45]

The preponderance of foreign investment in Chihuahua was in mining. In 1902, 45 American companies or individuals had invested \$US 21,277,518 in the state's mines.[46] By 1907 there were 212 American or British mining enterprises in Chihuahua (two-thirds of the 313 mining concerns in the state).[47] Foreign mining companies employed 76 percent of Chihuahuan mine workers and produced 80 percent of the value of its mineral production in 1909. Their share of employment and production rose steadily after 1904.[48]

A few large companies with production valued at more than 500,000 pesos each accounted for 75 percent of the state's total production in each year from 1906 to 1909. The number of firms this size shrank from 14 in 1907 to 10 in 1909. The connection of production is even more dramatic when we consider that the share of the five largest producers rose from 42 to 58.8 percent from

Table 4–2

Foreign Domination of the

Chihuahuan Mining Industry, 1904–1909

Year	1904	1906	1907	1908	1909
No. Active Mines	111	105	120	117	94
No. Companies	59	54	60	65	51
No. Employees	6,866	9,763	9,285	10,259	9,002
Production: Value (pesos)		16,906,917	23,979,810	21,990,164	20,576,848
American Companies	21	26	32	33	28
No. Employees	3,645	6,137	6,482	6,096	6,410
Empl.: Pct. of Tot.	55.4	62.8	69.8	63.7	71.2
Prod.: Value (pesos)	—	10,589,825	16,930,962	15,569,421	15,391,757
Pct. of Tot. Prod.	—	62.6	70.7	70.7	74.8
British Companies	4	3	2	5	3
No. Employees	570	440	310	499	448
Empl.: Pct. of Tot.					5.0
Prod.: Value (pesos)	—	1,779,971	1,165,838	1,491,624	1,171,600
Probable American or British	11	2	6	6	2
No. Employees	414	22	247	278	60
Empl.: Pct. of Tot.					
Prod.: Value (pesos)	—	4,700	770,000	54,000	110,000
Foreign Mining Cos.	36	31	40	44	33
Employees	4,631	6,599	7,039	6,873	6,918
Pct. of Empl.	70.4	67.5	75.8	71.8	76.8
Prod.: Value (pesos)	—	12,374,496	18,866,797	15,115,055	16,673,357
Pct. of Tot. Prod.	—	73.1	79.0	77.8	81.0
Mexican Companies	23	18(3)[a]	20	19(2)[a]	

Source: Chihuahua, México, Secretaría del Gobierno, Sección Estadística, *Anuario Estadístico del Estado de Chihuahua, 1905–1909.*

a. Origins of companies in parentheses are uncertain.

1906 to 1909. ASARCO, alone, accounted for more than a quarter of the state's production and employed 15 percent of the mining work force in 1909.

The depression furthered the concentration of mineral production. Newspapers, periodicals, and consular reports comment repeatedly on the shakeout of smaller mining firms, while the larger companies modernized and acquired new property.

Only in Sonora did foreign investment dominate as it did in Chihuahua. In 1910, 195 of 208 Sonoran mining companies were foreign owned, 186 of them by American firms. Chihuahua and Sonora together received more than 50 percent of all foreign investment in mining, which totaled nearly three hundred million pesos in 1910.[49]

Table 4–3
The American Smelting and Refining Company and
Affiliated Companies in Chihuahua, 1904–1909

Year	Production (kgs.)		Production (pesos)		Miners Employed	
	ASARCO	State	ASARCO	State	ASARCO	State
1904	46,852,950	394,074,953	—	10,378,816[b]	1,160	6,866
1905	50,000,000[a]	—	778,400[a]	15,832,049[b]	—	—
1906	—	592,857,298	1,946,068	16,906,917	2,058	9,763
1907	—	746,991,703	5,559,220	23,979,809	1,475	9,285
1908	—	831,016,491	5,457,496	21,990,164	1,350	10,259
1909	—	759,691,404	5,640,000	20,576,848	1,295	9,002

Sources: Chihuahua, Secretaría, del Gobierno, Sección Estadística, *Anuario Estadístico del Estado de Chihuahua, 1905–9.*
a. Jorge Griggs, *Mines of Chihuahua, 1907,* appendix 5. The figures are incomplete.
b. *Mexican Mining Journal,* February 1910, p. 33.

Next to mining, foreigners invested most heavily in Chihuahuan land. At one time or another during the *Porfiriato,* thirty-nine foreign proprietors owned more than one hundred thousand acres each. Five companies controlled more than a million acres apiece; the largest of these, the Palomas Land and Cattle Company, spread over two million acres on the New Mexico border.[50] The largest lumber operation, the Sierra Madre Land and Lumber Company, in its heyday employed two thousand men and supported a community of thirty-five hundred.[51]

In comparative terms, foreign landholdings in Chihuahua were by far the most extensive, though those in Sonora, Veracruz, and Oaxaca were more valuable in 1902. Only one company outside Chihuahua owned more than a million acres and only a handful more than one hundred thousand acres.[52]

In at least three instances, foreign landholders elicited bitter feelings from neighboring communities. The Corralitos Company in Chihuahua stole several thousand acres from villages in the Guerrero District, which became a hotbed of revolutionary activity in 1910.[53] The granting of the Richardson Construction Company concession set off the Yaqui wars in Sonora,[54] and the concession of key water rights to the British-owned Tlahualilo Company in La Laguna, Durango, moved a segment of the region's landholding elite to rebellion.[55]

Americans handled most of Chihuahua's business in farm implements, hardware, and general merchandise. Krakauer, Zork, and Moye, which operated on both sides of the border, was the state's leading dealer of hardware and mining supplies. Noake and DeSmith was the largest seller of buggies and carriages, and Ketelsen and Degeteau the largest wholesale-retail business in Chihuahua and one of the largest in Mexico.[56] The leading furniture and clothing stores in Ciudad Chihuahua were all owned by foreigners.[57]

Only in Sonora did commercial power of foreigners exceed that in Chihuahua. Their ranks swelled by nearly five thousand Chinese, foreigners owned almost 30 percent of the commercial establishments in Sonora. In some cities, such as Guaymas and Arizpe, foreigners owned half the firms. The representation of foreigners among the largest firms was even greater. Foreign-owned commercial enterprises were bitterly resented by native competitors. The Chinese in Sonora were especially harshly treated by Sonoran revolutionaries. Feelings ran high there because so many small stores were operated by foreigners, while in Chihuahua foreigners tended to own only the largest establishments.[58]

With such a large foreign presence in Chihuahua, it was impossible for the native elite, especially the Terrazas, to escape its profound effects. The arrangements worked out over several decades between foreign entrepreneurs and the native elite profoundly changed the rest of Chihuahuan society, and those changes helped ferment revolutionary discontent.

5

Elite and Foreign Enterprise

In Chihuahua, as in the rest of Mexico, there evolved during the *Porfiriato* a three-cornered system of relations between the regional native elite, the national elite, and foreign entrepreneurs that smoothed the path of economic development while at the same time preserving the delicate political balance of the Díaz regime. Three circumstances made these relations possible. First, the native elite (regional and national) controlled both the government and the natural resources. Second, the native elite was willing, though not in unanimity, to permit foreigners a wide scope of economic activity, even to the extent that they came to dominate key sectors of the Mexican economy, most importantly mining. Finally, foreign investors had the capital and technology, neither of which was available in Mexico, to develop the nation's resources. In short, foreign investment formed the basis of the Díaz regime.

The interests of the three groups did not always coincide, and each group suffered internal divisions. As a result, the system constantly changed to accommodate shifting political and economic circumstances. In the early years of the regime, when Díaz did not control the entire country, recalcitrant *caciques*, notably in the North, maintained considerable autonomy from the central government. Later, the dictator defeated, coerced, or bought off even his most powerful regional opponents. He constantly manipulated rival groups within the states, giving one faction a lucrative business concession and another political patronage. He juggled his governors, cabinet ministers, and generals so as to prevent the emergence of an obvious successor.[1] Relations between the national and regional elites varied accordingly. In Chihuahua, the dictator made and discarded alliances with *triistas* and *guerreristas* before he installed his own man as governor and eventually reached accommodation with the Terrazas. While denying the Terrazas political power for two decades, he allowed them to grow rich, a pattern he repeated in Sonora and Nuevo León, and in Coahuila, where he stripped the once-powerful Madero family of political authority, but permitted them to flourish economically.[2]

Relations between the national government and foreign entrepreneurs likewise changed over time. Initially, the bitter residue of the war of 1846, acrimonious border disputes, and the French Intervention hampered relations between Mexico and the United States and the European powers. But presidents Díaz and González mended these relations during the 1880s, and for the next two decades foreigners received preferred treatment. Americans were especially privileged until, in the early years of the twentieth century, the dictator began to see them as a threat to his authority. Under Díaz, the national government committed itself to economic development through foreign investment, for he and his advisers saw it as the quickest, most efficient way to modernize the economy while simultaneously maintaining the social and political privileges of the elite.

Relations between foreigners and the regional elites did not always proceed as smoothly as they did with the national elite, however. Frequently, the economic interests of regional elites and foreigners clashed, and on occasion the central government had to overrule local authorities, who acted in ways that hurt foreign investors.

In general, the native elites were subordinate to foreigners in the economic sphere. The former acted primarily as intermediaries or brokers, using their ownership or control of land and other natural resources or their political influence to obtain financial rewards, which came in the form of rents, sales proceeds, bribes, commissions, stocks, and employment. There were, nonetheless, regional disparities in elite behavior. The *científicos* and the elite families of Mexico City acted almost exclusively as intermediaries. In the peripheral regions, notably in the North, the elite acted not only in the traditional manner as intermediaries but also as independent entrepreneurs and active partners with foreign investors.

Dealings between foreigners and the native elite might begin when a foreign entrepreneur or corporation sought to purchase an *hacienda* or mine for development. The first order of business was to arrange the purchase or lease of the property. The foreigner would hire a well-connected lawyer or agent, a member of the regional or national (or perhaps one of each) elite, who handled the sale as well as the acquisition of government concessions, tax exemptions or favors, and other privileges. Usually, the native mine or land owner sold his property outright, but sometimes part of the sale price included stock in the company formed to exploit the property.

Because of the enormous amount of litigation over property boundaries and mining claims, it was wise for the foreign entrepreneur to retain the services of his elite intermediary to ensure continued favors from local authorities, particularly the courts. In larger enterprises, foreigners "required" the services of high-placed intermediaries, such as cabinet officers, generals, and relatives of Porfirio Díaz. Members of the native elite, especially on the local level, were not averse to using coercion to get commissions and bribes. Well-connected *jefes* could make the operations of foreign companies very difficult.

As a rule, foreigners were treated poorly before the mid-1880s, when local authorities subjected them to violence (lynchings were not uncommon) and extortion. Later, locals who troubled foreign companies fared better than small companies or individual businessmen because they often had more influential allies. ASARCO, for example, enjoyed direct access to Díaz. Smaller operators were more likely to be harassed.

Chihuahuan Variations

The native elite–foreign enterprise system in Chihuahua differed substantially from that in the rest of Mexico because of the unique position of the Terrazas-Creel family. Alone among the great regional families of the *Porfiriato*, the Terrazas, after 1902, controlled both the state government and regional capital resources. As we have seen, there were no rival factions left to challenge their political power after the Terrazas reached an accommodation with Porfirio Díaz, and the clan's financial resources and influence were unsurpassed. This meant that foreigners had to come to the Terrazas in order to do business in Chihuahua. Because the family had its own considerable capital, it did not have to accept a subordinate role in its dealings with foreign entrepreneurs. On the contrary, foreigners frequently borrowed from the Terrazas banks, and in many instances the Terrazas required from foreigners only technical expertise.

That is not to say the Terrazas did not act as intermediaries. In fact, their powerful political and economic position in Chihuahua greatly enhanced their value as middlemen. Many family members represented foreign companies before various governments and courts.

Chihuahua's location on the United States border also set the region apart in its relations with foreign entrepreneurs. It had a long history of commercial relations with the United States, so that the influx of investment and people from its northern neighbor was not as great a shock as elsewhere, and antiforeignism was not as widespread (although it certainly existed). A final difference lay in the extent of foreign investment and penetration, for foreigners invested more capital in nonrailroad enterprises in Chihuahua than in any other region in Mexico, permeating all levels of Chihuahuan society and economy.

The Early Years

As they did in other areas, the relations between the native elite and foreign entrepreneurs in Chihuahua varied according to the changing political and economic conditions, and they depended also on the size of the foreign enterprise and the extent of its connections with the national and regional elites.

From the late 1840s to the late 1880s, the lingering resentment toward the United States for losses in the war and the prevailing political and economic chaos created an unfavorable climate for foreigners. Many members of the Chihuahuan elite who had fought bravely in 1846 remained bitter.[3] As a result, foreign businessmen received little or no protection from local government.[4] In 1856 the governor demanded the recall of the United States consul in Ciudad Chihuahua because of his overzealous efforts to protect Americans from mistreatment.[5] During the French Intervention and the civil wars of the 1870s, foreign businessmen were often forced to loan large sums to various political factions, kidnapped, and imprisoned. Not even long-time residents like Henrique Müller were immune from these persecutions.[6] The United States consul in Ciudad Chihuahua complained in 1871 that "the rights of Americans were being constantly violated."[7] Americans regularly lamented abuses by local authorities.[8] Chihuahuans vented their hostility toward Americans during the 1880s by vandalizing the Mexican Central railroad.[9]

Cooperation and Conflict

The end of the Indian and civil wars, the construction of the Mexican Central, and the commitment of Porfirio Díaz to economic development through foreign investment altered the environment for foreign entrepreneurs. Although regional and local authorities often bridled at the incursion of foreigners and conflicts continued to arise, the dictatorship offered large foreign corporations a relatively free hand.

When Alexander Shepherd began his silver mining enterprise in Batopilas in 1880, he encountered stiff resistance from the local elite, which contested his mining claims. At one point the local *jefe* imprisoned the American, whereupon the governor quickly ordered his release. Shepherd assiduously cultivated the friendship of Porfirio Díaz—he was said to be one of the two Americans Díaz trusted—and of Luis Terrazas and Enrique Creel. Creel was appointed to the board of directors of the Batopilas Mining Company. Shepherd greatly profited from these connections by getting tax exemptions and a large degree of autonomy from local officials. When a local uprising in 1887 threatened Shepherd's properties, Díaz dispatched a small contingent of troops to protect them.[10]

The Guggenheims, who began operations in Mexico in 1890, also enjoyed direct access to the most influential members of the national elite, such as José Limantour and Joaquín Casasús. John Hays Hammond, the family's chief lieutenant in Mexico, had a warm friendship with Porfirio Díaz. The Guggenheims shrewdly hired as their representatives two of the dictator's close associates, Emeterio de la Garza and Bernardo Reyes, thus assuring cooperation from the two major factions within the national elite, the *científicos* and the *reyistas*.[11]

Despite their connections to the Díaz inner circle, the Guggenheims paid dearly for the right to operate in Chihuahua, because their company, ASARCO, competed with the interests of the Terrazas family. The Terrazas had dabbled in smelting for years, but were unwilling to invest the large sums required to build a modern facility in Ciudad Chihuahua, where there was heavy demand for one. In addition, the Madero family of Durango and Coahuila, kin and business associates of the Terrazas, owned the largest native-owned smelter in Mexico, which competed directly with ASARCO. Several times the Guggenheims had offered to buy out the Maderos, but they could not agree on a price.

After Creel became governor, he pressured the Guggenheims to construct a smelter near Ciudad Chihuahua, threatening to bring in a rival smelter if they refused. The Americans resisted for two years, but gave in when a renewed bid for the Maderos' operation fell through and the latter aggressively began to expand their mining activities in Chihuahua. The smelter was expensive. ASARCO had to purchase the state concession from the Terrazas (undoubtedly at a high price); General Terrazas sold ASARCO the land for the smelter, and Juan Terrazas obtained the concession to run the company store at the facility.[12]

Promoter William C. Greene, the owner of the Cananea complex in Sonora, expanded into Chihuahua in 1902. He too had excellent relations with the Díaz regime, receiving an enormous concession from the federal government to exploit mines and timber and build railroads in western Chihuahua. Nonetheless, the price of cooperation with the Terrazas was steep: the purchase of two mines from Enrique Creel for 830,000 pesos.[13]

The Hearst family, proprietors of the Hacienda de Bavícora in western Chihuahua, also bought special favors from federal authorities. Porfirio Díaz personally helped arrange the purchase of the estate in 1882. Reportedly, the dictator regarded William Randolph Hearst, the heir to the property, as a son. In 1908, Díaz sent federal troops to clear residents from a ranch Hearst had bought for oil exploration. Since Hearst rarely visited Bavícora, he had few dealings with the Terrazas, but his ranch manager, Jack Follansbee, was a friend and business partner of Alberto Terrazas.[14]

Some foreign operators prospered without influence in Mexico City. James

I. Long, the manager of the Hidalgo Mining Company, arranged his taxes personally with Governor Creel, who also helped in 1905 when Sonoran authorities sought to prosecute him for tax evasion.[15]

Of course, treatment of foreigners was not always favorable. In one instance, Terrazas kin Ramón Luján sued the Corralitos Company over ownership of twenty-two mines worked by the firm. After twelve years of litigation, during which the American company operated the mines, the Supreme Court ruled in favor of Luján.[16]

There were numerous notorious battles over mine titles. The Santa Eulalia Mining Company endured more than seven years of litigation over such titles during the 1880s.[17] Even as prominent a figure as Senator Henry Tabor of Colorado had to fight nine years to win his claim to the Santa Eduviges mines from the Siqueiros family, the local *caciques*. He finally obtained a favorable ruling in 1892.[18] The commander of the Second Military Zone, General Juan Hernández, in 1907 used his troops to evict American mining tycoon August Heinze from a disputed mine in Santa Eulalia. Not surprisingly, Hernández eventually acquired the property.[19] Santa Eulalia, where American investment was heavy, was well known for its number of lawsuits over mine titles and overlapping claims.[20] Given the large number of mining claims, the inherent imprecision of titles, and the high stakes involved, friction was inevitable. Influential Mexicans generally won out in these disputes unless the foreigner had connections to Díaz.

Another source of constant resentment for native mine owners and *hacendados* was the higher wages foreign companies paid their workers. There were continuous complaints about this problem, which was also acute in Sonora. Supposedly, landowners disgruntled by their loss of cheap labor sponsored Article 144 in 1908, which proposed to amend the constitution to forbid foreigners from owning mines.[21]

Clearly, there was a discernible difference in the treatment accorded large and small operators. American consul Lewis Martin complained in 1909 that "an American in this state seems to have the smallest chance for justice of any state in the Republic."[22] One American wrote to the *Engineering and Mining Journal* in 1905 that American mining companies were hounded by government tax collectors who meticulously inspected their books, while merchants escaped not only scrupulous audits but the taxes as well. He went on to say that foreigners were "harassed and blackmailed at every turn," and he bitterly attacked the injustice of high mining taxes when *hacendados* paid not a penny on their vast estates.[23] Neither man was describing the situation of the large corporations like ASARCO, which benefited from tax exemptions, but rather the plight of small companies and individual operators.

Conflict between the Terrazas and foreign entrepreneurs was rare, simply because the Terrazas were too powerful. Foreign businessmen generally steered clear of any enterprise that would compete directly against the family's interests. The clan had no serious competition in banking or in its industrial operations. The only disputes arose when the Terrazas had to sue to recover loans or enforce contracts.

Still the seeds of future conflict were sown when the Terrazas, after years of resting content to let foreigners dominate the mining industry, began to invest in a growing number of mining and smelting ventures after 1902. It could be expected that conflicts with foreigners would increase as the family expanded its mining interests to employ increasing numbers of grandchildren, nephews, and in-laws and to fulfill the broadening ambitions of Enrique Creel. By 1908, for example, Creel was speculating in oil exploration in Chihuahua, a venture which might have led to stiff competition with foreign companies.

The Elite as Intermediaries

The native elite in Chihuahua associated with foreigners primarily as sellers and lessors of property. In a typical case a peon might discover a promising mine site. One way or another (often by cheating the peon) an enterprising merchant or *hacendado* acquired rights to the property. In some instances, the mine in question was old and needed substantial investment in machinery to make it productive. It was not uncommon for the native owner to work the mine on a modest scale. After the easiest mining was completed, however, work stopped. The native owner had neither the capital nor the technical know-how to develop the mine further.

At this point a foreign company or promoter purchased the mine, employing the services of a local broker. This person was not always a Mexican, for over a dozen foreigners in Chihuahua lived by their wits, arranging transactions of this sort. Sometimes a broker bought an option on the property and tried to sell it to a large corporation. Other times the broker tried to organize his own company or worked the mine himself.

Native owners demanded high prices and payment in cash. Usually payments were made in installments, and it was not uncommon for a buyer to default and the property to revert to its original owners. Sometimes, native mine owners leased their properties for royalties. Such was the case in the 1890s when Enrique Creel leased a group of copper mines and a smelter at Terrazas Station to a foreign company for $US 100,000 and a 10 percent royalty and in 1907, when Pedro Alvarado, bankrupted by the depression, leased the legendary Palmilla mine for an immediate payment of $US 400,000 and 45 percent of production profits.[24] Neither arrangement lasted, for the lessors defaulted.

Whatever the particulars of these deals, foreign companies paid staggering amounts for mines in Chihuahua. There were numerous transactions that involved $50,000 to $200,000. The most spectacular sale involved Bernardo García and Buenaventura Becerra, who sold the Lluvia del Oro mine in Urique to a foreign company for $2 million. A French syndicate purchased another mine in 1910 for the same sum.[25]

Aside from selling and leasing mining property, the Chihuahuan elite profited the most from acting as intermediaries. They represented foreign companies and individuals in the acquisition of government concessions, contracts, and subsidies, in the arrangement of land and mine deals, and in litigation before federal and state courts. The most successful intermediaries were the members of "El Universal," the lawyers' clique headed by Francisco Terrazas, the general's grandson. One member, Manuel Prieto, represented ASARCO, and another Terrazas associate, Lorenzo J. Arellano, was attorney for William C. Greene.[26]

Elite members peddled their influence for bribes, commissions, lawyers' fees, and employment. In a letter in 1903, Grant Schley, the president of the Chihuahua al Pacífico railway, revealed the essence of the system. He complained to his general manager that he paid two Mexican members of the local board of directors, who performed no function. To make matters worse, they did not appear to have any notable influence in the government either. Moreover, Schley had to pay a large salary to a government inspector who did no inspecting. No less a figure than Porfirio Díaz had nominated the board members.[27]

Enrique C. Creel was probably the nation's most successful intermediary. Half-American, fluent in English, and Mexico's leading banker with access to the inner circles of both the national government and the Terrazas family, he was a much sought-after partner and associate. Alexander Shepherd was only one of many foreign entrepreneurs who offered Creel offices in their companies and memberships on their board of directors. The governor drew an estimated 50,000 pesos salary as a board member of the Mexican Central. He was vice-president of the Chihuahua al Pacífico, the KCM&O, and the Mexican Northwestern Railway. The first step that Arthur Stilwell, the organizer of the KCM&O, took when he arrived in Mexico was to see Enrique Creel. Stilwell eventually acquired one of the most lucrative railroad concessions ever offered by the Mexican government.[28] Creel, unlike many of his elite contemporaries, was worth every peso.

Partnerships

Partnerships between foreigners and the native elite were commonplace in Chihuahua. As usual, the Terrazas were the most adept at using foreigners to their advantage. In all their enterprises, except the railroads, the Terrazas were majority stockholders and managed everyday business. Foreigners provided minority capital and technical expertise. In some cases, the family took over foreign-owned concerns that faltered and made them profitable. Spaniards and Germans supplied technical expertise for their textile factories, Germans operated the brewery, and an American supervised the foundry. Often these men owned a part interest in the businesses they helped run.[29]

The Terrazas worked closely with a number of border businessmen. The Guaranty Trust and Banking Company of El Paso, for example, was a partnership of the Terrazas with such men as Max Weber, Britton Davis, Max Muller (also a partner in a Sonoran bank), Ben Degeteau, and Max Krakauer. Weber was also a stockholder in the Banco Minero and other Terrazas enterprises. Krakauer, head of the large hardware concern, was a board member of the Terrazas' electric company.[30]

Many foreigners married into the Chihuahuan elite, reinvigorating old families while establishing social status and political connections. The Müllers married into the Luján and Elías families, for example. The daughter of Buenaventura Becerra, the mining tycoon and political boss of Urique, married foreigner Martín Nesbitt, who took over the family's mining business after Becerra died and later succeeded him as *jefe* of Urique.[31]

National and Regional Elites

In other regions where foreign investment played a key role, the absence of a dominant elite faction produced differing relations between the native elite and foreign entrepreneurs. In Sonora, the sale of land and mines to foreigners was a major source of revenue for *notables* throughout the *Porfiriato*. The governor, General Lorenzo Torres, for example, secured his fortune through the sale of a large chunk of property in the Yaqui Valley. Sonoran *notables* also performed a wide variety of functions as intermediaries.[32] The elite operated in the same manner in San Luis Potosí as well. Governor Pedro Dieguez made a large profit in 1888 by selling his concession to build a railroad across the state to the Mexican National line.[33]

The most notorious intermediaries, and reputedly the most venal, were the *científicos*. Cabinet members and congressmen such as Pablo Macedo and Joaquín Casasús served on long lists of corporate boards. As agents for foreign firms seeking government contracts, their "commissions" often reached 25 percent of the prospective contract's value.[34]

The interlocking elite of Monterrey and La Laguna maintained considerable independence from foreigners. The shifting relations between Díaz and the regional political boss General Bernardo Reyes (and the changing rules of the game that this entailed) probably discouraged foreign investment in Monterrey after 1900. One part of this group, however, the Maderos, maintained close relations with *científico* leader José Limantour, the finance minister, whose cooperation was crucial in winning tariff protection for Monterrey's industries.[35] Many members of the elite of La Laguna, in fact, competed directly and bitterly with foreign companies. Cotton growers in the region clashed repeatedly over water rights with the British Compañía Tlahualilo. The Maderos, of course, were on-again, off-again rivals of ASARCO.[36] But neither the nascent Monterrey group nor the elite of La Laguna hesitated to enter into favorable arrangements with foreigners when the opportunity arose.[37]

Two sets of circumstances brought the Chihuahuan elite into business dealings with the national elite. The boards of all the railroads were staffed by *científicos*, relatives of the dictator, and prominent *capitalinos*. Casasús and various members of the influential Escandón family served on many railroad boards and Stilwell put Díaz's nephew and brother-in-law on his board.[38] Second, the far-ranging interests of the Terrazas brought them into constant contact with the inner circle in Mexico City. Creel's banking ventures brought together all the participants in the native elite–foreign enterprise system— foreign capitalists and regional and national elites. The Banco Central de México, which Creel organized, included as partners great European and American banks like the Deutsche Bank and J. P. Morgan and Company, French capitalists living in Mexico City, *científicos*, *reyistas*, and several prominent Mexico City families.[39] The Banco Hipotecario de Crédito Territorial Mexicano, also founded by Creel, included French, British, and American investors, as well as Olegario Molina, the *cacique* of Yucatán and Díaz's minister of development.[40]

The Terrazas were especially closely linked to the Maderos and other families of La Laguna elite. They were partners in two banks, the Banco de la Laguna and the Investment and Discount Company; a large soap company; a cement plant; and a glass factory.[41]

The best example of the interlocking economic interests of foreigners and the national and regional elites was the Compañía Nacional de Dinamita y Explosiva, established in 1902, which received a monopoly on dynamite sales in Mexico. Given the extent of mining in Mexico, this was an enormously lucrative venture. As a result, all factions of the national elite, several regional elites, and several foreign entrepreneurs made up its shareholders. The principals were the Compañía Jabonera de la Laguna, owned by the Maderos and the Terrazas; a syndicate of French investors; and the Societé Centrale de Dynamite of Paris. Originally set up to build a dynamite factory in Mexico City, in the interim it received exclusive rights to import and distribute the explosive. It delayed construction, in the meantime taking advantage of its monopoly to charge exhorbitant prices, to the detriment of the mining industry. Despite its damaging policies, the company continued to operate, protected by its powerful partners.[42]

Enrique C. Creel was the linchpin of the Terrazas' dealings at the national level in both financial and political matters. As he had labored during the 1880s and 1890s to reconcile the interests of his father-in-law and Porfirio Díaz, Creel worked after 1902 to bring together the various economic interests in the country. Alone among the advisers around Díaz, Creel enjoyed excellent relations with foreigners and had an independent political base. Only Olegario Molina rivaled him in this respect.

The Effect of the System

For the most part, the native elite–foreign enterprise system hurt the other sectors of Chihuahuan society and economic development. It foreclosed a broad range of opportunities for the emergent middle class, which could not compete against foreigners and elites who enjoyed unfair tax breaks and favored treatment before the courts. With no political influence or access to public office, the middle class could not share in the system's spoils. The working class bore the brunt of prices kept high by the closed system and suffered from the inequities imposed on them by elite-protected foreign companies. Small landholders also bore a disproportionate tax load and suffered the loss of their lands before corrupt government authorities and courts.

Perhaps most important, the system was unproductive. Proceeds from the collaboration with foreign businesses were not necessarily invested in productive enterprise. The Terrazas, of course, through the Banco Minero, invested their money in an array of enterprises, but even the Terrazas expended large sums in unproductive speculation, which was often more profitable.

The native elite–foreign enterprise system had its roots as much in the internal structure of Chihuahuan and Mexican society as it did in the world market. The Mexican elite saw foreign investment as a way to modernize the nation, make themselves rich, and sustain themselves in power. Together with export-led economic development, it provided them the means, in the case of Chihuahua, both to overcome their internal rivals and to retain their privileged position in society and the economy. But in the long run the price was steep. Rapid economic growth undermined the system laboriously constructed over thirty years of dictatorship. It was an inherently unfair system and thus proved brittle indeed.

6

The Rise of the Middle Class

Chihuahua's closed politics and economics weighed heavily on the middle class. Small mine owners, landowners, and merchants and shopkeepers, artisans, tradesmen, shift bosses, foremen, teachers, and nonelite professionals, whose numbers had all greatly expanded during the boom period between 1897 and 1907, were increasingly frustrated by the restraints on their political and economic ambitions, the privileged position of the Terrazas and their henchmen and foreigners, and the daily abuses of state and local government. Prosperity eased the pain of political and economic injustice for nearly a decade, but the depression of 1907 drove the middle class to desperation. Initially, they channeled their protests within the system in the hope that Governor Creel and his administration would rectify the widespread inequities. When they encountered first indifference and then hostility, the middle class began to organize political opposition to the Terrazas-Creels and Porfirio Díaz. Rallying behind Francisco I. Madero, in 1909, they set up Anti-reelectionist clubs in Chihuahua. When the Anti-reelectionists met repression from the authorities, they began to plot the overthrow of the dictatorship, and in 1910 the Chihuahuan middle class furnished much of the political and military leadership of the Revolution.

Like the working class, the middle class benefited enormously from the economic boom. Small landowners found markets for their cash crops in the burgeoning mining camps and cities, made accessible by the new railways and wagon roads. Small merchants, shopkeepers, and artisans sold their wares to a growing, relatively prosperous population. Muleteers and freighters transported ores and supplies to and from isolated mining camps, revitalized by foreign investment. Tradesmen found work in the thriving construction industry, and workers could win promotions to foreman or shift boss in the labor-hungry mines and on railway construction crews.

Although the evolution of the middle class is largely unexplained and the exact extent of its expansion—especially for the years before 1902—is difficult to measure, the existing evidence indicates substantial growth of this group. During 1905 and 1906 the number of retail and wholesale firms in Chihuahua increased by 12 percent. The trend was most notable in Galeana, Guerrero, and Iturbide districts, where railroad construction stimulated commerce.[1] The growth of small industrial establishments and artisan shops was especially striking. Seventy-five percent of all these establishments in 1907 were founded between 1898 and 1907. Thirty-seven percent began business in 1905 and 1906, the years of Chihuahua's greatest prosperity. Nearly as many started in 1906 alone as in all the years before 1898. Mexicans owned all these businesses, which seldom employed more than one or two persons. The most dramatic increase came in Ciudad Chihuahua, where 87 percent of artisan and small industrial shops began business between 1898 and 1906. In the rest of Iturbide District 77 percent opened their doors during these years, 78 percent of those in Hidalgo, 79 percent of those in Guerrero, and 86 percent in Rayón. Hidalgo, Guerrero, and Iturbide were to be centers of Anti-reelectionist and later revolutionary sentiment.[2] Some workers had obviously accumulated savings and used them to start their own shops.

Statistics concerning the number of small landowners are imprecise. There was, nonetheless, a discernible increase in the ranks of small holders in Chihuahua up until 1908. The largest increases were in Guerrero, Hidalgo, and Jiménez districts.[3] The terrible drought that struck in 1907 and 1908 and the early frost of 1909 took a heavy toll on these properties, and the number of small landowners may have declined as much as 20 percent.

Tracing the extent of small-scale mine ownership is even more difficult than assessing small landownership. Speculation in mining claims was widespread among merchants, mine superintendents, foremen, and ranchers, according to mining registrations. The varied occupations of the mining claimants—*agricultor, minero, empleado, empleado público, mecánico, operario,* and *labrador*—and the fact that registration of mining claims required a fee, start-up capital, and a knowledge of bureaucratic procedures were clear indication of working-class aspirations and ability to achieve middle-class status.

Although foreigners debated the quality of Mexican labor, there was a discernible trend during the economic boom to promote natives to positions as shift bosses and foremen, undoubtedly dictated by the severe manpower shortages.[4] There was also a substantial increase in the number of professional and public white-collar employees. The total number of professionals in Chihuahua rose by 43 percent from 1895 to 1910: the number of doctors increased by 59 percent, lawyers by 10 percent, and teachers (*profesores*) by

100 percent.[5] The number of public employees expanded by 30 percent between 1900 and 1910.[6] Moreover, the pool of potential white-collar workers also increased. In 1907 there were 60 percent more children in Chihuahuan schools than there were in 1900 (although very few went further than primary school). From 1895 to 1910 literacy rose from 19 to 28 percent.[7]

Thus, given the economic boom, job opportunities, and better education, upward mobility was certainly possible in Chihuahua during the first years of the twentieth century. The closed political and economic system, however, limited those opportunities, and the depression that struck in 1907 put an end to them.

Limits and Frustration

The great boom from 1898 to 1907 had a two-tiered effect on Chihuahuan society. On one level, it concentrated political and economic power and privilege among the Terrazas, their cronies, and foreign businessmen. On another level, economic expansion provided the opportunity for the middle class to grow. Despite the inequitable division of wealth and influence, the two groups could have coexisted and prospered as long as the boom continued. But when depression struck in 1907, the nascent middle sectors were largely ruined. The structure of Chihuahuan politics and society assured the survival of the Terrazas and the big foreign operators, but gave the middle sectors no such advantages.

The Chihuahuan middle class had always faced stiff competition from foreigners. In this competition, foreigners were abetted by favored tax status and discriminatory attitudes toward natives by both native and foreign employers. The number of foreigners in Chihuahua more than doubled from 1895 to 1910 (2,495 in 1895, 4,000 in 1900, and 6,641 in 1910).[8] But even these figures underestimate the effect foreigners had on the local economy, because the railroads brought businessmen from across the border.

Foreign competition had long been a fact of life for Chihuahuan merchants. American and German entrepreneurs established stores in the region in the mid-nineteenth century, and itinerant peddlers had long hawked their wares from across the border.[9] The construction of the Mexican Central during the 1880s brought a flood of commercial travelers, who undercut Mexican merchants because they paid no taxes.[10] The prejudices of American mining companies also worked against local merchants, for many of these firms imported all their needs from the United States. Often American miners ate canned goods, rather than buy locally. At Cananea they imported 70 percent of their foodstuffs and clothing.[11] United States consuls reported a bustling market for imported provisions and foodstuffs in Chihuahua.[12]

The Mormons were bitterly resented commercial rivals. By the mid-1890s, Colonia Dublán and Nuevo Casas Grandes had become important commercial centers. The Mormons of western Chihuahua peddled far afield to compete with local farmers and ranchers for the region's mining markets, supplying poultry, eggs, and dairy products. Since the Mormons were exempt from import taxes and duties on agricultural implements, they enjoyed a considerable advantage over their small-scale competitors.[13]

At the turn of the century, many foreign businessmen settled in the revitalized Hidalgo del Parral, and local merchants were forced to refurbish their stores to compete.[14] Always foreign stores had the advantage of tax exemptions, while small shops and stores run by natives paid disproportionately higher taxes. In one case in the Valle de Zaragoza north of Parral in 1907, *El Correo* reported the opening of a new store with "anti-constitutional" privileges that was wrecking the other local merchants, who had to pay taxes.[15]

In addition to the burden of unfair taxes, small shopkeepers, artisans, ranchers, and miners had to operate with little possibility of obtaining credit either to expand or sustain their enterprises. The Terrazas-controlled banks in Chihuahua lent money exclusively to members of the elite and foreign businesses. Furthermore, the Terrazas-run state government constantly limited alternative sources of capital, always under the guise of protecting Chihuahuans from the evils of usury.[16] The credit problem was to be especially acute during the depression.

Upward mobility was further hampered by discrimination against natives in the promotion practices of the railroads and mining companies. Foreigners occupied all management posts and often preempted middle and lower supervisory positions as well. Although there is some evidence that natives made advances in this area after 1900, it was not nearly enough, and whatever progress was achieved ended during the depression. This discrimination was the source of deep-seated resentment in Chihuahua. To make matters worse, foreign employees in the mining camps received far better housing, food, and medical treatment than the natives.

Small mine owners, whose labor-intensive operations were often only marginally profitable, were at a severe disadvantage against their larger contemporaries. They suffered discriminatory transportation and smelting charges, and bigger companies like ASARCO received substantial rebates.[17]

Professionals, especially lawyers, found it was impossible to earn a living without connections to the Terrazas inner circle. The lawyers' clique, "El Universal," controlled all the business before the courts in Chihuahua. The Terrazas controlled access to public jobs and political office, thereby foreclosing another traditional career path for attorneys.

The expanding railroad network, on the one hand, provided widespread economic opportunity, while, on the other hand, it thwarted the middle class by exposing it to foreign competition. Local shops, industries, and artisans were hard pressed to compete against cheap imported manufactures. Railroad construction also proved a mixed blessing. Many tradesmen set up small businesses to subcontract for the railroad. At least two future revolutionaries, Pancho Villa and Marcelo Caraveo, were railroad subcontractors.[18] Foreigners, however, were active bidders for this work and got most of the jobs; they also captured the lion's share of the most lucrative public works contracts and equipment sales.[19] Ironically, the construction of spurs, branch lines, and aerial tramways, which provided work for many Chihuahuans, severely cut into the opportunities of others, such as freighters and muleteers, whose occupations these innovations supplanted.[20] At least one prominent revolutionary, Pascual Orozco, Jr., was a freighter.[21]

Several leaders of the Revolution of 1910 provide excellent examples of middle-class frustrations that led to political opposition and then revolt. Abraham González, who was to be revolutionary governor of Chihuahua (1911–13), was born into a once influential family in western Chihuahua. Well educated in both Mexico and the United States, González lost out on a promising career in banking when the Terrazas took over the Banco de Chihuahua in 1896. Subsequent ventures in ranching and mining were stymied by the Terrazas and foreign competition. Frustrated by lack of success commensurate to his abilities and training, González joined the opponents of the Díaz regime in 1909 to form the Anti-reelectionist party in Chihuahua.[22] Pascual Orozco, Jr., the foremost military leader of the Revolution of 1910, was a muleteer, freighter, and owner of a small store in the Guerrero district who joined the rebellion at least in part because of his rivalry with another freighter, Joaquín Chávez, who enjoyed favored treatment from the Terrazas-Creels.[23]

Lawyers like Aureliano S. González, Pascual Mejía (both of whom were lower court judges in Chihuahua), Julio S. Jaurrieta, Luis G. Rojas, Tomás Silva, and Tomás Gameros joined the Anti-reelectionists in their frustration against the lack of opportunity in the Terrazas-Creel regime.[24] Among public employees, teachers were the most common revolutionaries (not only in Chihuahua but in other areas as well, such as Sonora). In Chihuahua, best-known examples were Abel S. Rodríques, who became governor during the Revolution, and Braulio Hernández.[25]

Several merchants also became Anti-reelectionists in protest against unfair taxes and other privileges held by foreigners and the elite. Juan B. Baca ran a store in Parral. After serving in the state legislature during the 1890s, he was shut off from political influence by the Terrazas and subsequently joined the Anti-reelectionists.[26]

All of these men were essentially reformers who sought only the chance to acquire their fortunes and run for political office on open and equal terms with their peers. Other than their expropriation of the Terrazas estates, which they believed were stolen from the people of the state, their program was moderate once they gained power. They sought to end the system of privilege, to make taxes equitable, and to return local politics to the people.[27]

Depression and Revolution

Whatever the inequities of the economic system and the dissatisfaction with political injustices, the boom did much to ameliorate middle-class resentment. But the depression that began in mid-1907 shattered economic advances and drove many of the middle class to contemplate desperate measures. As the economic crisis wore on, the middle class realized that it could find no relief within the Porfirian system.

Small merchants, shopkeepers, and artisans lost business when the depression threw thousands out of work and reduced the incomes of many others. The end of the construction boom virtually wiped out the tradesmen who had started their businesses over the preceding five years. The United States consul in Chihuahua reported in 1909 that merchants had lost between 10 and 30 percent of their business and were unable to meet obligations.[28] Notices of the bankruptcies of commercial houses appear in *El Correo* and the *Periódico Oficial* through 1910. The number of small industrial enterprises and artisan shops declined by 35 percent from the peak of 1906. The number of small businesses begun in 1907 and 1908 dropped precipitously, and only 25 percent of all the establishments founded in 1905 and 1906 survived the depression.[29]

The downturn hit hardest in Parral, which plunged into depression two or three years before the rest of the state and stayed until 1910. It is thus not surprising that Parral was a center of Anti-reelectionist activity. The Baca brothers, Juan, Guillermo, and Miguel, all merchants, were leaders of the Anti-reelectionists and later of the Revolution in the area.[30] Merchants in other mining areas hurt by the depression also became Anti-reelectionists, including Ignacio Félix and Ildefonso Manjarrez in Batopilas and Francisco D. Salido in Guazapares.[31]

Artisans and tradesmen became leaders of the Anti-reelectionist party in Chihuahua, especially those who had been active in mutualist societies. Of the artisans, shoemakers were the most active in the Anti-reelectionist movement. Jesús Ferrer, Policarpo López, and Mauricio Ortegón were officials of the Sociedad "Morelos" de Zapateros (shoemakers), who joined the Anti-reelectionists in Ciudad Chihuahua. Ferrer and López were officers of the club in the capital.[32] Shoemaker Gabriel Gardea was *jefe político* under Abraham González's revolutionary administration.[33] Anti-reelectionist club member Jesús Porras was a tinsmith.[34] Anti-reelectionists Longinos Balderrama and Alberto Talavera were officers in the Sociedad "Zaragoza" de Sastres (tailors).[35] Several officers of the Unión de Carpinteros (carpenters) Mexicanos, another mutualist society, became Anti-reelectionists, among whom were Juan Ortega, Francisco Salas, Miguel Sarabia, Francisco Jiménez, and Luis Esquivel, who was vice-president of the political club.[36]

The ranks of middle-class Anti-reelectionists were not made up solely of merchants, artisans, and tradesmen. Sebastián Quesada was a saloon keeper in Ciudad Chihuahua. Aniceto Flores was proprietor of a flour mill. Félix Terrazas was the owner of a lumber mill in Guerrero. Félix Valenzuela owned a stable in the capital. Rafael Martínez (the columnist "Rip-Rip" of *El Correo*) was a journalist.[37]

Small landowners and mine owners suffered the twin disasters of depression and drought. The price for cattle fell and the lack of rain ruined crops and killed cattle. An early frost in 1909 destroyed that year's crop in Guerrero District, the location of many small farms and ranches. The collapse of mineral prices forced many small operators out of business, and the drought, particularly in the sierras, dried up the streams that were crucial for working their mines. As a result of these economic stringencies, several small mine owners became Anti-reelectionists: José Barraza, Abraham González, Aureliano González, José de la Luz Blanco, Benjamín Saenz, and Antonio Sarabia.[38]

All of these small landowners and businessmen had no chance to acquire credit or government assistance. Instead, the banks and state government acted in a way that exacerbated their financial straits. In 1908 the prevailing interest rate jumped to 12 percent or more. By the first part of 1909, it had risen to between 18 and 24 percent.[39] No small entrepreneur could long afford those rates. If a small businessman had received a loan prior to 1907 (which was not likely), it was called in shortly after the depression struck in July 1907.[40]

The Terrazas-controlled legislature reacted to the economic crisis by increasing taxes on small and medium-sized firms. The state's freighters and muleteers, hard hit by a rash of mine closings, were confronted by a new tax on work animals. And in 1909 the *ayuntamiento* of Ciudad Chihuahua raised rents at the municipal slaughterhouse, forcing ten butchers out of business.[41] This, of course, squeezed out some of the Terrazas' competition in the meat business.

The evolution of the middle class from discontent to disillusionment and finally to revolution can be seen in the career of journalist Silvestre Terrazas (a distant cousin of Luis). As editor of *El Correo de Chihuahua*, based in the state capital, he steered clear of political controversy until 1905, after which he made the newspaper a sounding board for widespread complaints against local authorities in Chihuahua. Until 1907, Silvestre supported the official candidates on both the state and national levels. In 1903, for example, he warmly welcomed the return of General Terrazas to political power. In 1906, Silvestre began to criticize Governor Creel (see chapter 9) for his unconstitutional extension of Luis Terrazas's term. He then attacked Creel's candidacy in the 1907 gubernatorial election. Thereafter the editor became a vocal, persistent critic of the Terrazas-Creel regime. Silvestre endured constant harassment from local authorities, and his stance met with hostility from Creel, who twice had the editor jailed.[42]

Undoubtedly, Silvestre Terrazas opposed the Terrazas-Creels out of his sense of justice. He more than anyone else helped expose the growing excesses of their regime, and he justifiably feared the expanding influence of Americans in northern Mexico. But he also suffered from the restraints on economic opportunity imposed by the dominance of the Terrazas-Creels and the foreign entrepreneurs. When he sought to expand his printing business, Creel refused to loan him the necessary funds.

By 1909 it was clear to the editor that neither Díaz nor Creel would reform. Although his desire for journalistic neutrality made him decline office in the local Anti-reelectionist club, he held obvious sympathy for its goals. He was to spend a good part of the Revolution's early years in jail and eventually to become a key aide to Pancho Villa.

By the spring of 1909 such political and economic injustice had provoked many members of the fledgling middle class into opposition to the Terrazas-Creels and Porfirio Díaz. When the regime responded with repression, they sought recourse in violence.

A Comparative View

In other regions, the middle class followed a similar route to discontent and revolution, although alienation was, perhaps, more prevalent and intense in Chihuahua than elsewhere. Certainly the disgruntled middle class of Chihuahua proved more willing to challenge the Díaz regime by force of arms. Nonetheless, members of the middle class supplied much of the civilian leadership of the 1910 Revolution throughout Mexico.

The Mexican middle class had grown steadily with the economic growth of the *Porfiriato*. Its expansion was most rapid in the North, where opportunities lay in the building trades, commerce, services for the mining industry, mining, and ranching. In the Center, particularly in the larger cities and the capital, Mexico City, opportunities lay in government employment. The number of public employees in the Federal District increased by 68 percent between 1895 and 1910, while in Chihuahua the number decreased and in Sonora it increased by 30 percent.[43] Schoolteachers were the major exception to this trend, for their ranks doubled in the northern states, but increased at a lower rate in the nation as a whole.[44] The entrepreneurial nature of opportunities and advance in the North may account for the greater willingness of *norteños* to take the enormous risk of rebellion. The professionals and bureaucrats of the capital, dependent on the government, were more cautious, jumping on the revolutionary bandwagon after it defeated Díaz.[45]

As it did in Chihuahua, dissatisfaction among the middle class centered on two issues, economic and political opportunity. The entrepreneurial middle class, merchants, craftsmen, ranchers, miners, and servicers (such as muleteers) sought to eliminate the burdens of unfair taxation and corrupt courts, to gain access to credit, and to gain a say in local politics, where the rules that most concerned them were made. In peripheral states, such as Chihuahua and Guerrero, the issue boiled down to resistance to centralization and reassertion of the tradition of local autonomy. Thus the Figueroa brothers, of the state of Guerrero, merchants and manufacturers, led the revolution against centralization much as the González family did in western Chihuahua.[46] Such middle-class businessmen headed the Anti-reelectionist political party that opposed Díaz in 1910 in Yucatán, Sinaloa, Oaxaca, and Coahuila, often joining small groups of wealthy landowners who had political grievances against the Díaz regime.[47]

In central Mexico, the failure of the federal government to provide employment for a substantial number of professionals and other educated Mexicans after 1900, compounded by the depression of 1907, which dried up private employment, led to dissatisfaction. The political system was clogged with very old men, and the young professionals and bureaucrats wanted to clear them away. But they awaited action by their bolder contemporaries, who had weapons and a ready soldiery of *rancheros*, villagers, lumbermen, and miners.

7

Peasants to Arms

Small landowners (*rancheros*) and residents of landholding villages took arms in 1910 in response to the theft of their land by *hacendados* and speculators under the provisions of the Chihuahua Municipal Land Law of 1905. Beset by three successive years of drought and early frost that ruined their crops and killed their livestock, and deprived by the economic depression of auxiliary income from neighboring mines, factories, construction crews, or across the border, they rose, after years of futile protest, to defend their patrimony and regain what they had unfairly lost.

A Heritage of Conflict

The struggle of the *rancheros* and villages against the *hacienda* was old and bitter in Chihuahua, as it was throughout Mexico. The violence and hardship of the nineteenth century had imbued both sides with a distinctive toughness and resilience. At various times during the Apache wars, they had fought the Indians alone or together or joined with the Indians against the other.[1] Until the 1880s, the need for cooperation against the Apaches, the deep divisions in the state's elite, and the isolation of the region had enabled the *rancheros* and villages to hold their own.

By the end of the 1880s, however, strengthened by the enormous giveaway of public lands by the federal government, of which they were the main recipients, and by the cattle export boom, the *hacendados* gained the upper hand. At the same time, the end of both the national civil wars and the Apache menace ended the need for cooperation. By the early 1890s, factionalism in the Chihuahuan elite had been replaced by the hegemony of the Terrazas. The *rancheros* could no longer ensure their security by playing one faction of the elite off against another.

Two spurts of railroad building, the first from 1880 to 1884 and the second from 1897 to 1906, ended centuries of isolation, drove up land prices, and engendered wide-scale attacks on the holdings of *rancheros* and villages in Chihuahua. From 1872 to 1882, the price of public lands in Chihuahua remained at .12 pesos per hectare (2.47 acres). In 1883 the price jumped to .20 pesos. By 1891, the price ranged from .30 to .75 pesos, depending on the quality of the soil.[2] In the cities values rose precipitously too; in Ciudad Chihuahua land prices during the 1880s increased 50 percent.[3]

The policies of the Díaz government helped shift the advantage to the *hacendados* and concentrate vast tracts of land in very few hands. Under the provisions of the Law of Colonization of 1884, the national government granted concessions to favored companies to survey *terrenos baldíos*. In return, the companies received one-third of the land they surveyed. Another third was sold at a low fixed price, and the final third reverted to the government. Although the surveying companies were supposed to sell their lands in small parcels to industrious foreign farmers, the law was notoriously abused and served only to transfer huge tracts to influential officials or large landowners.[4]

Landholding villages and small landholders were despoiled of their property. Díaz interpreted the Reform Laws of the 1850s to prohibit communal landholding by villages. When the villages divided the land among their residents, the new owners quickly and easily fell prey to sharp lawyers and *hacendados*. In addition, the law enabled surveying companies to declare land "vacant" when its occupants held "defective" titles. The courts ignored protests, documentation, and decades of tenure to allow the companies to steal these lands. One historian has estimated that by one means or another villages in Mexico lost 2.25 million acres during the 1880s alone.[5]

In Chihuahua, former *presidios* in Galeana and Guerrero districts, with charters that dated back a century, and Tarahumara villages in western and southern districts were especially hard hit by the surveying companies. The American-owned Corralitos Company, for example, despoiled the village of Casas Grandes of 278,000 acres of land in 1885.[6] Luis Terrazas and Henrique Müller wrenched large sections from the common lands of Cruces (Namiquipa, Guerrero District), until by the end of the 1880s nothing was left of the grant made by Teodoro de Croix in 1778. They also stole land from the village of Galeana, despite an 1886 survey that upheld the village's claims.[7]

Indian villages in Andrés del Río and Hidalgo districts suffered similar outrages. In 1883 and 1884, the Tarahumara of Norogachic, Andrés del Río, rioted in protest against a land survey of the area. The local *jefe* had transferred Indian land to the Batopilas Mining Company.[8] The Tarahumara in Balleza, Hidalgo District, were so agitated by the surveying company, Compañía Ramón Guerrero, that *jefe* Anastasio Porras warned the state government that

Table 7–1
Other Great Landowners of Chihuahua

Estate	Owner	Location	Acres
Rancho Nuevo	Testament of Martínez del Río	Villa Ahumada	3,470,480
Madera Company	Mexico Northwestern Ry. Madera Company	Madera and Temósachic	2,589,037
Nogales/Wood-Hagenbarth	Wood-Hagenbarth/ Palomas Land & Cattle Co.	Janos and Ascensión	2,212,431
T. O. Riverside	Riverside Land & Cattle	Guadalupe, Ojinaga, Coyame	1,237,961
Canas, Rayón, and others	A. Asúnsolo	Escalón and Jiménez	976,045
Corralitos	Corralitos Land & Cattle	Casas Grandes, Galeana	880,634
Hacienda de Bavícora	Hearst	Temósachic, Guerrero	864,106
Los Angeles	Unknown	Unknown	688,055
García Tract	Development Co. of America (American-Mexican Lumber Co.)	Galeana and Guerrero	500,000
Hacienda de Santa Gertrudis	José María Luján Sold to Fleming 1910	Naica and Rosales, Camargo	498,882
Palotada, Alamos Altos	Luis Booker Sold to Warren Bros.	Janos, Ascensión	442,486
Hacienda de Santo Domingo	Santo Domingo Land and Cattle Co.	West of Villa Ahumada	438,148
Hacienda de Corrales	Luis Faudoa Sidney Lunhill	Allende, Jiménez	357,363
El Salitre	Benito Martínez	Batopilas	329,696
Tepehuanes and Saucito	Rafael & Ramón Saenz	San Andrés	303,667
Las Mesteñas	Cástulo Baca	Camargo	273,300
Hacienda de Dolores	Falomir	Aldama	270,011
El Sauz and others	Sánchez family	Zaragoza, Hidalgo	268,962
	Pine King Land and Lumber Co.	Mina	247,271
Hacienda La Providencia y Anexas		Namiquipa	247,270

Table 7–1 (continued)

Estate	Owner	Location	Acres
Ojitos, La Maquina	Santiago and Delaval Beresford. Sold to Warren Bros. Warrens owned total of 672,405 acres (see Palotada above)	Janos	229,919
Los Remedios	Marcos Russek	Escalón, Jiménez	216,905
La Santíssima	Shapleigh T. O. Riverside	Bravos	216,324
Ojo de Federico, Santiago	Pedro Prieto y Hermanos	Ascensión San Buenaventura	208,229
Hacienda de Santa Clara	Test. of Enrique Müller	Namiquipa	202,298 (346,805)[a]
	Casas Grandes Lumber Co.	west of Nuevas Casas Grandes	180,000 (125,000)[a]
San Pedro	A. B. Urmston purch. from C. G. Scobell	Janos	177,862 (282,000)[a]
San José and San Luis	Juan M. Salazar	Zaragoza, Hidalgo	173,524
	J. B. Haggui	Janos	173,524
Enramada	Pedro Erquicia	Camargo	160,510
	Parral & Durango Ry.		160,000
Hacienda de Samalayuca	Inocente Ochoa	Cd. Juárez	156,172
Corral de Piedra and others	Guillermo and Sabino Urrutia	Ascensión	154,003
Ojo Federico	Luis Booker Booker owned a total of 585,643 acres (see Palotada) until he sold Palotada	Ascensión	143,000
Las Delicias, Providencia, San Lucas	Sanatorio Miguel Salas	Camargo and Rosales	134,481
Palomas, Punta del Agua	Abel Baca	Villa López and Villa Coronado, Jiménez	134,481
Dos Hermanos	Enrique Visconti	Camargo	130,143
Guzman	Cruz González	Ascensión	130,143

Table 7–1 (continued)

Estate	Owner	Location	Acres
Pabellón	Muñoz Hermanos	Ojinaga	130,143
Batopilas Mining Co.	Alexander Shepherd	Batopilas	130,000
Hacienda Los Remedios	William Benton	Santa Isabel Iturbide	120,000
Saucillo, Ojo de la Morita	Rafael & Cipriano Urrutia	Rosales, Camargo	108,453
San Antonio and Cienequilla	Test. of Tomás Villegas	Zaragoza, Hidalgo	104,114
San Simón	Francisco Ochoa y Blancarte	Guadalupe y Calvo	104,114
Saucillo y Bernardo	Bruno Soto Chávez Probably included José de la Luz Soto Chupadero with 86,762 more	Escalón, Jiménez	104,114
Sierra Consolidated Mines		Ocampo	100,000
Realito de Tubares	Bernardo García	Batopilas	95,438

a. Alternative estimates.

any further incitement would lead to open rebellion and "bring ruin to the state."[9] And in 1892 the activities of surveying companies contributed to the uprising at Tomochi that resulted in the slaughter of the village's entire population by federal troops.[10]

Prolonged economic depression and drought in Chihuahua from 1890 to 1895 ended the cattle and land boom, and the despoilment of small holders and villages was curtailed for several years. The resurgence of political competition during the early part of the decade also afforded them a breathing period.

Conflict: 1902 to 1910

The unprecedented economic boom that followed the depression was accompanied by a railroad construction boom. Beginning in late 1896, several new railroad ventures extended the state's rail network east-west. During these years, the Rio Grande, Sierra Madre and Pacific, the Chihuahua al Pacífico, the Kansas City, Mexico and Orient, and the Mexican Northwestern all undertook major building projects, connecting the state's major population centers to Ciudad Chihuahua and opening up hitherto inaccessible mining, timber, and agricultural areas. As a result, land values in the regions served by the railroads increased enormously. Stimulated by the prosperity and growing population, urban land values rose even more sharply. Mining areas saw a boom in claim registrations. Land and mine speculation accompanied the spread of the railroads, pushing prices even higher.

In 1896 the price for a hectare of public land in Chihuahua stood at .75 pesos. With the first new railroad construction that year, the price jumped to one peso. It subsequently rose to $1.10 in 1902, $1.20 in 1905, and $4.00 in 1908, when most of the construction was completed.[11] Between 1898 and 1906 the value of property and rents in Ciudad Chihuahua increased 50 percent.[12] Prices for good farmland and urban lots were considerably higher than those of public lands. Farmland varied from 12 to 26 pesos per hectare, while pasture sold for 5 to 10 pesos. A city lot in Parral commanded as much as 60 pesos in 1905 at the peak of the boom.[13]

The railroads' effect was especially evident in the regions 100 to 150 miles east and west of Ciudad Chihuahua. The new lines stimulated wheat production east of the capital and fruit production in Miñaca, where the expansion of the KCM&O cut transportation costs by half. Landowners built wagon roads to the railroad and imported large quantities of new farm equipment in response to the new opportunities.[14]

Land became so valuable—in some areas values tripled—that latifundists and speculators yet again undertook to appropriate the lands of small holders, villages, and municipalities. Empowered by the Municipal Land Law of 1905, they began aggressively to acquire these holdings, which led to widespread tension and finally rebellion in 1910.[15]

There was a direct causal connection between the spread of the railroad network, the number of claims under the provisions of the Municipal Land Law of 1905, and the outbreak of agrarian discontent that led to revolution. The *rancheros* along the path of the railroads first peacefully protested the loss of their lands with petitions to the governor and president and letters to *El Correo de Chihuahua*. Eventually they turned to demonstrations and riots. Some of the protests were heeded, for Luis Terrazas and Enrique Creel mediated several disputes between large landowners and villagers or *rancheros*. Creel was able to arrange agreements in conflicts over *ejido* lands in Villa Ahumada, San Francisco de Conchos, and other areas,[16] but most protests fell on deaf ears, and trouble boiled. Some victimized landowners joined Antireelectionist clubs that sprang up in Chihuahua in 1908, 1909, and 1910. Later the former *presidios* would supply the soldiers and military leaders for the *maderista* revolution in Chihuahua in 1910.

Table 7–2
Adjudications of Municipal Land
in Chihuahua by District

	1905	1906	1907	1908	1909
Andrés del Río	9	26	24	25	35
Arteaga	0	0	0	3	5
Benito Juárez	11	63	107	65	95
Bravos	63	87	139	194	58
Camargo	31	56	49	169	44
Galeana	60	88	102	116	115
Guerrero	18	96	141	98	109
Hidalgo	49	102	100	57	13
Iturbide	74	260	623	441	133
Jiménez	1	5	48	10	11
Mina	0	0	1	0	3
Rayón	23	9	19	13	31
Unknown	2	6	24	1	3
Total	341	798	1,377	1,192	655

Source: Compiled from Chihuahua, Secretaría del Gobierno, Sección Estadística, *Anuarios, 1905–1909.*

Often the projected or actual presence of the railroad renewed old, bitter conflicts between large landowners and *rancheros*. The ex-*presidios* had seen much of their land stolen during the 1880s, and now the *hacendados* were back for more. The struggle grew desperate, especially after 1907, when the depression deprived the villagers and *rancheros* of any chance of alternate employment. Their backs were against the wall.

The pattern of railroad construction, usurpation of land, and resistance is clear in the case of the former military colonies in eastern Chihuahua that lay near the projected road of the KCM&O line. In one of these colonies, Cuchillo Parado, a local *hacendado* and member of the Terrazas inner circle, Carlos Muñoz, tried in 1903 to expropriate 43,000 acres from the community. Cuchillo Parado won its initial fight to keep the disputed land, but the conflict continued, undoubtedly spurred on by the increase in land values from the planned extension of the KCM&O to Ojinaga. Village spokesman Toribio Ortega was to be the first revolutionary leader to take up arms against the government in 1910.[17]

San Carlos, another former military colony, also lay close to the proposed KCM&O. It contested its borders with Governor Creel, who owned an immense tract nearby. The conflict deteriorated in 1909 to the point that *rurales* were dispatched to keep order.[18]

The effect of the railroad was more far-reaching to the west in Guerrero and Galeana districts. Former military colonies in Janos (Galeana) and Namiquipa (Guerrero) in northwestern Chihuahua lay along the route of the Mexican Northwestern railway that was to connect Casas Grandes with Madera. They too saw a renewed assault on their lands. Despite protests to Porfirio Díaz the move against Janos, led by two local *hacendados*, continued unabated.[19] Authorities called in the *rurales* to force the people off the land. One of the protesters who lost his land was Porfirio N. Talamantes, who was to become a colonel in Pancho Villa's revolutionary army.[20] Many villages in Guerrero suffered the consequences of the expanding rail network. There were numerous adjudications along the railroad route in Bachíniva, Temósachic, Matachic, and Tejolócachic.[21] In Namiquipa residents protested nearly three hundred adjudications, but with no more success than their neighbors to the north in Janos. It must have been especially upsetting to the rough independent people of this region that two of their most hated *jefes*, Luis Y. Comadurán and Joaquín Chávez, and their families were among the largest adjudicators of municipal land in the district.[22] In response to this attack on land, Namiquipa became a hotbed of revolution.[23]

The extension of the Parral and Durango railroad west and south of Hidalgo del Parral set off a wave of adjudications, especially in the vicinity of Villa Escobedo.[24] The construction of the railroad helped touch off bitter disputes in San Andrés, where a flood of adjudications led to riots in 1909.[25] Parral and San Andrés later became centers of the Revolution.

Land seizures also provoked discontent in areas of Chihuahua where the railroad had little effect. In 1904 Guadalupe in Bravos District was invaded by a surveying company. After four years the government finally resolved the dispute in favor of the former military colony, but it became a fertile recruiting ground for revolutionary soldiers.[26]

Residents of communities on the outskirts of Ciudad Chihuahua lost their land as a consequence of both railroad construction and the city's expansion. In Chúviscar and neighboring Barrio de Santo Niño, the rise in land values and numerous adjudications bred serious unrest. In the Barrio de Santo Niño, on the Hacienda de Tabaloapa, a community of factory workers lived for many years, paying only token rents, at the behest of philanthropist Laura Müller de Ketelsen. When the señora died in 1904, the new owners, the Terrazas-owned Compañía Industrial Mexicana, sought to evict the tenants from the valuable land. The company also began to charge a fee for passage through the tract. Complaints to the governor, of course, were ignored, and the community later became yet another center of revolutionary activity.[27]

Conflict also arose in San Lorenzo, Iturbide District, where Englishman

William Benton purchased an *hacienda* in 1908 that he converted from staple production to cattle breeding. He provoked considerable ill feeling in the area when he evicted tenants from the estate. Two years later, Benton widened the battle when he occupied land belonging to the nearby village of Santa María de las Cuevas. Surrounding himself with a bodyguard of twenty men and a detachment of *rurales*, he ran roughshod over the region. In 1914, Pancho Villa had the despised Benton shot.[28]

Villages and municipalities suffered also from a surge of mining speculation along railroad routes. Mining claims were registered on the common lands of Temósachic, San Carlos, Ojinaga, and Cuchillo Parado, which all became rallying points of the Revolution.[29]

Almost from its inception, the Municipal Land Law of 1905 drew angry complaints of secret dealings, favoritism, nepotism, and illegal procedures. Governor Creel had announced that the purpose of the law was to "modernize" land ownership and provide the lower classes opportunity to buy land. Like the Liberals before him, Creel thought community property holding obstructed economic development. Instead, the law worked to transfer communal lands to large landowners and speculators. *Jefes* gave their families and cronies preferred access to the land, easily circumventing the legal limit on adjudications by using frontmen and relatives. State government memoranda through the end of 1909 urged the *jefes* to comply with the law, but they were, of course, ignored.[30]

Water rights were another source of agrarian discontent, for the government granted *hacendados* and foreign companies the use of crucial water. When the Mormons of Colonia Dublán in Casas Grandes built a large irrigation project on the Casas Grandes River, other landowners heatedly protested.[31] There were other controversial grants on the Río Papigochi and Río Basuchil in Guerrero, on the Río Conchos in Nonoava, and on the Conchos in Ojinaga in 1908 and 1909, years when prolonged drought made water a matter of life and death.[32]

Drought, Harvest Failure, and Agrarian Unrest

To these outrages were added three successive years of crop failures from 1907 to 1909. Chihuahua had shown a definite pattern of crop failure and rebellion, especially in the Guerrero District, since the mid-nineteenth century.

Forty-five percent of Chihuahua is desert, 30 percent oak savanna, and most of the rest, pine forest and subtropical deciduous forest.[33] Even in the nineteenth century, Chihuahuans took reasonably good advantage of their limited agricultural possibilities. Chihuahua became a leading livestock region. Farmers tapped the precious few rivers, streams, lakes, and wells for

Table 7–3
Estimated Chihuahuan Staple Harvests

Year	Maize (hectolitres)	Wheat (kilograms)	Beans (hectolitres)
1856[a]	140,799	4,386,200	17,550
1879[a]	434,377	24,065,160	33,256
1883[a]	948,946	48,762,000	33,727
1889	253,323	27,492,525	
1890			
1891			
1892		1892–1900: estimated production of	
1893		wheat 149,513,966 or average of 16,612,000 per yr.	
1894	527,632	22,574,300	
1895			1892–1900: average of
1896	595,697	1,960,128	107,362
1897	243,891	4,345,649	1901–6: average of
1898	358,219	7,925,300	82,691
1899	506,483	13,833,969	
1900	421,182		
1901	486,978	1901–6: est. prod. = 113,988,801 or	
1902	410,515	average of 18,981,460 per yr.	
1903	392,364	11,601,150	71,245
1904	592,544		73,887
1905	863,720	35,207,023	153,171
1906	1,134,305	29,506,000	125,951
1907	1,021,752	24,090,991	117,098
1908	740,206	21,736,617	67,047
1909	644,644	14,908,942	62,499
1910			
1911			

Sources: Chihuahua, *Anuarios, 1905–1909*; Mexico, *Anuarios, 1894–1899*; *Periódico Oficial del Estado de Chihuahua*, 16 September 1906 and 20 April 1911; *Diario Chihuahuense*, 17 February 1900; *Revista Chihuahuense*, 1 (31 October 1909): 1–8; U.S., *Commercial Relations, 1891–1892*, p. 291; García Conde, *Ensayo Estadístico*, pp. 324–25; Chihuahua, Gobernador, *Memoria, 1892–1896*.
a. based on a fanega = ½ carga and a hectolitre = 1.75 fanegas.

irrigation water. Despite these efforts, the state's agricultural production, particularly of staple crops, was precariously at the mercy of cyclical and sometimes terrible drought. From the 1870s, political disruptions often accompanied these periods of suffering and hardship. The droughts hit hardest in Guerrero, where during the nineteenth century they coincided with rebellions. So it is not surprising that the drought led to political unrest and ultimately to rebellion in the period between 1907 and 1910.

Weather and harvest conditions, of course, were perhaps necessary but still not sufficient causes for unrest and revolt. In almost every case, political disputes ignited the discontent brought on by adverse weather. In 1877 and 1879, already ruined by Indian raids and nearly two decades of civil war, Chihuahua suffered through crop failures and in the latter year revolt broke out in Guerrero.[34] Poor harvests again victimized the state in 1884 and 1885, keeping staple prices and the cost of living high until 1887.[35] In 1886 there was a violent political struggle in Cusihuiriachic. The following year the legislature broke up, throwing state politics into chaos. Although in neither case were agricultural conditions the primary cause of unrest, they exacerbated existing discontent.[36]

From 1890 to 1895, Chihuahua suffered a prolonged drought, accompanied by a 56 percent increase in the cost of living in two years.[37] Seven rebellions erupted in the state during this period. Guerrero again was the major source of unrest. The most serious broke out in Tomochi, where a handful of residents held off a federal army, killing hundreds of soldiers before being overrun and massacred in September 1892. There was another uprising in Santo Tomás (Namiquipa) in March 1893. Six months later, a rebel group sprung up in northwestern Chihuahua near Palomas, Galeana. In 1895 and 1896, other rebels raided in extreme eastern Chihuahua, near Ojinaga. Finally, the Tarahumara Indians rioted in Agua Amarilla (Guadalupe y Calvo) in May 1895.[38]

Poor weather ruined the crops in 1901 and 1902, sending up the cost of living again.[39] The devaluation of the peso at the same time brought on a nationwide recession. But neither unrest nor rebellion ensued, for the harvest failures and recession were not severe enough or long enough, and there was no outstanding political issue to spark a revolt.

The combined drought and early frost from 1907 to 1909 differed from earlier weather disasters in that it followed the most successful harvests in Chihuahuan history. Although the harvests of 1908 and 1909 were not terrible by Chihuahuan standards, there were more mouths to feed and after years of low staple prices the effect was devastating. The succession of boom and bust hit particularly hard in Guerrero District, where both the corn and wheat harvests doubled in 1906 and remained high in 1907. Wheat production dropped in 1908 and corn production fell drastically in 1909. Crop failure and rising staple prices pushed the Chihuahuan peasantry, already besieged by land-stealing *hacendados* and speculators, to the brink.

The massive assault on the land of *rancheros* and villages, coming at a time of widespread unemployment, drought, and general hardship, drove the peasants to rebellion. The independent small holders and residents of the former *presidios*, who had shed blood for their land, would not surrender their patrimony without a fight.

A Comparative View

There were four types of revolutionary peasants in Mexico in 1910–11, only one of which was present in Chihuahua. The first was the "modern" peon of La Laguna of Durango. These highly paid agricultural workers, who resided and picked cotton on the region's large estates, fought under their *hacendados*.[40] Most peons resident on *haciendas* in Mexico and Chihuahua did not join the Revolution. Many, like the slaves of Yucatán's henequén plantations, were too oppressed to rise. Others, imported by *hacendados* to work lands expropriated from neighboring villages, enjoyed relatively privileged status and were isolated from or at odds with the local *campesinos* (country people).[41]

The second category included the tribal Indians of the North, most notably the Yaquis of Sonora, who allied themselves with revolutionary *hacendados* José María Maytorena and, later, Adolfo de la Huerta. They fought to regain lands lost during the nineteenth century.[42]

The third comprised the residents of landholding villages on the central plateau who had lost their lands to the *haciendas* after the railroad boom of the 1880s. These villagers, typified by the Zapatistas of Morelos, found themselves in 1910 beset on all sides by encroaching *haciendas*, economic depression, and successive bad harvests. Desperate, they fought in 1910.[43]

The final group was the *rancheros*. These small landowners led the Revolution in Chihuahua, seeking to regain despoiled lands. In other regions they fought to regain local political control, as in the state of Guerrero.[44] In areas where the railroad had not disrupted land tenure, such as Oaxaca, the small holders did not rebel.[45]

Few of the men who led the peasant revolutionaries were "true" peasants. They invariably had wider contacts and experiences. The peasants of La Laguna had almost all come from the central plateau, lured by high wages. They were alienated from traditional ties of family and village. Many of the *morelense* rebels, including Zapata himself, had worked in Mexico City or even in the United States. The Yaquis had fled deportation into slavery and worked in the United States. The small landowners of northern and western

Chihuahua had the most extensive links to nonpeasant society. Many worked to supplement their agricultural income in northern mines, lumber camps, and railroad construction crews and in the United States. Other Chihuahuan peasants diversified into commerce and other pursuits. As they did elsewhere (Tlaxcala-Puebla, for example), these "peasant workers" proved early revolutionaries. These men were often exposed to radical ideologies and union organizations.[46] In some cases it is difficult to categorize men like Pascual Orozco, who was a *ranchero*, storekeeper, and muleteer. Class in western Chihuahua in particular was fluid. It is perhaps no coincidence that the peasants with the widest outside contacts, the *rancheros* of Chihuahua, were initially the most successful revolutionaries.

Whatever their backgrounds or traits, peasants, led by middle-class civilians, malcontent *hacendados*, or their own, were the shock troops that won the Revolution's first victories. Later, their leaders and allies abandoned them. But some continued the fight well into the 1920s to regain the land they loved and claimed.

8

The Origins of Working-Class Discontent

Disaffected workers, mostly miners, lumbermen, and railroadmen, played a critical role in the Revolution in Chihuahua, though a lesser one than the middle class or peasants. With the exception, perhaps, of textile workers from the Tlaxcala-Puebla region and Sonoran miners, workers were more active in Chihuahua early in the Revolution than they were anywhere else.

From the colonial era, workers in Chihuahua were more independent, more mobile, and less bound by traditional ties of family and geography than their counterparts in central Mexico. Moreover, because of the region's chronic shortage of labor, they were a privileged group relative to others in Mexico.[1] Wages and working conditions were almost always better in the North. Chihuahuan labor was different, too, in the extent to which its well-being was linked to the export economy and world market conditions. When world demand for Chihuahuan minerals was high, an insatiable demand for labor drove up wages in all sectors. When mining declined, it brought widespread unemployment and suffering. After 1900 new opportunities for employment across the border in the booming southwestern United States forced employers all over northern Mexico to raise wages and improve working conditions to compete for scarce labor. Exposure to better wages and working conditions and nonpaternalistic employers in the United States accentuated the trends that already set northern workers apart from their brethren to the south.

These tendencies were magnified during the heady boom days between 1898 and 1907, when Chihuahuan workers enjoyed unprecedented prosperity. Taking their cue in part from their experience across the border, Chihuahuan workers took advantage of the tight labor market to organize mutualist societies and unions and seek even better wages and working conditions. At the height of the boom, they instigated a number of strikes for higher pay, shorter hours, and an end to discrimination against native workers. These efforts met solid resistance from both employers and local authorities. Then the depression that began in mid-1907 with its widespread mine closings and unemployment ended nearly a decade of advancement. The following two years of joblessness and misery led a significant number of Chihuahuan workers to join the political opposition to the Díaz-Terrazas regime, and many of these men took arms with the revolutionaries in 1910.

The Prerailroad Age: 1821–1880

Despite political chaos and Indian depredations, the scarcity of labor on the northern frontier assured laborers of relatively high wages and favorable working conditions, although both stagnated after 1830.[2]

Then in the 1860s a brief resurgence of the mining industry improved working conditions once again. Whereas early in the decade miners earned between 37.5 and 50 centavos a day, by 1868 mines in Urique in extreme western Chihuahua offered as much as a peso a day to attract miners to the isolated region.[3] In an effort to increase the work force, the Chihuahuan legislature passed a law in 1867 that limited the amount of indebtedness a worker could incur to three months' salary.[4] Despite this measure, the shortage of labor persisted. Mining companies in Santa Eulalia had to rely on convicts supplied by the state government.[5] But the boom collapsed in 1873, and Chihuahuan workers had to wait another decade for their plight to improve again.

Despite the hard times, Chihuahuan workers, miners in particular, showed an early tendency to resist oppressive conditions. In 1874, for example, thirty-six employees of the González, Herrera, and Salazar Company got an *amparo* (writ of protection) against their employers to prevent their paying wages in scrip and charging exorbitant prices at the company store.[6] Workers also founded two mutualist societies during the 1870s, the Sociedad Mutualista de Trabajadores de Parral in 1877 and the Sociedad de Obreros de Chihuahua in 1878.[7]

The Boom-and-Bust Mining Economy

The revitalization of the mining industry (and the rest of the Chihuahuan economy) substantially improved wages and working conditions from 1880 to 1910, especially during the 1880s and from 1902 to 1907, after extensive railroad construction. The growing railroad network opened new job opportunities and gave workers considerable mobility. Between these two booms were two major depressions when wages stagnated or fell and unemployment was rampant.[8]

After 1900 there were three categories of workers in Chihuahua, *peones*, miners, and industrial workers. The largest number of Chihuahuans, of course, worked in agriculture throughout the era. In absolute terms the number of agricultural workers increased steadily, but their proportion slightly declined.[9] Wages and working conditions on the *haciendas* depended to a large degree on the peon's status or occupation (resident, temporary worker, tenant, sharecropper, *vaquero*, shepherd). Generally, the closer the *hacienda* was to the railroad or the nearer it was to the United States border, the higher the wages were. In isolated areas of the state very harsh conditions sometimes prevailed.[10]

Because miners, the second most numerous category of workers, were in short supply and constant demand, they enjoyed the highest wages and greatest chance of upward mobility. Although their pay varied according to skill, miners in Chihuahua (and the Northwest) consistently earned more than their counterparts elsewhere in Mexico.

The nonmining industrial work force included railroad workers, construction laborers, and textile workers. Railroad workers were generally the highest paid, especially the skilled or semiskilled, who plied their trades in the maintenance shops. (Other supervisory and skilled positions went to foreigners paid twice the native scale.) There was also a large number of seasonal workers who built or repaired the lines.

The construction trades boomed after 1902, when the state government and the largest municipalities embarked on extensive programs of public works. As with miners and railroad workers, construction labor's pay depended on the level of skill. The highest wages were paid in the state's major cities, Ciudad Chihuahua and Ciudad Juárez.

The expanding economy also provided more jobs in textiles, as manufacturers sought to clothe the growing population. Women made up the bulk of the work force in the textile industry and received less for their efforts than men. Male textile workers earned more than agricultural laborers but less than miners, though hours in the textile factories were longer than in the mines.

The 1880s and 1890s

As we have seen, the resurgence of mining during the 1880s brought an acute labor shortage that in turn sharply raised mining wages. By mid-decade miners' wages ranged from seventy-five centavos to three pesos a day.[11] The arrival of large American corporations in Batopilas (Andrés del Río District) and Palmarejo (Arteaga) in mountainous, isolated southwestern Chihuahua

caused large wage increases in those areas.[12] Foreign companies, constantly
in need of labor, continued to offer attractive wages, but shortages persisted.[13]
And the availability of jobs made it possible for miners to demand improved
conditions so that when some mine owners continued old abuses, the miners
balked. A British firm in Pinos Altos tried to pay its workers partly in scrip,
and in 1882 they struck in protest. Local authorities ended the strike by shooting the ringleaders.[14]

Agricultural workers did not share in the first postrailroad boom. Peons in
some areas around the state capital and in the western districts still earned
only twenty-five centavos a day, no more than fifty years before.[15] In some
areas, *hacendados*, confronted with stiff competition for labor from the
mines, chained their peons to the *hacienda* with steep debts.[16]

Comparative statistics available for the 1880s indicate that all categories of
Chihuahuan workers were better off than their brethren in other parts of the
country. Even agricultural workers earned 50 to 100 percent higher wages.
Skilled and semiskilled labor earned two to five times as much in Chihuahua
as in Mexico City, San Blas (Nayarit), Monterrey (Nuevo León), or Mata-
moros (Tamaulipas). Only in Sonora, where wages rose 30 percent from 1878
to 1884 and miners earned a peso or more daily, did the rise in workers' wages

Table 8–1

Composition of the Chihuahuan Work Force

Sector	1895	1900	1904	1906	1907	1908	1909	1910
Agriculture	64,293	78,972	35,002	44,732	45,788	43,255	32,988	86,721
Industry (total)	13,566	17,108						24,333
Mining	5,525	8,749	6,866	9,763	9,285	9,566	9,002	11,609
Manufacturing	7,466	7,222		4,326	2,988	3,738		
Construction	575	1,127						1,624
Services (total)	14,503	14,073						19,983
Commercial	3,161	4,592	1,175	1,081				5,253
Transportation	669	724						1,177
Public Service	785	524						708
Personal Services	501	1,352						4,399
Armed Services	622	1,241						1,268
Professional	2,547	2,096						3,643
Domestic	6,218	3,544						3,535
Other	10,673	8,757						13,553
Miscellaneous								
occupations	8,843	12,572						14,442
Total Work Force	101,205	122,725						145,479

Source: SHMM, *Estadísticas Económicas*, pp. 38–60.
Note: Some columns do not total because of missing categories.

rival that of Chihuahua.[17] Sonorans were burdened with a 10 percent increase in food prices during this period and a far higher cost of living throughout the decade.[18] Although it was more expensive to live in Chihuahua than in Mexico as a whole or the rest of the North (with the exception of Sonora), higher wages more than made up the difference.

The depression and drought of the early 1890s brought widespread unemployment and high staple prices. But recovery in 1896 brought renewed demands for labor, and wages rose again. Increased employment and bumper crops brought relative prosperity to Chihuahuan workers in 1896, 1897, and 1898.[19]

Miners continued to receive the best wages, which rose by approximately 30 percent during the decade. But wages for peons stagnated again.[20] During six of the ten years of the decade, the cost of living in Chihuahua was lower than in Mexico as a whole. In nine of the ten it was lower in Chihuahua than in the rest of the North. Mining wages were higher than in any other state except possibly Sonora, Baja California, and Querétaro.[21] Agricultural and nonmining industrial wages remained 25 to 50 percent higher in Chihuahua than in the center of the country.

Mining wages continued to rise in the first three years of the new century. Jobs were plentiful, as American companies absorbed hundreds of new workers.[22]

The Great Boom: 1902 to 1907

From 1902 to 1907, Chihuahuan workers enjoyed unprecedented prosperity. Employment boomed. Railroad construction provided thousands of jobs and opened new areas for mining, agriculture, and lumbering. A massive public works program by the state and larger cities also provided a large number of jobs. Most important, the flourishing economy of the United States Southwest created a huge demand for unskilled and semiskilled workers at double the wages paid in Mexico.[23] Record corn, wheat, and bean harvests pushed down the cost of living.

Writing in the *Engineering and Mining Journal*, a reporter observed in 1907 that the Mexican worker had risen from virtual slavery in the 1890s, when a peon earned one peso a week augmented by two-thirds of a bushel of corn and a miner earned fifty centavos a day, to the point where they earned a peso a day as field hands and up to three pesos a day in the mines.[24] The United States consuls in Chihuahua noted that wages had risen from 10 to 20 percent between 1897 and 1907 with most of the increase coming after 1902. Compensation had improved to the extent that workers were buying lots on the installment plan and building their own homes.[25] Protestant missionary Alden B. Case remarked in 1906 that "in no part of Mexico are the masses in so good circumstances materially" as in Chihuahua.[26]

Although the Chihuahuan work force as a whole increased by nearly 50 percent from 1895 to 1910—the mining force almost doubled from 1895 to 1907—it did not satisfy demand. Employers constantly complained of labor shortages. Demand for labor reached its peak from 1905 through the first half of 1907. Both the Mexican Central and KCM&O began major construction projects, the American Smelting and Refining Company started a new smelter in Ciudad Chihuahua, and several large public works got under way. Labor shortages had grown so acute by 1906 that a mining company official in Santa Eulalia urged that the state government ban outside hiring agents to prevent them from luring workers to other areas with the prospect of better wages.[27] Other states with similar labor scarcities had already adopted such laws. The KCM&O could not attract native workers at 1.25 or 1.50 pesos a day and as a result had to fill many of its 2,500 jobs with imported Chinese.[28]

Demand for labor in the United States Southwest and northern Mexican mines produced a continuous northward migration. Workers came first from the central plateau to labor in Chihuahuan mines and on the railroads. They then left for more lucrative wages across the border in the United States. One expert estimated that from 1902 to 1907 at least sixty thousand Mexicans a year passed through Ciudad Juárez. For Mexican workers the migration acted as an "agent of something approaching social revolution."[29] Once the migrant crossed the border, his real wages doubled. (Although wages in nominal terms were the same on both sides, American employers paid in dollars worth twice the Mexican peso.) Workers on large railroad construction projects in the Southwest often received free lodging and transportation to the place of employment as well. Because of the demand for labor, wages of migrant farm hands rose 25 percent from 1903 to 1907. A cotton picker could earn three dollars a day and a family perhaps five dollars. Some workers accumulated savings. Most important, Mexican laborers became accustomed to a better standard of living. Paid in cash and divorced from the traditional paternalistic relations between employer and employee, they acquired a new independence that they did not lose when they returned to Mexico. The seemingly unending flow of labor northward exacerbated the shortage of labor in Chihuahua. One company official complained that his firm had imported labor from central Mexico, only to lose 80 percent of it to employers in the United States.[30]

The massive influx of foreign investment into Chihuahuan mining after 1902 boosted wages, for foreign companies were willing to pay over the going rate. In some instances, the arrival of a foreign company had dramatic results on nearby competition. During the two years after William C. Greene's Greene Gold and Silver Company began operations in the Sierra Madres of western Chihuahua, wages in the region jumped 25 percent.[31] One rival mine owner complained that "wages have been raised by the entry of Colonel Greene to such an extent that I cannot hope to pay; in fact the miners . . . simply dictate what they should be paid, or they will not work." [32] When a foreign firm took over the Lluvia de Oro mines in Andrés del Río, wages quadrupled. [33] The *Mexican Herald* reported in 1906 that because of the presence of American companies, wages had doubled in the past ten years. [34]

Although agricultural wages always lagged well behind those of miners, who were more in demand, they rose substantially after 1900 and were higher than elsewhere in Mexico. Through the 1890s agricultural workers earned 37.5 centavos a day. By 1905, they generally earned 50 centavos daily, a rise of one-third. Some temporary workers received as much as a peso a day. [35]

As we saw earlier, *vaqueros*, the most privileged workers on the *haciendas*, who earned seven or eight pesos a month in 1902, had doubled their wages by 1913. Some *vaqueros* were permitted to augment their income by raising their own cattle on *hacienda* land. Furthermore, if a cowboy became a foreman (*caporal*), he could draw as much as thirty pesos a month. [36]

Sharecropping arrangements were also more favorable in Chihuahua than elsewhere in Mexico. The *hacendado* took between one-third and one-half the crop in return for use of the land and some equipment, while in the Center and South he took two-thirds of the crop. [37] Some *haciendas*, like Corralitos, provided schools and medical services as well. [38]

The high wages paid in the mines, on railroad construction crews, and lumber camps lured small landowners and peons from the countryside. Some left permanently, for the percentage of the total work force in agriculture declined from 24.5 to 21.4 percent from 1895 to 1910. Many others worked seasonally, returning to their land at planting and harvest. There were reports that some villages in western Chihuahua almost wholly migrated during slow periods in agriculture. [39] Such "peasant-workers," some of whom had lost their lands to usurping *haciendas*, were noted also in Tlaxcala, where the textile industry attracted labor. But they remain the subject of speculation. Neither proletarians nor true peasants, they were profoundly affected by the depression of 1907 and made up a significant part of the revolutionary working class in 1910. [40]

Miners' wages rose markedly between 1904 and 1906, when demand for labor peaked. In Santa Eulalia increases ranged from 25 to 50 percent. At ASARCO's giant Tecolotes complex some workers won a 75 percent raise. [41] Moreover, mine owners had to pay their workers more often and in cash. In Santa Eulalia, a camp notorious for abuses of its company stores, miners no longer had to buy staples at these stores, and their standard of living improved accordingly. [42]

Wages were highest near the United States border. The Candelaria Mining Company, for example, paid a minimum wage of four pesos a day to its almost entirely native work force.[43] Wages also remained high in isolated camps, while in other camps near the railroad lines like Parral and Santa Bárbara, where miners could live less expensively in town, pay was lower.[44] Employees of the biggest companies in the more densely populated areas earned the poorest wages. ASARCO paid workers in its ore treatment plants (*haciendas de beneficio*) 55 percent less than other companies in Chihuahua.[45]

Because native-owned companies are underrepresented in wage data, it is unclear whether foreign companies generally paid more than native companies. Although to the consternation of local *hacendados* and mine owners some American firms paid substantially above the regional norm, most American operations went along with local customs: they paid as little as possible.[46] Americans were sometimes reluctant to run company stores, unless the mining camp was in an isolated area and the store would be the most efficient way to supply necessities.[47] In a few cases, the companies avoided this unpleasant institution by contracting the store to others. Treatment of workers varied according to the individual company and local conditions. Testimony before the United States Senate in 1919 (the Fall Committee) indicated that Americans were more considerate of their workmen and Mexicans allegedly preferred to work for them.[48] But in 1908 United States consul Lewis Martin of Ciudad Chihuahua reported that American companies treated their employees unjustly.[49] It was more advantageous to work for large foreign companies because they generally worked the entire year, while smaller operations shut down for several months, leaving their employees without work. There is also some evidence that during the boom native workers increasingly won promotions to lower-level supervisory positions.

In some instances, native companies offered better long-term job security. The big companies were prone to introduce labor-saving capital equipment, especially during the depression of 1907. With less capital, the operations of Mexican firms were more labor intensive. Pedro Alvarado, the fantastically successful owner of the legendary Palmilla mine in Parral, refused to mechanize because it would have put many long-time employees out of work.[50] And the smaller companies were less likely to show the blatant favoritism to foreign miners that one found in the larger concerns.

Nonmining industrial workers, particularly in the construction trades, may have benefited even more than miners from the great boom. Many tradesmen set up their own shops in Ciudad Chihuahua and other cities, moving upward into the middle class. Between 1905 and 1906 the average minimum wage for industrial workers (nonmining and nonconstruction) rose from $.9392 pesos to $1.4848 for males and $.5163 to $.748 for females, increases of 58 and 43 percent, respectively.[51]

Whatever the variation in wages according to district, company size, or ownership, the peons, miners, and industrial laborers of all types were generally better off in Chihuahua than elsewhere. Agricultural workers were the highest paid anywhere in the nation.[52] Real wages for industrial workers in Mexico slipped or stagnated during this period, but rose in Chihuahua. In 1907, Chihuahuan miners earned more than their counterparts in other regions with the exception of Sonora and, perhaps, Coahuila and Querétaro. Construction workers earned more than their contemporaries other than those in Hermosillo, Sonora.[53] Nonmining industrial workers also earned the highest wages in the nation.

And from 1903 to 1907 the cost of living in Chihuahua was substantially lower than in Mexico as a whole. Although there was a major rise in the cost of living in the state in 1905, it was still cheaper to live in Chihuahua than elsewhere. Maize prices were lower in three of the five years, while wheat and bean prices were lower in all five.

Discontent

Better wages and improved working conditions, however prevalent, did not end traditional abuses of and impediments for native labor. But after 1900, taking advantage of the tight labor market and often influenced by exposure to union activities in the United States or American workers in Mexico, workers grew increasingly militant and willing to protest injustices. They objected, in particular, to preferential pay and treatment for foreigners, payment in scrip instead of cash, as mandated by law, unfairly high prices charged by company stores, deductions from pay for nonexistent or inadequate medical services, and harassment by company police.

The history of workers' organizations in Chihuahua dates to the early 1870s. There were two types of organizations. The earliest, mutualist societies, were usually associations of artisans who sought to protect their economic and social position through cooperative programs of savings, insurance, and pensions. They also offered a range of cultural programs.[54] Although they did not push economic issues and were not aggressive, their formation indicates at least an incipient class consciousness. The second type was, of course, the labor union.

The first recorded strike came in 1881 in Paso del Norte, when Mexican workers protested a reduction in wages by the Mexican Central. Subsequently, local authorities intervened and the wages were restored.[55] Strikers were not so fortunate two years later at Pinos Altos, where authorities executed strike leaders. During the 1890s, attempts to organize workers at the Batopilas complex failed.[56] In 1890 workers founded the Sociedad Juárez de Obreros. Ten years later, the new national railroad brotherhood, Unión Mecánicos Mexicanos, established a branch in Chihuahua, and it moved its headquarters to the state the following year.[57] The Sociedad Cooperativa, a mutualist society, was founded in Parral in 1900. Another railroad union, the Sociedad de Hermanos Caldereros (steamfitters), was formed in 1903. In the next four years, fifteen new mutualist societies and unions sprouted up. By 1907, seventeen mutualist societies had 1,150 members.[58]

Chihuahuan workers deeply resented the preferential treatment and pay given foreigners and struck several times during 1906 and 1907 over this issue. Even the more benevolent American employers discriminated against natives. None of Alexander Shepherd's top fourteen employees, for example, were natives.[59] Some Americans worried that the mutualist societies would become vehicles for anti-American sentiment.[60]

The most persistent and onerous abuse of workers was the illegal payment of all or part of their wages in scrip (the *boleto*) redeemable only at the company store. In most cases, the store charged exorbitant prices for staples sold more cheaply at local merchant houses. Workers commonly could use their scrip at other stores, but only at a less than face value.[61] There were company stores in every mining camp in the state; Santa Eulalia alone had three hundred.[62] All of the major foreign operators had them, including ASARCO, Batopilas, and Greene. In 1905 and again in 1908, the state government tried to curb the *boleto*, but without success.[63]

There were related complaints from workers about the infrequent payment of wages. In an extreme case, the Greene company paid its workers only every forty-five days in 1908 after it had fallen on bad times. Later, it did not pay them at all.[64]

The Cananea Strike in Sonora in early June 1906 set off a wave of strikes in Chihuahua aimed at rectifying these injustices and winning higher wages. Carpenters, railroad mechanics, streetcar operators, and biscuit factory hands all walked off their jobs. The streetcar line and biscuit factory were both owned by the Terrazas family, indicating that workers had indeed grown bold.[65] Governor Creel warned President Díaz that he feared workers would join the uprisings in the North led by the Partido Liberal Mexicano (PLM).[66] Labor unrest reached such a point that the federal government sent a detachment of forty *rurales* to Chihuahua to reinforce troops already there.[67] In 1907 there were new strikes of Ciudad Chihuahua street cleaners and textile workers, and railroad trainmen, engineers, and firemen.[68] Many more workers, dissatisfied with wages or working conditions, did not go on strike but left for other employment.

During the initial period of labor militancy in 1906 and early 1907, workers in Chihuahua, as elsewhere in Mexico, looked to the government, especially state governors and the dictator Díaz, to intervene on their behalf.[69] In fact, the president settled several strikes with some advantage to workers under his framework of "peace and order," and in Chihuahua a strike of railroad mechanics in February 1907 was settled through the mediation of Luis Terrazas.[70] Still, the brutal repression of a January textile strike at Río Blanco in Puebla gave the unions cause to reevaluate their strategy. Even so, workers continued to seek government intervention in labor disputes in 1909 and 1910, when union activities renewed, and several governors intervened at this time to alleviate some of the most serious abuses in their states.[71]

After the Puebla strikes, with the exception of urban transit workers, who struck for and won a pay raise in July 1909, the Terrazas took a hard line.[72] They fired striking employees of the La Estrella biscuit factory. When textile workers at the family's mill in Ciudad Camargo struck in July 1907 for a ten-centavo raise, the manager adamantly refused and discharged the workers.[73]

DEPRESSION AND RECOVERY, 1907–1909

The plight of the working class in Chihuahua changed drastically in the second half of 1907. A financial crisis in the United States caused mineral prices to plummet, and investment in the state's mines stopped abruptly. Many mines closed. At the same time, the depression dried up employment opportunities across the border.

The first sign of disaster appeared in late 1906, when ASARCO lowered the wages of construction workers at its new smelter outside Ciudad Chihuahua.[74] In November 1907 two of the largest mining complexes in Mexico, Velardeña in Durango and Cananea in Sonora, closed, throwing thousands of miners out of work.[75] Simultaneously, the Río Tinto mines at Terrazas Station shut down, leaving five hundred unemployed.[76] ASARCO ceased mining at both Santa Bárbara and Santa Eulalia, adding another thousand men to the jobless.[77] Almost every mine in Hidalgo del Parral closed.[78] Those mines that continued to operate in Chihuahua did so with fewer workers, who labored for reduced wages.[79] A United States government ban on Mexican migrant workers touched off a crisis along the border, as thousands of unemployed workers congregated in Ciudad Juárez. The state government provided some of the returnees with train fare in an effort to forestall potential violence.[80]

The depression wiped out the gains of a decade. In Hidalgo del Parral the biggest companies cut their work force by half or more. The same was true in Palmarejo and other isolated districts. The Candelaria Mining Company cut the number of its employees from 490 in 1907 to 132 in 1908. Half the mining operators listed for Chihuahua in 1907 were no longer in business in 1909. Many companies substantially reduced wages.[81]

Poor harvests in 1907, 1908, and 1909 sent prices for staples skyrocketing. The price of maize jumped 55 percent from 1907 to 1908, while beans rose 40 percent.[82] The cost of living in Chihuahua underwent the largest single-year increase in two decades. Real (if not nominal) wages fell as a result. Thus unemployment and inflation combined to strike a doubly heavy blow at Chihuahuan workers.

Although the depression ended the tight labor market that had spawned worker militancy and impeded union organization in Chihuahua, it did not end all organizing and strikes. The employees of the Parral and Durango railroad struck in July 1907.[83] Early in 1908 railroad workers on the Mexican Central walked off their jobs to protest the firing of one of their fellow workers for union activity and the favoritism shown foreign labor.[84] Miners at reopened Velardeña struck in February 1909.[85] The Gran Liga de Electricistas was founded in April 1909, with the aim of becoming "strong, powerful, and respected in society."[86]

A scattered recovery began in 1909. At a few of the big companies hiring levels reached predepression peaks. The Candelaria Company actually exceeded its pre-1907 numbers.[87] But even by August 1909, ASARCO's Tecolotes works still employed only half its old number of workers.[88] Key mining areas such as Parral and Guadalupe y Calvo remained in the throes of depression well into 1910.[89] El Correo remarked in March 1910 that there was a marked increase in the number of beggers in Ciudad Chihuahua due to the lack of jobs,[90] and in July reported a large number of vagabonds in Batopilas.[91] The failure of the harvest in 1909 and continued high staple prices added to the misery.

Still, many had returned to work by 1910. A Canadian company reopened Greene's lumber operation in western Chihuahua, supplying jobs for hundreds in the Guerrero District.[92] A dam project in Santa Rosalía employed four hundred.[93] Some areas again endured labor shortages, and employers had to raise wages to attract workers.[94] Generally, wages returned to predepression levels.[95]

MILITANCY RENEWED

Chihuahuan workers emerged from hard times with a renewed spirit of militancy. As the *Mexican Herald* observed in April 1910, Mexican workers, employed again, were no longer content with "just *frijoles* [beans] and tortillas."[96] Carpenters and bricklayers at the Veta Colorado Mining company struck in August 1910, complaining of abuses by the company store.[97] Laborers on the new dam struck the same month for better wages and after the intervention of the local *jefe político* got a 33 percent wage increase.[98]

There is considerable evidence that unemployed workers joined the revolutionaries in 1910. The PLM and later both the Anti-reelectionists and rebels received considerable support in Parral, the hardest-hit mining area. Cástulo Herrera, the vice-president of the steamfitters' union in Parral, founded the city's Anti-reelectionist club and was one of the early revolutionary leaders.[99] Jobless workers joined the PLM disturbances in northwestern Chihuahua in 1908.[100] According to the local *jefe*, workers in Casas Grandes loudly voiced their support of Francisco Madero, the leader of the opposition to Díaz, in 1910.[101] Railroad workers impeded the movements of federal troops in late 1910 after the first revolutionary outbreaks.[102] Miners and lumbermen were subsequently identified as composing a large segment of Madero's army that captured Ciudad Juárez in April 1911, the Revolution's greatest victory.[103]

After the victory of Madero's revolution in May 1911, Chihuahuan workers unleashed their pent-up protests. Long frustrated by the excesses of the company store, employees of the Madera Company, a huge lumber enterprise in the Guerrero District, struck in June.[104] A month later, miners in Naica struck against the *boleto* system and payroll deductions for nonexistent medical care. They won a 20 percent raise (to $1.50), but remained unhappy because labor elsewhere earned more for similar work.[105] In July, too, there was a strike in Cusihuiriachic, when three hundred miners staged a job action.[106] At the same time, employees at ASARCO's smelter protested the high prices at the company store (run by Juan Terrazas) and demanded higher wages.[107]

A Comparative View

A similar pattern emerged throughout Mexico: rising labor militancy, then union activity, with the unions soon frustrated by a lack of government response to protested injustices, followed by tremendous suffering during the depression of 1907 to 1909, and finally the workers joining forces with the political opposition to Díaz in 1909 and 1910. During these years, the thirty or more groups of workers were affiliated with the political opposition to Díaz in the Federal District, Puebla, Aguascalientes, Veracruz, Zacatecas, and Jalisco. These groups comprised, for the most part, textile workers, but their ranks included railroad laborers, electricians, miners, and typographers. Many workers had been mobilized to opposition by the violent repression of strikes at Cananea and Río Blanco. Sonoran miners, some of them refugees from the massacre at Cananea, took active roles in the Revolution in that state. Textile workers in Puebla who had witnessed the slaughter at Río Blanco joined the Anti-reelectionists and later the revolutionaries. Uprisings of textile workers in May and June 1910 actually antedated the general revolt, although they were unsuccessful. A band of factory workers attacked the army barracks at Orizaba in November 1910, the date of the nationwide upheaval, and in February 1911 groups of workers gathered in bands to fight the regime in Puebla and Tlaxcala.[108]

For the most part, workers acted as individuals in joining the opposition. They joined in greatest number perhaps in the North in the initial stages. Few workers became revolutionary leaders.

During the *Porfiriato*, the real wages of Mexican workers had stagnated or declined. Many in the agricultural sector were actually worse off in 1910 than their ancestors had been a century before.[109] This was not the case in Chihuahua. Although miners, tradesmen, peons, and factory workers suffered through vicious cycles of boom and bust, engendered by the dependence of the economy on mining and erratic harvests, they were better off in Chihuahua from 1902 to 1907 than ever before. Life was hardly utopian, and by all contemporary accounts it was not nearly up to the less than comfortable standards of late-nineteenth-century industrial America, but Chihuahuans consistently earned the highest wages and enjoyed the lowest cost of living of any Mexican workers.[110] Not only were they relatively well paid, but they were geographically and socially mobile as well. The highly competitive market for labor in the northern mining regions and across the border in the United States kept Chihuahuan workers in better circumstances than their brethren elsewhere in the country.

Given their relatively high standard of living, the depression of 1907 hit Chihuahuan workers especially hard. Their expectations raised and then suddenly crushed, Chihuahuan workers first looked to such leaders as Terrazas, Creel, and Díaz for succor. When they received no satisfaction there, they turned to the opposition.

9

The Restoration of the
Terrazas, 1903–1911

The return of the Terrazas to power in 1903 upset the balance of politics in Chihuahua, for the family, no longer in conflict with the national government and without serious local rivals, ruled unchallenged. Its unending efforts to centralize power and inattention to day-to-day political affairs led to widespread abuses and increasing unrest in Chihuahua. This political crisis combined with effects of the depression and the unrest that arose from illegal land seizures to foment revolution.

As we have seen, the rival local factions that had contested and checked the Terrazas' power for decades had all collapsed by the end of the 1890s. With Porfirio Díaz no longer in opposition, the Terrazas, unrestrained, transformed the state into a family fiefdom.

At the same time, day-to-day leadership of the family passed from General Luis Terrazas to his son-in-law Enrique C. Creel. The change was one of both style and substance. The general had been an exceptional nineteenth-century *cacique*, as much at home in the tough milieu of the western *serranos* and the northern *presidios* as in the world of business and society in Ciudad Chihuahua. He had been a hero of the Indian wars and a patriot who supported Benito Juárez in the darkest days of the French Intervention. His successor was a banker, half-American, and a *científico* modernizer, concerned less with rough ex–Indian fighters than with the intrigue of Mexico City and the intricacies of international finance. Luis Terrazas had rarely left Chihuahua, for tumultuous conditions there would not permit him the luxury. Creel, who became governor, was away from the state as often as he was at home, serving on several banking commissions, later as Mexican ambassador to the United States, and finally as secretary of foreign relations in the Díaz cabinet. Governing Chihuahua was not a part-time job.

The family's return to power and the change in leadership unsettled long-time political arrangements. The clan's monopolization of political office and its closed control over much of the state's economy led to widespread resentment among the growing middle class. Moreover, Creel's efforts to modernize and centralize the state government produced considerable unrest in a region that had for centuries fiercely guarded local autonomy. And the lack of substantial opposition created a less politic, less responsive regime. Because of Creel's extended absences and frequent use of interim appointments in key administrative posts, the family lost touch with the state's political problems and saw a diminishing of its control over local officials. Ultimately, the Terrazas could not or would not control their subordinates.

The Creel Administration, 1904–1910

Under the terms of his agreement with Porfirio Díaz, Luis Terrazas succeeded Colonel Miguel Ahumada as governor, and after being suitably honored by popular election in 1903, he stepped down in favor of Enrique Creel, who took over as interim governor in August 1904. He completed the general's term and won election in his own right in October 1907, serving until January 1911.

Creel set about to reform and streamline the state government and modernize and expand its infrastructure. He supervised a complete revision of local legislation, reforming penal and sanitary codes and issuing new laws for public finances, municipal administration, and education. He established a registry of deeds and mortgages with regional offices and reestablished the statistical section of the state government. Creel also introduced a seniority system, insurance, and annual vacations for public employees and installed electricity in public buildings.[1] One of the governor's particular concerns was education. He streamlined educational administration, increased expenditures for public instruction, and founded or subsidized new vocational, agricultural, and normal schools.[2]

During his administration, the state embarked on an unprecedented program of public works. Creel initiated or continued the construction of a new prison, new water and sewer systems for Ciudad Chihuahua, a dam on the Río Chúviscar to supply the capital with potable water, and several wagon roads. In addition, he encouraged the state's municipalities to sponsor similar projects. As a result of his program, state government debt tripled and municipal debt rose sharply.[3]

To these efforts, Creel added a far-ranging program for the Tarahumara Indians. Through a law passed in 1906, he sought to protect the tribe, ensure its food supply, and inculcate it with twentieth-century values. Toward these ends, the state appointed a protective commission to oversee the Tarahumara and set up schools for them. Creel also acquired a large tract of land to divide among the tribe in the hope of making them into small farmers.[4]

Another of Creel's innovations was a law that provided homes for the working class. The scheme set aside a large tract of municipally owned land in Ciudad Chihuahua for division into small homesteads to be sold to workers at much reduced prices. Local lending institutions were encouraged to furnish credit for the purchase of the lots, and the property was to be exempt from taxes for ten years. Worker-owners could not sell or mortgage the property without the state government's permission.[5]

The governor crusaded fervently against alcoholism, which he, like other *científicos*, felt was the bane of the Mexican lower classes. Creel saw to it that the business hours of saloons were severely restricted. In 1906 he tried to organize a private charitable corporation to purchase all the saloons in Chihuahua.[6]

Creel expended much energy promoting the state's economic development. Under his auspices, it established a permanent mining exhibition. He also actively encouraged new businesses, especially foreign, to invest in Chihuahua, and his efforts created many new jobs.[7]

Creel showed other evidence of at least paternalistic concern for the lower classes. During the drought of 1907 and 1908, he recommended to all Chihuahuan municipalities that they purchase supplies of staple crops and resell at cost to the poor of their districts.[8] Creel was one of only three Porfirian governors willing at least to discuss the needs of labor and possible solutions to pressing problems. When railroad workers struck in 1906, Creel responded sympathetically, criticizing the Mexican Central for its low pay and discrimination against native labor. Later, however, when family enterprises were struck, he refused to negotiate with the unions.[9]

Despite all these progressive programs and benevolent projects, Creel presided over a morass of corruption and governmental abuse. He and his father-in-law came to symbolize the tyranny against which the revolutionaries of 1910 fought.

The Origins of Political Discontent

Political discontent in Chihuahua between 1903 and 1910 centered around five issues. First, the Terrazas virtually monopolized government at every level, controlling the governorship and installing family members and close associates in the legislature, judiciary, and local offices. Second, Enrique Creel himself became controversial both because he was half-American and because of his extended absences from Chihuahua. Third, corrupt and tyrannical local political bosses ran roughshod over their constituents. Fourth, both the police and the judiciary were notoriously venal and arbitrary. Finally, state government policies flagrantly discriminated against the native middle and lower classes, especially in taxation, and favored foreign entrepreneurs and members of the Terrazas inner circle.

STATE GOVERNMENT

The Terrazas thoroughly controlled the Chihuahuan state government. Family members occupied the governor's chair from 1903 to 1911, during which years the state legislature was a private club of family members and close associates. Until that time, the *porfirista* governor Miguel Ahumada had carefully maintained a balance in the legislature between various local factions. After the 1902 agreement between Díaz and Terrazas, however, the latter eliminated all opposition.[10]

Simultaneously, the Terrazas took control of the state judiciary. In the two-year court term before the reconciliation (1901–3), there were no Terrazas family members or allies among the nine *magistrados* of the Supremo Tribunal de Justicia de Chihuahua, and only four among the nine *suplentes* (alternates). Thereafter, the clan maintained a clear majority on the court.[11] The control of the judiciary went still further, for Francisco Terrazas (the general's grandson) headed a group of lawyers popularly known as "El Universal," the lawyers' clique that monopolized the business before the courts in Chihuahua.[12] Upon their return to power, the Terrazas also appointed their allies to crucial posts as *jefes políticos*. In 1903, Governor Terrazas replaced nine of eleven *jefes*.[13] In addition, family members held a wide variety of state administrative offices, ranging from state treasurer to director of primary education.[14]

The Terrazas and their local henchmen resorted to widespread vote fraud to ensure their political control. Silvestre Terrazas charged that vote fraud was rife in the gubernatorial election of 1907.[15] Terrazas allies like the Mápula family of Janos maintained their hold on local politics through fraudulent manipulations.[16] When elections were won by candidates unacceptable to the regime, the legislature overturned the results and imposed more satisfactory officials. Indeed, the legislature increasingly manipulated local government during 1909 and 1910 when discontent and political opposition arose.[17]

CREEL

Enrique Creel became a political lightning rod in 1906, when Silvestre Terrazas, the editor of *El Correo de Chihuahua*, made him a symbol of the inequities of Chihuahuan society. Silvestre (a distant relative of Luis Terrazas), later a hero of the Revolution and governor of Chihuahua, first criticized Creel in June 1906 for what the editor of *El Correo* believed to be the illegal extension of General Terrazas's term as governor.[18] Thereafter the newspaper became a sounding board for complaints against the Terrazas-Creel regime.

The newspaper vigorously opposed Creel's candidacy for governor in 1907. Silvestre Terrazas steadfastly insisted that, despite Creel's considerable talents, he was ineligible to be governor of the state because he was not a Mexican citizen.[19] Silvestre considered the issue of citizenship far more than a legal technicality, for he feared that Americans would consider Creel's governorship a precedent to take over northern Mexico politically as they had economically. The editor's fear struck a responsive chord among mine owners, small shopkeepers, and miners, who had long resented the favoritism shown foreigners in Chihuahua. Moreover, Silvestre believed that Creel's candidacy was typical of the disdain the Terrazas-Creels had for the state's constitution and laws. The effect of *El Correo*'s opposition is clearly indicated by the vote totals for the gubernatorial election of 1907. Creel received barely thirty thousand votes, one-third less than Luis Terrazas had polled four years before and lower than any winning gubernatorial vote total in a quarter of a century.[20]

The editor continued to oppose and criticize the Creel administration. He protested bitterly when Díaz named Creel ambassador to the United States, arguing that during the governor's long absences, interim governors would rule, in effect depriving the people of their right to an elected governor.[21]

The Banco Minero robbery in March 1908 catalyzed the growing dissatisfaction with the Terrazas-Creel regime. News of the affair dominated the front page of *El Correo* for months. Creel personally headed the investigation, placing himself squarely in the middle of the sordid affair. Government outrages against a succession of suspects angered Chihuahuans to an unprecedented degree.[22]

The scandal heightened the unpopularity of the entire family. Enrique Creel's brother Juan was widely suspected of having masterminded the robbery to cover gambling debts. The obvious violation of even the most basic civil rights of the accused showed clearly the Terrazas' contempt for the law. To many Chihuahuans, victimized by the corruption and abuses of the clan and its henchmen, the affair typified the whole regime.[23]

LOCAL GOVERNMENT ABUSES

Of all of Creel's policies and programs (except the Municipal Land Law of 1905, discussed in chapter 7), his elimination of local government autonomy drew the most widespread and profound protests. The local governments had already suffered a severe blow in 1888, when the *guerrerista* state government had ended the popular election of *jefes políticos*, having them instead appointed by the governor. In 1904 the legislature, under the auspices of Governor Creel, further centralized authority, adopting the Law for the Organization of the Districts, which replaced the *presidentes municipales* and *presidentes de secciones*, the most important popularly elected local officials, with new officials, *jefes municipales*, to be appointed by the governor. These *jefes* presided over municipal councils (*ayuntamientos* or *juntas*), exercising extensive legislative and police power.[24] From 1905 to 1910 complaints about local officials filled the pages of *El Correo*. Localities which for decades had guarded their independence deeply resented the loss of autonomy and the imposition of outsiders as *jefes municipales*. Many appointees proved unfamiliar with and insensitive to their constituencies, and allegations of the corruption, incompetence, and arbitrariness of the *jefes* were commonplace.[25]

The areas where there were repeated and frequent abuses by local authorities were the same areas where the Flores Magóns' Partido Liberal Mexicano drew its heaviest support. Oppressed citizens from these localities later formed Anti-reelectionist clubs in 1909 and 1910 to oppose the Terrazas-Creels. These regions also produced the first uprisings in 1910 and 1911 and provided many of the leaders for the Revolution. After more than a year of futile complaints against local authorities citizens of Ciudad Camargo set up an Anti-reelectionist club in September 1910.[26] Numerous complaints against the *jefe* in Villa López, Jiménez, led to Anti-reelectionist activity there also.[27] In 1909 complaints to Governor Creel about the *jefe* of Bocoyna, Benito Juárez District, elicited no response. A few months later inhabitants established an Anti-reelectionist club. The village was one of the first to take up arms in December 1910.[28] In the Valle de Zaragoza near Parral, the *jefe* was the object of heated protests from 1907 to 1910. When Parral pronounced for the Revolution of 1910, the call came from Valle de Zaragoza.[29] In Nonoava, Benito Juárez District, the actions of the *jefe* provoked the founding of another Anti-reelectionist club, led by Delfino Ochoa, who had written many letters of protest to *El Correo*.[30]

Complaints against local authorities were especially vocal in the Guerrero District, where the people were well known for their independence and the loss of local autonomy was deeply resented. Bachíniva, for example, suffered the rule of the hated *jefe* Luis Y. Comadurán.[31] In Temósachic continuous protests against municipal authorities finally led to the ouster of the *jefe* by the state government in 1909, but his replacement proved no better.[32] In 1908 fifty citizens of Namiquipa went to Ciudad Chihuahua to demonstrate against the tyrannical abuses of their *jefe*.[33] All three of these municipalities were centers of revolutionary activity in 1910. Bachíniva was the scene of one of the first revolutionary uprisings. One of the leading revolutionaries, José de la Luz Blanco, was a native of Temósachic. Pascual Orozco, the first great general of the Revolution, came from nearby San Isidro.[34]

THE JUDICIARY AND POLICE

The Chihuahuan judiciary was a morass of corruption and incompetence. After a year campaigning on the pages of *El Correo* for desperately needed reform, Silvestre Terrazas in November 1908 declared that justice in Chihuahua was a "fiasco" and liberty dead. The situation had not improved by 1910.[35]

The police were another source of bitter resentment. There were frequent complaints of despotism, corruption, and inefficiency from every part of the state. The state rural police (*rurales*) were a hated instrument of oppression. Formed by Governor Creel in 1904 to "guard the country and persecute wrongdoers," the *rurales* acted instead to enforce the will of large landowners. In 1908 they were used to harass the people of Janos, who protested illegal land seizures. Joaquín Chávez, the chief of *rurales* in Guerrero and Rayón districts, became a symbol of Terrazas oppression in western Chihuahua.[36]

LOCAL CACIQUES AND COMPANY TOWNS

As we have seen earlier, the Terrazas preferred to establish working arrangements with firmly entrenched local *caciques*. Often these men and their families ruled their municipalities and districts for decades. In Urique, for example, the Becerra family managed to capture every local, state, and federal office for themselves, with the concurrence of the Terrazas.[37]

Other municipalities were controlled by large mining, lumber, or cattle companies. Conditions were particularly oppressive in Naica, Dolores, Corralitos, and Madera, where local officials were in the employ of these large firms. Often company police terrorized the population. Such abuses led to revolutionary discontent. Madera, for example, was an early center of the Revolution. One of the first acts of the revolutionary administration of Governor Abraham González was to place these towns under state jurisdiction and turn them over to local residents.[38]

Creel tried to eliminate some of the most notorious abuses. He issued circulars in 1907 that expressly forbade *jefes* from using shady tactics to steal municipal land and ended the common practice of multiple officeholding at the municipal level. Under popular pressure, the governor dismissed several incompetent or oppressive *jefes*. Creel fired both the *jefe* and the local judge in Bocoyna between 1907 and 1909, but abuses persisted. District *jefes* often ordered investigations of citizens' complaints, but rarely were actions taken against local officials. Mostly, the state government ignored local protests.[39]

Whatever sympathies the Creel regime showed disappeared after 1908, when the uprising of the PLM in the northwestern part of the state and the furor surrounding the Banco Minero affair soured the governor on trying to please the electorate. The emergence of opposition political groups in 1909 increased the family's intransigence. Creel, who headed Díaz's secret police along the border, hounded local Anti-reelectionists. He cracked down hard on *El Correo*, jailing its editor, Silvestre Terrazas, twice.[40]

TAXATION

The tax laws administered by Creel elicited loud outcries, especially from the middle class. Without exception the tax structure favored large landowners, big merchants, and foreign corporations at the expense of the native middle class and workers. To finance Creel's ambitious public works program, the state borrowed nearly two million pesos between 1903 and 1911.[41] To repay these debts, the legislature had to raise taxes. Since the oligarchy and foreigners enjoyed tax exemption, the burden fell on shopkeepers and small mine owners, landowners, and service businesses. These found themselves encumbered by unfair taxes that not only absorbed their incomes but also put them at a disadvantage against their bigger, more influential competition.[42]

In 1904, Creel sponsored a new tax law that laid the burden of taxation squarely on small landowners, small businessmen, and manual laborers.[43] Those affected did not feel the full impact during the heady boom days of 1905 and 1906, but when the depression hit, taxes proved intolerable. *El Correo* was flooded with protests against unfair taxes and favoritism to foreigners.

The state legislature added another troublesome burden in 1908 when it levied taxes on the dues of members to mutualist societies. The effect was to threaten the existence of these organizations.[44] At the same time, the state raised other taxes 300 to 400 percent. Again, the burden fell hardest on the middle and lower classes.[45] Another law passed two years later placed a levy on all work animals (horses, burros, mules), but demanded nothing from *hacendados* with their thousands of livestock.[46]

Chihuahuans stood up against these unfair impositions. A man from Temósachic protested that taxes were three times what they should have been and had made conditions even worse in the midst of depression. Temósachic became a hotbed of the Revolution.[47] The residents of San Andrés rioted to protest unfair taxes in 1909. The taxes especially galled them, because the tax collector also managed the local undertaxed properties of Enrique Creel. San Andrés produced three of the Revolution's most prominent leaders, Pancho Villa, Ceferino Pérez, and Cástulo Herrera.[48]

Politically, the Terrazas had grown arrogant in power. They had by 1910 largely forgotten the lessons of their long struggle to achieve hegemony in Chihuahua. In their victory lay the seeds of their ultimate fall.

10

Revolution

The destabilizingly rapid economic development, the depression and harvest failures of 1907 to 1909, the widespread expropriation of small landholdings, and the restoration of Terrazas rule furnished the volatile fuel for the Revolution of 1910. But two additional sets of circumstances were required to kindle armed rebellion. First, the three major groups alienated by the events and conditions of the preceding decade, the middle class, small landowners, and workers, had to conclude, once and for all, that their only recourse to settle their grievances was violent opposition to the Porfirian regime. Second, the three disparate groups, whose aims often conflicted, needed the positive, unifying force of a charismatic leader. They found that in Francisco Madero. In Chihuahua, of course, the Terrazas provided a powerfully negative unifying force; whatever the goals of the revolutionaries, they all hated the Terrazas. Ultimately, the rebellion emerged, persisted, and won because of the weakness of the Díaz-Terrazas regime. Its coercive mechanisms, particularly the army, were corroded, its elite divided, and its leaders incompetent to meet the challenge of the revolt.

The Rise and Fall of Loyal Opposition

Loyal political opposition to the dictatorship emerged during 1908, backed by some disaffected state elites, including *hacendados* whose economic interests the government's policies had damaged, members of families ousted from political power by Díaz years before, and a venturesome sector of the middle class. Peasants and workers provided scattered additional support.

The dictator himself spawned political competition by his own words. In an interview with American reporter James Creelman, published in *Pearson's Magazine* in February 1908, Díaz stated his determination "to retire at the end of his current term, and . . . not accept reelection." He went on to encourage the formation of political parties to contest the forthcoming elections.[1] Although Díaz quickly retreated from his imprudent statement, allowing himself to be "persuaded" to run again by the end of May, he acted too late to forestall the ensuing political storm.

The brief possibility that Díaz would retire exacerbated the deep split within the inner circle of the dictatorship. On one side were the *científicos*, led by José Y. Limantour, the minister of finance, and Ramón Corral, the incumbent vice-president; on the other were the anti*científicos*, who rallied around General Bernardo Reyes, the governor of Nuevo León.[2] After Díaz decided to take another term, the infighting centered on the vice-presidency, which gained added meaning because the eighty-year-old president was not expected to survive his new six-year term. Corral and the *científicos* won out—he was renominated as vice-president—but the repercussions of the struggle were far-reaching. Although they had emerged victorious, the *científicos* were increasingly mistrustful of the president, and there was a growing feeling among them that he was more a hindrance than a help to their plans. Many of the defeated *reyistas*, moreover, set about to oppose the dictator. And although their ostensible leader never moved into formal opposition, they began to organize a political movement in his name.[3]

In the meantime, another group, the Club Central Antire-eleccionista, organized by Coahuilan *hacendado* Francisco I. Madero and forty-five others in May 1909 and encouraged by the Creelman interview, began a nationwide campaign against the dictator's reelection.

Initially, Díaz and Corral concentrated their efforts on crushing the *reyistas*, who posed the greatest threat to the regime. The government cracked down hard and by late summer destroyed Reyes as a potential danger. The beaten general meekly accepted a diplomatic post abroad. Only then did the regime turn its attention to the *antire-eleccionistas* and their emerging leader, Francisco Madero.[4]

During 1909, Madero had in a national tour become spokesman for the political opposition to Díaz, and the *antire-eleccionistas* nominated him as their candidate for president in April 1910. But the government had already moved to harass and suppress his movement. The previous January, for example, Madero had been denied a platform to speak from (and a bed to sleep in) by authorities in Sonora. Police and *porfirista* thugs harassed him and his followers. Forewarning what was to come, Madero protested sharply to old family friend Limantour: "We have the right to hope that since we are working loyally, so will the Díaz government treat us. We have confided in the patriotism of General Díaz and those who surround him . . . because if the public is not left free to exercise its rights at this time, and has no hopes of exercising them during the administration of Corral, the idea of conquering these rights by force will be seriously entertained in the heart of every Mexican who is anxious for liberty." [5]

Ignoring Madero's complaints and threat, Díaz's henchmen acted strongly to suppress opposition organizations in Yucatán, Morelos, Sinaloa, and Coahuila, where there were hotly contested gubernatorial campaigns. In Yucatán authorities jailed the opposition candidate for governor.[6] Several states banned Anti-reelectionist activities. As the June elections approached, Anti-reelectionists were imprisoned and shot. In mid-June, Madero was jailed, and the dictator won the primary election on 26 June.

Before being released on bond in late July, Madero began to plan rebellion. Amid growing unrest—minor uprisings broke out in several states—Madero fled across the border to the United States on 6 October. From exile he proclaimed the Plan de San Luis Potosí, declaring war on the Díaz regime. Usually a man of peace, Madero had tried to work within the system and had found the effort futile. He was not alone.

Disgruntled Chihuahuans, particularly among the battered middle class, early joined the opposition to Díaz. They greeted Madero enthusiastically when he spoke in the state in January 1909. As it did elsewhere, his visit spurred the organization of an Anti-reelectionist club in Chihuahua. Abraham González and others founded the Club "Benito Juárez" Antire-eleccionista in July 1909. Clubs quickly sprung up in Parral and elsewhere.[7] In February 1910, the Chihuahuan clubs were the first to come out in favor of Madero as the *antire-eleccionista* presidential candidate.[8]

Like Madero, Chihuahuans who organized the Anti-reelectionist clubs in Ciudad Chihuahua and elsewhere began as a loyal opposition and became rebels only in the face of the escalating repression, climaxed by the imprisonment of Madero himself.

At first, the Terrazas-Creels regarded the fledgling Anti-reelectionist movement with mere scorn, but as it gained momentum and a wide following in Chihuahua, they stepped up their repression. Local authorities beat up, imprisoned, and fined active Anti-reelectionists. In Batopilas the local *jefe* tried unsuccessfully to get the American-owned mining company to fire employees who belonged to the local Anti-reelectionist club.[9] Creel, who as head of Díaz's secret police along the border well knew the extent of the political opposition, increased the number of police and the level of harassment of local authorities. Protests against the abuses of local *jefes* reached their peak in 1909 and 1910.[10] With the government in tight control of the election process (soldiers were stationed at many polls), the results were a foregone conclusion. Angered by Madero's imprisonment and frustrated by the election, Chihuahuan Anti-reelectionists began to organize the rebellion, and they became the force behind the Revolution of 1910.[11]

The Partido Liberal Mexicano

That the nation was not ready for armed revolt until 1910 was evidenced by
the failure of the Partido Liberal Mexicano (PLM) in its attempt to foment
rebellion in 1906 and 1908. Led by Ricardo and Enrique Flores Magón, the
PLM had agitated and plotted from various places on the border since 1900,
publishing radical newspapers and staying barely ahead of Creel's secret police network. They drew strong support in the North, especially in depressed
mining districts like Parral (which had been in depression since 1904), among
unemployed miners.[12]

Seeking to capitalize on the extensive antiregime feeling engendered by the
suppression of a 1906 mining strike at the Cananea complex in Sonora (which
they had helped foment), the PLM planned uprisings in Sonora, Chihuahua,
and Veracruz for September, but the government discovered the plot and
quickly snuffed it out. An attack planned on Ciudad Juárez was thwarted by
police in October.[13]

Undaunted, the PLM tried again in June 1908, with attacks in northwestern
Chihuahua and Viesca, Coahuila. Both, of course, failed. The group continued to fight, however, and succeeded in mounting substantial guerrilla activities in Coahuila and Veracruz. Nonetheless, despite an excellent organization and a large number of sympathizers, the PLM was unable to trigger a
general uprising.[14]

Although the PLM failed to arouse organized rebellion, violence neverthe-
less spread in Chihuahua and the North. Bandit gangs marauded in southern
Chihuahua and La Laguna (reminiscent of the 1870s). Even *haciendas* were
attacked. Unemployed miners and agricultural workers presented a constant
threat to public security. Wealthy families hired private guards. Crime increased precipitously, and the number of vagrants in the urban areas rose
sharply.[15] Occasionally, as in San Andrés in 1909, riots erupted. But this all
was spontaneous, scattered, individual, and unorganized.

Francisco I. Madero

Then in 1909 and 1910 dissidents from all classes rallied around Francisco I.
Madero, the scion of a wealthy Coahuilan family with interests in guayule,
cotton, and industry in Durango, Coahuila, and Nuevo León. The family's
smelter at Torreón was the largest native-owned smelter in Mexico. Short,
slight, undistinguished in appearance, and an uninspiring speaker, Madero on
the surface hardly met the usual criteria for charismatic leadership. Nonetheless, his persistence and great courage in confronting the dictatorship when

his personal safety was in obvious peril, his hard work, and his dedication to democratic principles won for him an extensive national following.[16]

Initially, leadership of the opposition had fallen to him partly by default. Bernardo Reyes had shied from breaking with Díaz. Other governors, like Teodoro Dehesa of Veracruz, though rivals of the *científicos*, were too closely tied to the dictatorship. Of all the vocal opponents of the regime, only Madero had the necessary funds to embark on a speaking tour and a national reputation—won with his book *The Presidential Succession of 1910*—to draw crowds.[17] When it came time for the opposition to choose a presidential candidate, he was the obvious choice.

Madero appealed to a cross-section of disgruntled Mexicans. For dissatisfied *hacendados*, he was one of them. For the middle class, his desire to open the political system coincided with one of their most cherished goals. For peasants and workers, his reputation for benevolent treatment of his employees stood him well.[18] While strident in its demands for political reform, his program was sufficiently vague on labor and agrarian issues to appeal alike to worker and industrialist, villager and *hacendado*.

Whatever his personal or ideological appeal, Madero was the central figure, the unifying force, of the heterogeneous group that initiated the Revolution of 1910.

The Chihuahuan Revolution

The Revolution erupted first and most successfully in Chihuahua in great part because of its unique alliance of the middle class, peasants, and (to a somewhat lesser extent) workers. Because the Chihuahuan elite was so monolithic, there were no disaffected elements of the elite to slow down the fermenting of revolution. In Sonora and Coahuila, for example, *hacendados* like José María Maytorena and Venustiano Carranza took command of the Revolution. Extreme caution and self-interest marked the movements in both states, but in Chihuahua there were no "good" *hacendados*.[19] The omnipotence of the Terrazas had polarized Chihuahuan society. The adversarial relationship, particularly between the middle class and the Terrazas, precluded the kind of alliance that ameliorated social conflict elsewhere in Latin America.[20] The entrepreneurial middle class in Chihuahua, substantially bolder than their counterparts in other regions, were not restricted by any alliance with the elite.

Moreover, the middle class in Chihuahua had a distinctly close relationship with the state's small landowners. Class lines between the middle class and these peasants were often blurred, especially in western Chihuahua. Pascual

Orozco, for example, was a small landowner, store owner, and muleteer. Other ranchers owned lumber mills. Even members of the urban middle class, like Abraham González, were able to cooperate to a high degree with the tough *rancheros* (among whom were many relatives). The difficult life of the frontier may have reduced the gap between rural and urban society, and the middle class and peasants shared common political and economic goals. Both sought restoration of local political autonomy, and both generally respected private property and regarded radical land reform with suspicion.[21]

The gaps between worker and peasant and worker and middle class were also smaller in Chihuahua than elsewhere. Many workers were peasants who supplemented their incomes by labor in the mines and mills. Other workers had only a short time before left rural areas for more lucrative jobs in the camps and factories. In addition, many peasants and workers had the common experience of migratory labor in the United States, where both underwent a similar socialization, shedding traditional ties and paternalistic employment. The relatively privileged position of workers and relatively favorable possibilities for upward mobility in the North narrowed the gap between the working and middle classes. During the boom years, many workers had ascended to the middle class and then dropped back when the depression struck. Class was more fluid in Chihuahua than in central and southern Mexico.

Thus the three classes were thrown together, united by their desire to overthrow the Terrazas and by the unique social and economic conditions that blurred the lines between them. Although their interests later diverged sharply, the three groups came together in 1910 to defeat the Terrazas-Díaz regime.

In no other region, except Morelos, was the polarization between elite and nonelite as complete. In both Sonora and Coahuila the middle class allied with revolutionary *hacendados*.[22] In Sonora peasants fought with revolutionary *hacendados*, as they did under different circumstances in La Laguna.[23] Workers fought with the Revolution in Durango and Sonora.[24] Nonetheless, the extent of involvement and cooperation among the nonelite classes in Chihuahua was unequaled.

Moreover, each of the three groups—middle class, workers, and peasants—had a long tradition of independence and a familiarity with violence, and this stood them in good stead when they confronted the national government. All were at home with guns, even the middle class. Muleteers, such as Orozco, used guns in their work. Tradesmen and supervisory personnel had worked in the rough-and-tumble world of the mining and lumber camps and construction crews. The *rancheros*, of course, had fought the Apaches for decades. Chihuahuans were especially well prepared to do battle. When it came time to take up arms, they had a leadership and general population thoroughly familiar with weapons and military action.

The final ingredients for armed uprising were access to arms and ammunition and a terrain suited for guerrilla warfare. Chihuahua had both: the nearby border made it easy for the rebels to get weapons, and the state's mountains and desert were ideal for small-scale war. With the support of the native population and knowledge of the land, the rebels enjoyed a major advantage over federal forces sent to subdue them.

The Old Regime Falters

Still, the key to the revolutionary victory in 1911 was the weakness of the Díaz regime. By 1910 it was severely enfeebled by internal dissension and old age. Its instruments of coercion, the *rurales* and the army, were undermanned, poorly trained, and atrociously led.[25]

The delicately balanced structures between the national government and regional elites and within the regions themselves were badly disrupted by the economic depression and the political storm following the Creelman interview. Seemingly, Díaz had lost his magic touch. From the beginning the dictatorship had depended as much on astute political maneuver as force. Díaz's regional alliances had produced more than a decade of peace. Nonetheless, there were still elite groups in the states waiting for any symptom of weakness to resume opposition. After 1900, Díaz permitted the development of political imbalances in crucial states. Where once he had played off several factions, after the turn of the century he let the Terrazas-Creels in Chihuahua and the Torres-Izábal-Corral clique in Sonora become too powerful. In Morelos he imposed a new governor incapable of dealing with a complex and explosive political crisis.[26]

Nationally, the deep split between *científicos* and anti*científicos* widened. When the dictatorship was endangered by the *maderista* uprising in early 1911, the *científicos* were more than willing to abandon Díaz, playing a crucial role in the negotiations that led to his ouster. Dissatisfied with Díaz's economic policies, the *científicos* saw Madero as an acceptable (if, perhaps, temporary) alternative.[27] The anti*científicos* first toyed with *reyismo*, then cautiously waited and, finally, joined the opposition, tipping the balance against Díaz. Carranza and others of this group eventually jerked the reins of the rebellion from the original revolutionaries.[28]

The greatest weakness of the regime was the army. Much of its strength was only on paper, for its real manpower level was barely half its advertised thirty thousand soldiers. Moreover, most of its soldiers were draftees, dragged into service as punishment for minor crimes or because they had fallen into disfavor with local *jefes*, who used them to fill their quotas of "recruits." Porfirian generals stole their soldiers' pay, as well as funds earmarked for supplies and equipment. When sent into the field against the tough Chihuahuan guerrillas, many federal troops deserted. Led by decrepit generals, the federal army was unable to crush the rebels quickly and thereby let them gain strength until the final victory at Ciudad Juárez.[29]

In many ways the situation in Chihuahua duplicated that in the nation as a whole. The problem, however, was not so much old age as officials who had lost touch with the populace and a lack of competent leadership in the Terrazas family other than Enrique Creel. Even this would not have been critical had Creel not been overburdened with his duties in the United States as Mexican ambassador and in Mexico City as adviser to Díaz. General Luis Terrazas, of legendary vigor but over eighty in 1910, could hardly have supervised the daily affairs of the far-flung Terrazas empire or led troops in battle against the rebels, as he had done often in the past.

Creel had made a concerted effort to place younger members of the clan in responsible positions and train them. He also saw to it that members of "El Universal" played a growing role in the legislature and government office. (This also, of course, eliminated the restlessness rampant among the younger generations of the elite elsewhere.) The results of this gradual changeover were not always efficacious. Kinsman Martín Falomir failed in his short tenure as *jefe político* of Iturbide District. Even a bigger blunder was the appointment by Díaz of Alberto Terrazas, the general's youngest son, then forty-one, as governor in January 1911, when the rebellion in western Chihuahua was at a crucial stage. Alberto misjudged the strength of the revolt and then fought with the federal military commander over strategy. Díaz peremptorily removed him in a matter of weeks in favor of Miguel Ahumada.

These problems would have loomed far less large had Creel devoted his full attention to the growing unrest during 1909 and 1910. He had easily crushed the PLM in 1906 and 1908 by closely supervising government actions against the rebels. His secret service continued to provide extensive intelligence on rebel agitators throughout the North,[30] but he was out of Chihuahua eleven of the fourteen months between November 1909 and December 1910, and his substitutes could not handle the crisis.[31]

The Terrazas did not have an army of their own, as they had during the 1870s. Creel had set up a state rural police force, but it was not capable of counterinsurgent warfare. The Terrazas thus had to rely on Díaz to put down the rebellion, but Díaz was neither able nor willing to commit the necessary troops. And to make matters worse, the Terrazas and Díaz quarreled over strategy.[32]

The Revolution Wins

The rebels planned their rising for 20 November 1910. In the beginning it did not go smoothly. Madero had crossed the border the day before, but discouraged by the failure of an army to meet him, he had returned to the United States. A premature revolt in Puebla had been crushed. Small scattered bands scored quick victories, only to lose their gains with the mobilization of the federal army. It appeared that the rebellion would fail.[33]

But in Chihuahua the revolutionaries won a series of victories and managed to persist despite the concentration of federal troops in the region.[34] Pascual Orozco captured Ciudad Guerrero in early December. Even after he withdrew from the city, he continued to harass government forces. Eventually rebel chiefs like Pancho Villa and José de la Luz Blanco, who had previously fought more or less independently, joined forces with Orozco and made him their commander. Madero joined the rebel army in February.

Madero took over military leadership briefly in March, heading an unsuccessful attack on Casas Grandes that nearly proved disastrous for the rebel cause. Thereafter he left the battle to the Chihuahuan *rancheros* and their chief, Orozco. In April *maderista* forces besieged Ciudad Juárez, which led to negotiations with Díaz. When talks broke down, Orozco, against Madero's orders, stormed the city on 7 May. Three days later it fell. In classic guerrilla style (as Díaz had come to power in the 1870s), the revolutionaries had stayed in the field until the frail structure of the regime began to crack.[35] Encouraged by the persistence of the Chihuahuan rebels, others revolted in the South. The aura of invincibility that had protected the regime was shattered. As the number of outbreaks multiplied, the army was overwhelmed. Díaz's only hope had been a quick victory. When his army failed, he was doomed.

The Treaties of Juárez signed on 21 May 1911 ended the *maderista* revolt. Díaz and Corral left Mexico. After a five-month interim government, Madero was elected president and took office in November. In Chihuahua, the *terracista* legislature reluctantly elected Abraham González governor in June. But within two years both Madero and González were dead at the hands of assassins (within days of each other in February and March 1913). There followed a decade of counterrevolution, civil war, and foreign invasion. The Chihuahuan rebels broke into personalist and class factions, and the state's violent politics harked back to the pre-Porfirian era.

In 1920 Chihuahua, as it had a half century before, stood in ruins. It awaited a new elite to rise and rule over the mines and the grasslands. Chihuahua had come full circle.

11

Conclusion

This book has examined three closely related historical phenomena: the accession of the Terrazas family to unprecedented political power in Chihuahua, the development of an economy in Chihuahua based on the export of cattle and minerals, and the creation of discontent in Chihuahua that led to revolution in 1910. The first two interacted in such a way as to produce the third. In this last chapter I will summarize my explanations of these phenomena, compare Chihuahuan developments to those in other Mexican states, and, finally, tie the Chihuahuan case to wider theories of economic development and revolution.

The Terrazas won unchallenged political power in Chihuahua over the course of four decades because better than any of their rivals in the state (and better than any other regional elite in Mexico with the possible exception of the Molina-Montes clan of Yucatán) they mastered the opportunities presented by the export economy. The family used the enormous financial resources it earned from selling cattle and acting as intermediaries for foreign investors to overcome rancorous subregional political rivalries, forge a homogeneous regional elite, and successfully resist the centralizing intrusions of the Díaz dictatorship. The Terrazas employed these resources to gain control of the state's banking institutions, build the world's greatest landholding, and create one of Mexico's largest and most diverse industrial and commercial empires. They could afford, literally, to make business associates, marriage partners, or employees of a considerable portion of the Chihuahuan elite.

The rise of the Terrazas proceeded in three stages. In the first, Luis Terrazas emerged from the subregional political conflicts of the 1850s as a compromise governor with strong backing from Conservatives, most of whom were kin, and a liberal faction from the Guerrero District. He established himself as a powerful regional *cacique* during the French Intervention and the presidencies of Juárez and Lerdo. During these two and a half decades (1860–84),

Conclusion

Luis Terrazas brilliantly manipulated subregional politics and employed the limited financial and military resources of the state government to augment both his political power and personal wealth. The *cacique* solidified his links to the Conservatives, forged strong ties to subregional factions in rapidly growing Ciudad Juárez (then Paso del Norte) and in the western mining districts, and formed his first lucrative associations with foreign entrepreneurs.

In the second stage, 1876 to 1902, the Terrazas family and the regime of Díaz struggled for ascendancy in the region. The Terrazas successfully resisted Díaz initially, gave way during the 1880s, and resurged during the 1890s, forcing Díaz to a stalemate and eventually to reconciliation in 1902. The key to the Terrazas' comeback and triumph was the enormous financial windfall the family earned from the cattle export boom of the mid-1880s. These funds enabled the Terrazas to support a constant state of rebellion against Díaz in Chihuahua throughout the late 1880s and early 1890s. Moreover, the same moneys buffered the family from the severe depression that lasted from 1890 to 1896 which destroyed the financial base of its most formidable political rivals, the *guerrerenses*.

The third stage, 1902 to 1911, brought the restoration of the Terrazas to political power in Chihuahua. They turned the state into a family fiefdom.

Two simultaneous political struggles took place in almost every Mexican state from 1821 to 1911 (and continued until the late 1930s). Subregional elites battled within the states, while regional elites fought against the centralizing tendencies of national regimes. During the administrations of Benito Juárez and Porfirio Díaz, subregional factions looked to the central government for support against their opponents. The national government in turn used its support as a wedge to establish its influence and eventually its control at the state level. In state after state during the 1880s and 1890s, Díaz installed allies in control of governorships. Taking deft advantage of subregional intra-elite rivalries, Díaz brought Sonora, Coahuila, Nuevo León, and Guerrero under his thumb. The dictator saw to it that excluded political groups did not go empty handed, for he ensured that they became rich through land grants, concessions, and tax breaks. Only in Chihuahua did Díaz's opposition, the Terrazas, fight him to a standstill. No other regional elite group participated so successfully and for such a sustained period in the export economy. Thus, no other regional elite had sufficient resources to withstand the pressures of centralization.

In the other two northern border states where foreign investment underwrote the development of a mining export economy, Sonora and Coahuila, the pattern of politics differed markedly from that in Chihuahua. In neither state did any single elite family or political faction successfully resist the Díaz regime or effect the degree of homogeneity in the elite imposed by the Terrazas. Instead, weaker coalitions in intimate alliance with the national government established far more tenuous control. Three men, Luis Torres, Rafael Izábal, and Ramón Corral, dominated Sonoran politics from 1879 to 1910. Lacking the Terrazas' great financial resources, the Triumvirate, as they were called, substituted an early and close relationship with the central government. While Luis Terrazas, supported by a political network built during fifteen years as governor, revolted and overthrew Díaz's henchmen in 1879, the Torres-Izábal-Corral clique chose to collaborate and, consequently, won their first political victories. Thereafter, federal patronage and troops formed the backbone of their rule in Sonora. Like the Terrazas, the Triumvirate judiciously distributed the bounty of the export economy, acted as intermediaries for foreign investors, and extended wide their family ties. Nonetheless, they never matched either the depth or breadth of the Terrazas' control, for they neither amassed the enormous financial resources of the Terrazas nor overcame the entrenched subregional political and economic rivalries that afflicted Sonora. The Ciudad Chihuahua–Paso del Norte (Ciudad Juárez) axis came to dominate Chihuahua, but in Sonora no city or combination of cities gained the upper hand. Controlling the state government and access to credit, the Terrazas virtually dictated the terms of their arrangements with subregional groups. Conversely, the Triumvirate had to permit a wider range of local autonomy. Thus, throughout the *Porfiriato*, dangerous rivals remained unsubjugated, to reemerge at the regime's first show of weakness in 1911.[1]

Subregional rivalries were virulent throughout the Díaz era in Coahuila, where three major factions, or *camarillas*, grouped around the Madero, Garza Galán, and Cárdenas families, competed for political power. As he had in Chihuahua during the late 1870s and 1880s, Díaz intervened on the side of successive factions in search of a reliable and effective collaboration. Political turbulence forced Díaz to dispatch his most trusted general, Bernardo Reyes, to reestablish order in the late 1880s. Diverted by his duties as *cacique* of neighboring Nuevo León and the intensifying struggle with the *científicos* in Mexico City for influence with the aging dictator, Reyes, and his henchman Governor Miguel Cárdenas, never could overcome old political rivalries or the increasingly important conflicts over economic policy, especially regarding water rights in the Comarca de la Laguna. Although the "outs" among the Coahuilan elite, like those in Sonora, grew rich from the favors of the Díaz regime, they, too, never accepted their exclusion from political power. The most powerful economic group, the Madero family, pushed out of state government by Díaz for two decades, never reconciled itself to this situation and ultimately led the opposition to the regime in both Coahuila and the nation as a whole.[2]

Díaz was far more successful in imposing his rule in the two states, Nuevo León and Guerrero, where foreign investment had less overall impact. He employed the same general strategy as in Chihuahua, Sonora, and Coahuila during the 1880s, seeking allies among competing subregional elites and eventually sending a loyal general to establish order.[3] In Nuevo León rivalries between political factions led to virtual civil war in the mid-1880s, whereupon Díaz dispatched General Bernardo Reyes to the state. From 1886 to 1909, Reyes ruled the state as its *cacique*. The Monterrey commercial and industrial elite, which had the resources to challenge Reyes, instead cooperated with the regime and became rich, helped immeasurably by tax exemptions, subsidies, public works, and protective national tariffs. These businessmen saw Reyes as just the latest in a long line of *caciques* with whom they had to come to terms. Fortunately for them, Reyes was a *cacique* with close ties to the national government. The Monterrey elite was content with their riches.[4]

The state of Guerrero, too, was torn by subregional rivalries, though for several decades the great *cacique* Juan Alvarez and his son Diego ruled with little challenge. During the 1880s, Díaz again sought allies among the opponents of Alvarez and eventually brought in an outsider, General Francisco O. Arce. Despite continuous opposition to centralized control, which produced a revolt in 1893, no one faction could muster the resources or allies to resist Díaz. More so than in most states, the dictator's famed policy of "divide and rule" seemed to work in Guerrero.[5]

Through various means—alliance with reliable subregional factions, importation of outsiders of unquestionable loyalty, military force, division of regional power between governors and military zone commanders—Díaz brilliantly created his Pax Porfiriana. Subregional rivalry and political violence, nonetheless, were never very far below the surface, as is evidenced by the manifold rebellions and heated election campaigns of 1892 and 1893. Consequently, in many states dissident elites bided their time. The most notable exceptions to this were Chihuahua, where the Terrazas had homogenized elite interests, Nuevo León, where elite businessmen avoided overt involvement in politics, and Yucatán, where the Molina-Montes family controlled the elite through their monopoly of the henequén trade.

Yucatán is the example closest to that of Chihuahua. For there the moneys supplied by the Molinas' activities in the export of henequen enabled them to dominate the state politically. Unlike the Terrazas, though, the Molinas did not at any point oppose Díaz. Moreover, the Molina family never controlled subregional politics in Yucatán as the Terrazas did in Chihuahua—the *Casta Divina* was left to rule in the municipalities as they saw fit—because there was no need. Through their alliance with International Harvester, the largest consumer of henequén, the Molinas, controlled the market for the fiber and thus controlled the Yucatecan elite. But while Chihuahua was the seedbed of the Revolution in 1910, the Revolution was imposed on Yucatán by outsiders only in 1915.[6]

Díaz, then, sat majestically on a political powder keg. His regime remained secure as long as he possessed sufficient coercive power to crush recalcitrant foes and sufficient economic resources to buy the cooperation of those more flexible. But in 1910 he would be found lacking in both. One of the great ironies of the *Porfiriato* was that Díaz purposefully permitted his army to deteriorate in order to assure that neither it as an institution nor any of its leaders would challenge his power. As a formerly ambitious young general who had overthrown his predecessor, Díaz knew better than anyone the dangers of an over-mighty military. Unfortunately for the shrewd dictator, this meant that his regime was based in part on a bluff. When he needed the army to defeat the rebels of 1910–11, it proved unequal to the task.[7] Even the dissolution of the coercive power of the dictatorship would not have been fatal, however. In what must be termed the greatest irony of the Porfirian regime, the nature of the economic development that had maintained it longer than any previous government since independence robbed it of the ability to satisfy all of the key elements of Mexican society.[8] This is best seen in Chihuahua, where the export economy enabled the Terrazas to construct an unparalleled political and economic empire while it also set loose the economic and political forces that undermined their regime.

Unlike that in other regions in Mexico, the export economy in Chihuahua developed in two sectors, one, cattle, controlled by the native elite and the other, mining, dominated by foreigners. The Terrazas were the state's largest cattle exporters, generating huge profits from a boom in sales to the United States market that lasted from 1883 to 1904 (with the exception of the depression of 1890 to 1896 when the McKinley tariff excluded Mexican livestock). These profits underwrote the construction of the Terrazas' economic empire and their successful resistance to the Díaz regime. Cattle exports provided the Terrazas with economic resources that enabled them to maintain a degree of autonomy from both the national government and foreign entrepreneurs that other regional elites could not match. At a time when the justification for massive foreign investment in Latin America was the lack of private native capital, foreign entrepreneurs were borrowing large sums from the Terrazas. On one level, then, the Terrazas were not dependent on foreigners.

The cattle business could not alone, however, satisfy the burgeoning needs and ambitions of the Terrazas. They had to continue to expand and diversify their economic holdings in order to meet the demands of family employment obligations and co-optation of subregional elites. Here again the clan's financial resources afforded a degree of independence, but they nonetheless required foreign technology and management skills in their mining and industrial pursuits. The Terrazas, moreover, vastly augmented their fortunes by serving as intermediaries for foreign investors, especially in the mining sector. This activity, too, provided resources for co-opting political rivals. Since there was more nonrailroad foreign investment in Chihuahua than anywhere else in Mexico, the Terrazas had the most spoils to distribute.

Conversely, the mining sector was for the most part beyond the control of the Terrazas. And this ultimately would prove the family's undoing. Chihuahua's prosperity depended almost entirely on the mining industry. Whatever autonomy and riches the cattle boom afforded the Terrazas rebounded primarily to their own benefit. The engine that powered Chihuahuan development was mining, an industry controlled by foreigners. The mining economy, markets, prices, day-to-day decisions—all lay outside the areas of Terrazas hegemony.

The fortunes of the Terrazas had always partially rested with the booms and busts of the export mining economy. Until the depression of 1907, the family was actually able to take advantage of both ends of the cycle, using the unrest brought about by the depression of the 1890s to further its political goals in opposition to Díaz and using the booms to expand and diversify its economic holdings. But the crisis that began in 1907 led to its downfall.

The difference between 1907 and earlier crises was that the export boom in mining during the preceding ten years had set in motion developments that were to create widespread discontent and opposition to the Terrazas. The mining export economy destabilized Chihuahuan society by creating a new class, ruining an old, proud class, and expanding another, all of which, alienated or victimized by the exigencies of this economy and the unchallenged power of the Terrazas, subsequently allied to overthrow the Terrazas empire.

The economic boom stimulated by the export economy that lasted from 1897 to 1907 produced exceptional opportunities for the rise of a Chihuahuan middle class. The members of this class, however, soon realized that the closed political system imposed by the Terrazas and the predominant economic position held by the Terrazas and foreign entrepreneurs severely limited their mobility. In the depression of 1907 middle-class Chihuahuans saw many of the advances of a decade ruined, a situation they blamed on the Terrazas.

During the years of greatest prosperity from 1905 to early 1907, some members of the middle class spoke up to protest the inequities of the existing structure, seeking fairer treatment and a more just share of the economic and political pie. They sought these goals within the existing system, feeling that men like Enrique Creel and José Y. Limantour, with whom they shared many values, would be sympathetic to their needs. Instead they encouraged indifference and ultimately repression.

The middle class's first concern was the lack of political opportunity. These men believed that access to politics and government would in time bring economic gains. They were appalled by local-level political abuses and the corruption and favoritism characteristic of all levels of government. Silvestre Terrazas expressed these aspirations and attitudes of the middle class on the pages of his newspaper *El Correo de Chihuahua*.

The prosperity of the decade before 1907 had largely masked the worst effects of the Terrazas system, but the depression of 1907 exposed them harshly. Coming after years of rising living standards and upward mobility, the economic crisis drove the middle class to desperation.

The middle class in Chihuahua had little recourse within the Terrazas system. In Sonora and Coahuila disaffected elements of the middle class had dissident elite factions with whom to ally; in Chihuahua the Terrazas had eliminated or co-opted all elite opposition. The system was closed right down to the municipal level. When, in 1908, Díaz offered to open the political system to free competition and then abruptly reneged on his offer, middle-class frustration reached its height. When the dictatorship—personified by the Terrazas in Chihuahua—proved unwilling to bend and share even a small portion of its power, the middle class turned to rebellion. They turned for allies in Chihuahua not to disgruntled elites but to the small landholding class. Together the two brought on the Revolution.

While the expansion of the export economy initially benefited both the middle and working classes in Chihuahua, it hurt small landholders. The east-west expansion of the state's railroad network from 1896 to 1908 set off a large-scale attack by the elite on the landholdings of *rancheros* and villages. Empowered by the Municipal Land Law of 1905, the assault reached its peak in the midst of the depression. As it did in Morelos and Tlaxcala, pressure on shrinking land resources increased as men returned home unemployed from the mining camps and factories and from across the border in the United States. Drought in 1907 and 1908 and an early frost in 1909 ruined the harvests and killed the cattle of these peasants. As they followed years of record-breaking crops and prosperity, depression and drought struck a doubly cruel blow. The peasants were thus twice victimized by the export economy. First, the booming economy had pushed up land values, precipitating the attack on their landholdings. Second, the cyclical boom and bust of the export economy cost Chihuahuan peasants work elsewhere and increased the burden on their shrinking ranches and farms.

Like the middle class, the *rancheros* and villagers initially channeled their protests within the system. They petitioned the courts, the governor, and Porfirio Díaz himself. In rare cases they received satisfaction. Mostly they encountered repression. Hardest hit by the renewed assault on the land and the drought were the inhabitants of the former *presidios*. These tough, armed men had reached the end of their patience in 1910. They rose to protect their patrimony, providing much of the military leadership and many of the soldiers for the *maderista* revolt. The disadvantageous circumstances brought about by the export economy brought these men to revolution, but they were predisposed to fight by their long tradition of independence and violence and their military expertise. The combination of their heritage and current conditions pushed them over the line.

Throughout Mexico, during the same era, where the commercialization of agriculture and the accompanying spread of the railroads combined with the sharp downturn in the export economy in 1907–9, serious unrest arose. The virtually nationwide drought added to the discontent. Pressed by sugar planters responding to the growing market for sugar by expanding their estates and deprived of alternative ways of making a living by the economic crisis, *morelense* peasants revolted under the leadership of Emiliano Zapata.[9] Yaqui peasants seeking to regain lands stolen by the Triumvirate joined the Revolution in 1911.[10] Small landowners in Tlaxcala rebelled in 1910 and 1911 after years of futile protests against unfair taxes on their property.[11] Like those of Chihuahuan small holders and *morelense* villagers, their major alternative sources of income—working in factories and the service sector in the cities—disappeared during the depression.

In each of these regions—Chihuahua, Sonora, Tlaxcala, and Morelos—the peasants who rebelled were not the worst off. In addition, they often worked at other economic pursuits. Yaquis, reputedly the best workers in northern Mexico, were much sought after for work in northern and United States mines. Chihuahuan *rancheros* also crossed the border, worked in western Chihuahuan lumber camps and mines, ran small stores, and were muleteers. Tlaxcalan peasants labored in the textile mills, as muleteers, and as domestics. In each instance these peasant-workers and peasant petty bourgeoisie were exposed to outside influences and ideologies.

Most country people, of course, did not rebel. The most oppressed—the slaves of the henequén plantations of Yucatán, for example—the better-off resident peons on the *haciendas*, who were often outsiders and hated by the local villagers, and small owners unaffected by the intrusions of the export economy did not join the *maderista* revolt. The railroad pushed the peasants of Chihuahua, Sonora, and Tlaxcala to rebellion. The commercialization of agriculture, which resulted in the expansion of the sugar plantations, moved the *zapatistas* to revolt.[12] But in Oaxaca small landowners, undisturbed by land speculation brought on by railroad construction or the expansion of export crop production, remained at peace.[13] In Yucatán the coercive system of the *henequeneros* kept the peons in their place long after the Revolution had triumphed elsewhere.[14]

The working class in Chihuahua, too, experienced unprecedented prosperity between 1898 and 1907. The state's laborers, especially miners, were highly mobile and divorced from traditional ties of geography and family. Some had been exposed to union organization across the border or in mines and factories in Mexico. During the boom period, like the middle class, they began to protest the inequities of the Terrazas-Díaz system, frequently striking in 1906 and 1907. They met with hostility from the elite.

The depression, caused by a drop in mineral prices, struck the workers hard, especially the miners, who had enjoyed a decade of rising wages, improving living standards, and opportunities for upward mobility. Thousands were thrown out of work, and many starved. The failure of three successive harvests drove up the cost of living, exacerbating an already desperate situation. As a result, a significant, though small, number of unemployed workers, mostly miners and lumbermen, joined the Anti-reelectionists and later the Revolution. They too had fallen victim to the boom-and-bust export cycle.

Miners in Sonora and textile workers in Tlaxcala and Puebla were also among the early revolutionaries. Both groups had participated in bloody strikes put down by federal troops in Cananea and Río Blanco, respectively.[15] The Terrazas repressed strikers in Chihuahua, but because none of the strikes ever reached the size of Cananea and Río Blanco, no bloody incidents took place. What all three regions had in common was the fluidity of movement between rural and industrial occupations. The Yaquis moved easily between *hacienda*, small holding, and mines in Sonora.[16] Tlaxcalan peasant-workers went back and forth between agriculture and textile mills.[17] Even if the move from the country was permanent, they maintained ties to their villages. We have previously seen how Chihuahuan peasants often augmented their incomes in the mines and lumber camps. These peasant-workers were doubly victimized by the events of 1907 to 1909. Because they were often alienated from traditional ties and exposed to radical ideologies and because they had a heritage of independence, mobility, and violence, they too joined the Revolution, though in smaller numbers than the peasantry, from whom they were not always easily distinguishable.

Only in Chihuahua did the middle class, peasants, and workers join together against a common enemy—the Terrazas. Because there were no dissident elites in Chihuahua, these groups did not ally with *hacendados*, as they did in Sonora, Coahuila, and Durango. Sonoran Yaquis fought under their protector, *hacendado* José María Maytorena.[18] Durangan resident agricultural laborers fought under their *hacendados*.[19] The Coahuilan middle class looked to the Maderos and Carranzas, large landowners, for their leadership.[20] Thus, the very omnipotence of the Terrazas not only produced discontent but united the dissidents. The unique alliance of revolutionary classes in Chihuahua was also facilitated by the peculiar composition of Chihuahuan society. Socioeconomic lines between classes were often blurred. As a result, the three groups—peasants, middle class, and workers—were not far apart in background, goals, or outlook. The middle class in the state had exceptionally close ties with small landowners, especially in the western districts. Many of the middle class had only recently been members of the working class. Many workers had only recently been peasants or still worked the land, supplementing their income in the mines or factories. Both peasants and members of the middle class respected private property and sought redress of their grievances through access to local politics. The three groups were often indistinguishable. Pascual Orozco was a *ranchero*, muleteer, and small storekeeper. Abraham González was a small landowner, miner, and promoter. Toribio Ortega was a *ranchero* who worked on the railroads in the United States. Family ties intertwined the groups further.

The Revolution began in Chihuahua because of the singular nature of its elite and the special configuration of the nonprivileged classes. Peasants, middle class, and workers in other states were inhibited by alliances with dissident elites, who cautiously awaited a crack in the Díaz regime because they had too much to lose from precipitous action. The exception to this was, of course, Francisco Madero, who constantly outpaced his own family in his course to rebellion.[21] The Chihuahuan revolutionaries, their lands stolen, their upward mobility blocked, and their proud tradition of local autonomy trampled, had no such stake in the Terrazas system or the *Porfiriato*.

The blurred class structure of Chihuahua, the impact of the export economy, and the omnipresence of the Terrazas all combined to create the circumstances for revolution in Chihuahua. But why did the Revolution take place in Chihuahua in 1910, and not before? Depression and drought and political unrest had coincided three times before, in 1877–79, 1884–86, and 1891–95. Violence had erupted, but no revolution had ensued. Illegal land expropriations had occurred during the 1880s, but they had not caused widespread resistance.

The depression of 1907 was more severe than its predecessors, however, because more people were employed in nonagricultural occupations that were directly affected by the downturn. The impact of the downturn was magnified because it came after a long period of rising living standards. Furthermore, the economic boom from 1898 to 1907 had created a middle class whose progress was crushed by the depression. This group proved willing to articulate its disappointment and frustration. The effect of the drought was similar. The failure of three successive harvests, after two years of abundance, intensified its impact. By 1910, too, the Terrazas regime in the state had grown haughty and unresponsive, its power so great that it forgot the lessons of four decades of struggle. Creel's centralizing innovations conflicted with the proud tradition of local autonomy. The omnipotence of Terrazas control left the middle class and small landowners no recourse but to rebel.

Most important for the actual start of the Revolution, the small landholders of Chihuahua were driven to rebel. Hard hit by drought, depression, and land expropriations and capable of military action, their decision to fight struck the spark of revolution.

The Revolution in Chihuahua succeeded because of two outside factors, the rise of a leader around whom various dissidents could rally, Francisco Madero, and the collapse of the coercive power of the Porfirian regime. When the Chihuahuan *rancheros* successfully stayed in the field through the winter of 1910–11, the carefully woven fabric of the Díaz regime unwound.

Although there are, of course, marked limitations on the conclusions to be drawn from an individual case study, *Capitalists, Caciques, and Revolution* contributes to the ongoing theoretical debates over economic development and revolution. Chihuahua during the *Porfiriato* is an excellent example of a regional export economy, for the most part financed and managed by foreigners, of the kind that emerged throughout Latin America at the end of the nineteenth century and the beginning of the twentieth century as the area became incorporated into the world capitalist economy. Chihuahua, too, provides a superb case for examining the determinants of social upheaval, for it was there that the Mexican Revolution, the first great social revolution of the twentieth century, began. Underscoring the importance of the Chihuahuan case, Mexico was the only country in Latin America where export-oriented economic development led to revolution in this era. (Bolivia and Cuba were later examples.)

Mexico, in and of itself, affords an excellent opportunity for comparative study. Several regions in Mexico underwent the transformations of export-led economic development with divergent results. Moreover, there were several different Mexican revolutions. Since only a handful of the nation's twenty-one states or territories erupted in revolt in 1910–11, we have a useful control for our observations. Those regions where revolution took place produced widely diverse movements. As I have emphasized throughout the study, Mexico was far from a nation in 1910. Though Porfirio Díaz had imposed a degree of centralized authority, it was neither universal nor deep. In some ways, then, Mexico was a confederation of regions. Some of these regions developed export economies. Others did not. Some regions revolted in 1910. Others did not.

For the past two decades dependency theory has dominated the debate over economic development. In brief, its proponents hold that the past and current economic backwardness of Latin America (and other Third World nations) results from their inequitable position in the world capitalist economy as providers of primary commodities. The industrialized nations at the center of this system have drained and continue to drain resources and capital from the less developed nations, or periphery, stymieing their economic development.[22]

This exploitative system required the collaboration of the native elites of Latin America (and the Third World), who controlled the governments and owned the resources of these countries. Latin American elites collaborated not only because it enriched them but because this type of development enabled them to maintain the social and political status quo. The last decades of the nineteenth century were consequently the heyday of the oligarchies of Argentina, Chile, and Brazil.[23]

At the same time, however, the development of the export economy set in motion profound changes unanticipated by the Latin American elites. The export economy created a new, vocal middle class that stridently sought to participate in the political system and a new working class that pursued a fairer share of the bounty of economic development. In addition, in Mexico the export economy engendered an alienated, disgruntled peasantry. The elites of all the major exporting nations in Latin America confronted the same dilemma in the first decade of the twentieth century: how to deal with these rising classes. By 1910 it was clear that the elites would either have to change the system to accommodate these groups or repress them. In Argentina and Chile the elites accommodated.[24] In Mexico, the elite did not compromise but was not strong enough to crush the dissidents.

The Chihuahuan case, especially when compared with other regions in Mexico, suggests some refinements or alterations in dependency theory and points to some of the complexities overlooked by the theory, but does not challenge its basic tenets. The cases of the Terrazas and other northern elites —particularly the Monterrey industrialists—indicate that dependency theorists have underestimated the entrepreneurial traits of native elites, overestimated the subordination of these elites to foreigners in the export economy, and oversimplified the position of the native elite within the native elite–foreign enterprise system.

Although historians have dispensed with the notion that Latin American elites were nonentrepreneurial parasites addicted to conspicuous consumption, dependency theory implies a degree of passivity or loss of control by these elites.[25] The Terrazas, to the contrary, were never subordinate to foreigners in any business endeavor. They were almost always the major stockholders and managers of their enterprises. The family used several networks of investors that included foreigners (the French community of Mexico City, American businessmen of the border area) to raise money for its ventures, but family members retained control. Even when the family was not the major shareholder, as in the two banks founded by Creel in Mexico City, it had much to say about management.

The Terrazas were, moreover, venture capitalists, willing to risk their own moneys in capital-intensive industry. They built their own railroads initially (as did Argentine, Chilean, and Brazilian elites) and invested in urban utilities and heavy industry. They shied away from smelting, but this was a logical strategy in view of the overwhelming position of the smelters' trust, ASARCO, in this industry. As time went on, the clan moved into mining and oil, both of which involved competition with foreigners.

Because the Terrazas had both their own credit resources and political power, they maintained the upper hand in most dealings with foreigners. Not infrequently, large foreign companies came to the family for capital. Foreigners, moreover, did not always get their way easily or cheaply in their dealings with the Terrazas. As British historians of their countrymen's investments in Latin America have pointed out, it was not always clear who got the best of whom.[26] William Greene, for example, paid Enrique Creel nearly one million pesos for two mines in return for help in getting a huge timber and mining concession in western Chihuahua. It is doubtful "Big Bill" even realized a fraction of that sum in profits from the concession.

Monterrey entrepreneurs exhibited a similarly venturesome spirit and ability to keep foreign investors at a distance. Even more than the Terrazas, they invested in heavy industry, including smelting.[27] The Molina-Montes family of Yucatán, while hardly the risk capitalists that the Terrazas or the Monterrey group were, managed to best the giant International Harvester Company in its henequén dealings.[28]

All of this is not to say that the Terrazas or any of the other regional elites did not act as intermediaries, or *compradors*, in the classic mode. The Terrazas were in fact the most successful intermediaries of all the Mexican elite.[29] But the example of the Terrazas and the Monterrey group (and the examples of the pioneer Chilean nitrate miners and individual entrepreneurs like Mauá in Brazil) demonstrates that there was (and is) no stereotypical Latin American elite.[30] Some were indeed parasites who lived off the fees and bribes of foreigners. Many others, however, engaged in capitalist entrepreneurship.

The varied makeup of native elites in Latin America leads to the further point that the relationships between these elites and foreigners were themselves complex. Relations depended not only on what kind of elite the foreigner dealt with but also on the time period and conditions in the particular region. Such relations were not static but changed over time to reflect changing conditions. Not all native elite groups welcomed foreigners. Sonoran *hacendados* bristled when the infusion of foreign capital drove up wages.[31] Coahuilan *hacendados* objected to concessions given a foreign company in the Comarca de la Laguna which deprived them of water.[32] The native elite– foreign enterprise system did not work the same in Chihuahua as it did in Nuevo León or Mexico City or Chile or Argentina.

The relations between native elites and foreigners should be seen not as dealings between two monoliths but as arrangements on several levels that varied according to the relative strengths and circumstances of the participants. In Mexico the system was triangular, involving relations between native elites at the regional and national levels and foreign entrepreneurs. This was probably the case in Brazil and perhaps Argentina as well.

A regional breakdown reveals much about the effect of export-led economic development and the native elite–foreign enterprise system on nonelite sectors of society. Export development created a middle class and a relatively privileged working class in the North. Even those peasants who worked for wages saw their lot improved. In the North, of course, labor was scarce. In Yucatán and other tropical regions the export economy brought a tyranny, reducing labor to virtual slavery. In Argentina the working class associated with the export of cattle and agricultural commodities also benefited. There, too, export development engendered a middle class. The impact of the export economy depended, as much as anything, on the ability of the native elite to coerce other classes. Competition of scarce labor undermined the coercive power of the elite in northern Mexico, however, and so the working class flourished. In the South the elite retained its coercive strength (partly because of geographical considerations—there was no escape); consequently they reinstituted slavery.[33]

Three tenets of dependency theory are supported by the Chihuahuan case. First, foreign-owned mining companies most certainly drained capital and resources from the region. This was, however, limited to the largest companies, like ASARCO, which dominated the mining industry. The smaller operators provided stronger economic linkages and stimulated the local economy. Second, to a great extent the control of the economy lay outside the region (and the country). The market for Chihuahuan minerals was in the United States and western Europe, and the largest foreign companies were run from New York City and other places outside of Mexico. As we have seen, even the Terrazas could not control the ultimate fate of the Chihuahuan economy. Third, the cyclical nature of the capitalist economy—the world market for Chihuahuan products—was inherently destructive. Beginning in the 1880s each decade saw successively harsher depressions that tore at the fabric of Chihuahuan (and Mexican) society.

Perhaps the greatest weakness of dependency theory has been the lack of empirical data, especially for the era 1880 to 1920. As might be expected, evidence gleaned from case studies can potentially alter the theory. The Chihuahuan case, juxtaposed with other Mexican regions, suggests some of these alterations, but does not challenge its basic premises.

Theories of revolution are difficult to construct. There are wide, probably unresolvable, disagreements over definitions and methods. Moreover, the rarity of the phenomenon and its dispersed historical occurrence render comparisons, the bedrock of theory, uncertain.[34] In light of the small sample with which theorists have to work, it is puzzling that, with only a few exceptions, they have afforded little attention to Mexico, which underwent the first great revolution of the twentieth century.[35]

Recent studies of the Revolution in several Mexican regions indicate that the composition of the various regional movements, their goals, and their outcomes differed widely. For the most part they were autonomous movements (tied rather tenuously in the initial stages by the charismatic leadership of Francisco Madero) with local origins. They ranged from the peasant revolution of Morelos, the dissident elite–peasant alliance in Sonora, the revolutionary *hacendados* of Coahuila, to the middle class–peasant–worker coalition of Chihuahua.

When compared with other Mexican regions, the Chihuahuan case offers interesting insights into the phenomenon of revolution. First, it sheds light on the role of elites and the state in the revolutionary process. Almost all theories of revolution attribute importance to the breakdown of the coercive power of elites and the state resulting from intra-elite divisions or disputes between the elite (or sectors of the elite) and the state. At first glance the Chihuahuan case seems to be an anomaly, for the Terrazas were the strongest regional elite in Mexico. A closer look, however, reveals that the very omnipotence of the Terrazas worked against them, because it brought together their opponents, middle class, peasants, and proletariat. Hatred of the Terrazas was a powerful unifying force. The Chihuahuan case also hints that the roles of the elite and the state must be examined at different levels. It was possible, and such was the case in Chihuahua, to have a powerful regional elite but a weak national state (and elite), the Díaz dictatorship. In Coahuila and Guerrero the regional elite was fragmented and weak.[36] In Yucatán the elite was strong and prevented the Revolution because it was not dependent on the national government for coercive resources.[37] Finally, a persuasive argument can be made for the Chihuahuan case as an example of conflict between elite and state. The state, the Díaz dictatorship, acted not as a representative of elite interest but as an autonomous entity. From its inception the regime juggled different elite interests to sustain itself. This conflict is evident in the continuous squabbling between Díaz and the Terrazas during the spring of 1911 and the ultimate removal of Alberto Terrazas as governor. The Sonoran and Coahuilan cases also point toward elite-state conflict. In both regions the national government pursued economic policies damaging to a large sector of the elite, who subsequently revolted.[38]

Second, we must consider the fact that the Revolution began in the region of Mexico most affected by economic development financed by foreign investment and directed toward the export market. Moreover, revolution broke out in other regions where the amount of foreign investment increased most rapidly after 1900. States where foreign investment was stagnant or negligible did not erupt. There is in the Mexican case a positive correlation between a large influx of foreign investment and the development of the export economy on one hand and revolution on the other. The major exception, of course, was Yucatán, where the elite was very strong and the region isolated from revolutionary activity elsewhere.

One theory of revolution claims that dislocations (disequilibrium, dissynchronization, and so forth) arising from economic development, particularly rapid economic development and especially when a long period of advancement is followed by a sharp downturn, lead to a potentially revolutionary situation. Critics of this theory have charged that its proponents cannot identify those groups alienated from the system nor can they prove the mental state of the disgruntled sectors.[39] Yet there is sufficient empirical evidence from Chihuahua, Morelos, and other Mexican regions to identify who the revolutionaries were and why they revolted. Moreover, we can see the progression. A middle-class storekeeper or artisan started his small business in the boom days of 1900 to 1906, was adversely affected by the depression of 1907, wrote a letter protesting inequitable taxes to *El Correo*, joined the Anti-reelectionists, and finally joined the Revolution. While we do not have a huge sample of such cases, we have sufficient examples to give the theory credence. The evidence is available for the peasants as well in both Chihuahua and Morelos. Peasants who lost their lands petitioned the courts, then the governor or president, wrote a letter to *El Correo*, joined the Anti-reelectionists, and then revolted. (One must remember too that in Chihuahua there were never more than a few thousand revolutionaries, and the initiators were even fewer in number.) The process of dislocation and revolution is more vague in theory than in actual practice.

Third, it is clear from the examples of Chihuahua and other Mexican regions that peasants play a (perhaps *the*) crucial role in the formulation of revolution. Of all the Latin American nations where export-led development brought substantial social and political transformations at the end of the nineteenth century and the beginning of the twentieth century, only Mexico had a large peasantry. Only Mexico experienced a revolution. Neither Argentina nor Chile had significant traditional, sedentary Indian populations.

The Chihuahuan (and Mexican) case also points to the fact that it was a particular kind of peasant that revolted, the small landowner with strong ties to his village community.[40] This most certainly was the case in Morelos.[41] The Chihuahuan case varies somewhat, but supports this general thesis. Chihuahuan peasants had their feet in two worlds because they were not isolated but instead often worked in cities, mines, and across the border in the United States. On one hand, they were separated from traditional values, learning new nonpaternalistic employer-employee relations, being exposed to new ideologies. On the other, they retained links to their villages and, most important, their love of their land. This was the most dangerous type of peasant; not only did they have the internal organization and autonomy to revolt but they had substantial exposure to the nonpeasant world.[42]

This factor has further importance in that it facilitated the alliance between peasant, worker, and middle class in Chihuahua. In every other Latin American nation the middle class has joined the elite in times of political crisis. Only in Chihuahua of all the Mexican regions did the middle class and small landowners join together against the elite. This was possible in great part because the peasants were not an isolated class.

Finally, the Chihuahuan (and Mexican) case points to the importance of drought and economic depression in the fermentation process of revolution. In every great revolution, including the French and Russian revolutions, drought (or harvest failure) and economic depression were present and helped create unrest. Mexico had a pattern of drought-induced violence from the colonial period. During the nineteenth century another pattern emerged of cyclical economic downturn and violence. In Chihuahua major violence took place during the depressions of the late 1870s, mid-1880s, early 1890s, and 1907 to 1910. There is a consistent, if not perfect, correlation between drought and depression and political upheaval. But drought and depression are necessary but not sufficient to engender revolution. They must be accompanied by a major political crisis. When political crisis merely involved temporary use of violence as part of an ongoing bargaining process between interest groups, the combination of drought, depression, and political crisis did not lead to revolution. When there was a major political crisis that led to a breakdown of the coercive mechanisms of the elite, then revolution ensued.[43]

Epilogue

After Madero's victory, the Terrazas attempted to apply their time-tested strategy of conciliation and pressure. They maintained their contacts with the Maderos. But in 1912 the Terrazas financed the revolt of Pascual Orozco, who had grown disgruntled with Madero for not according him the proper honors due the Revolution's victorious general. The failure of Orozco's rebellion forced much of the family into exile in the United States.

Luis Terrazas lived in El Paso, Texas, for seven years, moving to Los Angeles in 1919 after his wife died and he suffered a stroke that partially paralyzed him. In 1920, the general returned to Chihuahua, where he died 12 June 1923.[1] His son Alberto fought the revolutionaries until 1914, when, badly wounded, he too fled to the United States. He also returned to Chihuahua in 1920, but left again three years later, dying in El Paso in 1926.[2]

Enrique C. Creel lived in Los Angeles during the Revolution, returning to Mexico in the 1920s to become an adviser to the Obregón administration. He headed a banking firm, Creel Hermanos, until he died in 1931.[3]

General Terrazas took five million pesos with him into exile.[4] He later received thirteen million pesos from the Obregón government in compensation for land expropriated during the Revolution.[5] His progeny used this money to buy new lands and rebuild the Terrazas economic empire during the 1920s. By the 1930s, Luis's grandchildren had become great cattlemen, and today the Creels rank among Mexico's greatest industrialists.[6]

No family member has held high political office since the Revolution, but like the Conservatives of the nineteenth century who were discredited by the French Intervention, the Terrazas have continued to exert influence through family ties and their powerful economic position.

Appendix

The Terrazas Family Tree

Juan José Terrazas
m.
Petra Fuentes

Luis Terrazas m. Carolina Cuilty Bustamente
Jesús Terrazas Fuentes—Unmarried
Zeferina m. Magdaleno Cabral
Dolores m. Toribio Ramírez
Rosa m. Francisco Molinar
Bertha Terrazas Fuentes—Unmarried

Gabino Cuilty
m.
María de la Luz Bustamente

Carolina Cuilty Bustamente m. Luis Terrazas
Paz Cuilty m. Reuben Creel
Alejandro Cuilty
Enrique Cuilty
_____ m. Carlos Moye
_____ m. Pedro Zuloaga

Luis Terrazas
m.
Carolina Cuilty Bustamente

Adela	m. Jesús Muñoz
Luisa	Vicente Guerrero
Juan	María Luján
Carlota	Miguel Márquez
Angela	Enrique Creel
Luis	Teresa Bobadilla
Elena	Rafael Horcastias
Elisa	Bernardo Urueta
Federico	Genoveva Falomir/Margarita Muñoz
Celestina	Julio Laguette
Alberto	Emilia Creel
Amada	Federico Sisniega
Guillermo	Unmarried

Enrique C. Creel m. Angela Terrazas
Juan A. Creel m. Julia Muñoz   m. Concepción Rodríguez
Beatriz m. Ing. J. Lino Ramírez

Reuben Creel — Carlos
m. — Reuben
Paz Cuilty — Ermine m. Walker Peters
María m. Christian Helmus
Paz
Carolina

Angela
Adela
Margarita
Adela Terrazas — Guillermo Muñoz
m. — Carolina m. Ignacio Cuilty
Jesús Muñoz — Jorge Muñoz m. Rosa Terrazas Luján
Luisa
Nieves
Elena

Luisa Terrazas
m. — Carolina Guerrero m. Lic. Manuel L. Luján
Vicente Guerrero

Juan Terrazas
m. — Rosa Terrazas Luján m. Jorge Muñoz Terrazas
María Luján — Francisco Terrazas Luján

Rosa Terrazas — Consuelo M.(uñoz) de Madero
m. — Leonor Muñoz de Picard
Jorge Muñoz — Juan Francisco Muñoz
Rosa María Muñoz de Félix

Adela Creel m. Joaquín Cortazar, Jr.
Emilia Creel m. Alberto Terrazas
Angela Terrazas — Luis R. Creel m. Teresa Luján
m. — Eduardo J. Creel m. Carlota Algara
Enrique C. Creel — Enrique Creel m. Leonor de la Barra
Salvador Creel m. Carolina Sisniega

María
Carlota
Sara
Carlota Terrazas — Bertha
m. — Eva
Miguel Márquez — Miguel
Benjamín
Hortensia

Appendix

Luis Terrazas, Jr. m. Teresa Bobadilla	Guillermo Terrazas B. Esther m. Luis Robinson Sara Ema Luis Terrazas B. Juan Terrazas B. Adela Teresa Abel Terrazas B. Carolina Alicia Elvira
Elena Terrazas m. Rafael Horcasitas	Rafael Horcasitas Clementina m. Francisco Ramos José María Horcasitas Pablo Horcasitas Amalia Elena Luis Horcasitas Teresa Carolina
Elisa Terrazas m. Bernardo Urueta	Eduardo Urueta Esther Carlos Urueta
Federico Terrazas m. Genoveva Falomir	Federico Terrazas Gracia Genoveva
Federico Terrazas m. Margarita Muñoz	Alfonso Terrazas María Luisa
Celestina Terrazas m. Julio Laguette	Ema Eugenio Laguette Luis Laguette Julio Laguette
Alberto Terrazas m. Emilia Creel	Alberto Terrazas Enrique Terrazas Luis Terrazas Gustavo Terrazas Blanca

Amada Terrazas
m.
Federico Sisniega

María Luisa
Federico Sisniega
Carolina
Carlos Sisniega
Amada
Lourdes

Notes

ABBREVIATIONS

AERM   México, Ministerio de Fomento, Dirección General de Estadística, *Anuario estadístico de la República Mexicana*, 1893–1907.

AGNRR   Archivo General de la Nación, Ramo de Gobernación (Revolución), Mexico City

AGNRP   Archivo General de la Nación, Ramo de Estado Mayor Presidencial, Obregón-Calles

AGPD   Archivo de General Porfirio Díaz, ed. A. M. Carreño

BSAM   *Boletín de la Sociedad Agrícola Mexicana*

BSCEH   *Boletín de la Sociedad Chihuahuense de Estudios Históricos*

CR   U.S., Department of State (or Commerce) *Commercial Relations of the United States with Foreign Countries*

EMJ   *Engineering and Mining Journal*

EPDT   *El Paso Daily Times*

EPMT   *El Paso Morning Times*

EPT   *El Paso Times*

FR   U.S., Department of State, *Foreign Relations of the United States*

HAHR   *Hispanic American Historical Review*

JMC   John McNeely Collection, University of Texas at El Paso

LARR   *Latin American Research Review*

MMJ   *Mexican Mining Journal*

NARG 59   U.S., National Archives, Record Group 59, General Records of the Department of State

NMHR   *New Mexico Historical Review*

POC   *Periódical Oficial del Estado de Chihuahua*

SAJ   *South American Journal*

SHMM   El Colegio de México, Seminario de la Historia Moderna de México

STC   Silvestre Terrazas Collection

STP   Silvestre Terrazas Papers

INTRODUCTION

1. Bernstein, "Regionalism in the National History of Mexico," pp. 389–94; Drake, "Mexican Regionalism Reconsidered," pp. 401-15; Love, "An Approach to Regionalism," pp. 137–55; Carr, "Recent Regional Studies of the Mexican Revolution," pp. 3–15. For the special characteristics of the North see León-Portilla, "The Norteño Variety of Mexican Culture," pp. 77–113, and Carr, "Las peculiaridades del norte mexicano," pp. 320–46.

2. Mariano Otero, in his *Consideraciones sobre la situación política y social de la República Mexicana en el año 1847* (Mexico: 1847), p. 42, was moved to say: "In Mexico that which is called national spirit cannot nor has been able to exist, for there is no nation." Charles Hale concludes that this sentiment was widespread in the aftermath of the defeat by the United States. Hale also quotes Jesús Reyes Heroles, *El Liberalismo mexicano*, 3 vols. (Mexico: UNAM, 1957–61), 1:358, who contends that the Mexican Constitution of 1824 "did not disunite the united, but rather . . . joined together what had been disunited." The provinces recreated a central government, but continued to hold the upper hand (Hale, *Liberalism*, pp. 14 and 81).

3. The terms *caudillo* and *cacique* have engendered considerable historical and anthropological debate. For my purposes in examining nineteenth-century politics, *caudillo* refers to a national leader, while *cacique* refers to a regional political boss. For a bibliography of the debate see Joseph, "The Fragile Revolution," pp. 60–62, 41–43. Stuart Voss has used the term *notable* to describe the elite families of Sonora in his "Porfirian Sonora." Voss, Diana Balmori, and Miles Wortman, "Notable Family Networks," have applied the term to all Latin America.

4. Jacobs, "Rancheros of Guerrero," pp. 76–80; Díaz Díaz, *Caudillos y caciques*.

5. González Navarro, *Raza y tierra*, pp. 63–75.

6. Voss, *On the Periphery*.

7. Sinkin, "Modernization and Reform in Mexico," pp. 209–28; Perry, *Juárez and Díaz*, pp. 89–151. Juan Alvarez died in 1867. Juárez and Lerdo deposed Diego for a time, but Díaz restored him in 1876. Almada, *Juárez y Terrazas*; Cosío Villegas, *La república restaurada: La vida política*, vol. 1 of the *Historia Moderna de México*.

8. Coerver, *The Porfirian Interregnum*, pp. 75–95; Cosío Villegas, *El Porfiriato: La vida política*, 2 pts., vol. 9 of the *Historia Moderna de México*, 2:54–124. For more detailed examinations of individual states see Haden, "The Federalist," Saragoza, "The Formation of a Mexican Elite," Bryan, "Mexican Politics in Transition," and Voss, "Porfirian Sonora."

9. Katz, "Villa: Reform Governor of Chihuahua," pp. 25–46; D. A. Brading, "Introduction: National Politics and the Populist Tradition," and Alan Knight, "Peasant and Caudillo in Revolutionary Mexico, 1910–1917," in Brading, ed., *Caudillo and Peasant*, pp. 1–16 and 17–58.

10. Bailey, "Revisionism and Recent Historiography of the Mexican Revolution," pp. 62–79; Katz, "Labor Conditions," pp. 1–47; D. A. Brading, *Miners and Merchants in Bourbon Mexico*; Jan Bazant, "Landlord, Labourer, and Tenant in San Luis Potosí, 1822–1910."

11. Love, "An Approach to Regionalism," pp. 141–45. Most of the studies of the Mexican economy divide the nation into larger blocks: North, Gulf of Mexico, Pacific North, Pacific South, and Center.

12. Olegario Molina in Yucatán also exercised enormous economic and political power, with his stranglehold over the henequén trade and his governorship, but his economic empire was not nearly as extensive as that of the Terrazas. Wells, "Henequén and Yucatán," pp. 100–122.

13. The literature on elites is large and stems primarily from two sources: the classical elite theorists, Pareto and Mosca (and their disciples), and Karl Marx. The classical theorists divide society into two classes, the rulers or elite and the ruled. For Marx the ruling class consisted of those who controlled the means of production. Neither approach is totally satisfactory, for politics and economics are too closely linked in Mexico (and all the underdeveloped world) to separate the elite in the way of either the classical theorists or Marx. See discussions of elite in Bottomore, *Elites and Society*, pp. 1–17; Putnam, *The Comparative Study of Political Elites*, pp. 1–19 and throughout; Geraint Parry, *Political Elites*; Smith, *Labyrinths of Power*, where chapter 1 includes an extremely useful evaluation of the studies and theories of elites.

14. Safford, "Bases of Political Alignment in Early Republican Spanish America," pp. 97–99; Cardoso and Faletto, *Dependency and Development*, xiv–xvii, 22, 26, 27; Wasserman, "Foreign Investment in Mexico," pp. 3–21.

15. Here I am talking about, of course, the application of the framework provided by dependency theory. There is no "unified theory of dependency . . . ," according to Chilcote, "A Question of Dependency," p. 55. In Cardoso, "The Consumption of Dependency Theory," pp. 7–24, one of the originators of dependency theory anguishes over the so-called testing of this framework and even objects to its use as a theory. All this confusion persists after more than a decade of lively, intense debate. Several points can be made that bear directly on this study. First, the clear implication of the dependency approach is that "underdevelopment in Latin America is a consequence of foreign penetration" (Chilcote, "A Question of Dependency," p. 56). Second, it is evident that there is no one dependency, because dependency changes over time. And third, whatever the definition of dependency, all agree that "a wide range of political, economic, and social conditions can be explained by the interaction of the forces of world capitalism and the internal dynamics of class relations" (Jackson, et al., "An Assessment of the Empirical Research on *Dependencia*," p. 13). *Capitalists, Caciques, and Revolution* is concerned with what Cardoso calls "the historicosocial process through which certain classes impose their domination over others," and the "crisis" of export political system brought about by the transformations it causes (Cardoso, "The Consumption of Dependency Theory," p. 16, and Cardoso and Faletto, *Dependency and Development*, pp. 77 and 102).

CHAPTER I

1. The best sources on the geography of Chihuahua are Almada, *Geografía del estado de Chihuahua*, and Schmidt, *A Geographical Survey of Chihuahua*.

2. Chevalier, "The North Mexican Hacienda," pp. 95–107; McBride, *Land Systems of Mexico*, pp. 25–81; Whetten, *Rural Mexico*, pp. 90–107.

3. West, *The Mining Community of Northern New Spain*, pp. 57–76; León-Portilla, "The Norteño Variety of Mexican Culture," pp. 110–12.

4. Katz, "Labor Conditions," p. 31; Chevalier, "The North Mexican Hacienda," pp. 95–107.

5. Harris, *Sánchez Navarro*, pp. 58–78, 205–30.

6. León-Portilla, "The Norteño Variety of Mexican Culture," p. 110.

7. Chevalier, "Conservateurs et Liberaux," pp. 457–74; Carr, "Las peculiaridades del norte mexicano," pp. 322–23; Powell, "Priests and Peasants," pp. 296–99.

8. Sinkin, "Modernization and Reform in Mexico," pp. 209–33; Acuña, *Sonoran Strongman*.

9. West, *The Mining Community of Northern New Spain*, pp. 57–76.

10. Voss, *On the Periphery*; Moorhead, *New Mexico's Royal Road*.

11. Clark, "Mexican Labor in the United States," pp. 466–522; Martínez, *Border Boom Town*.

12. Except where otherwise noted, for the history of colonial Nueva Vizcaya and early independence era Chihuahua I have synthesized from Almada, *Resumen de la historia*, pp. 5–246; Almada, *Gobernadores*, pp. 7–194; and Jordán, *Crónica*, pp. 25–315.

13. Almada, "Votos para la fundación de Ciudad Chihuahua," pp. 6–17.

14. Kennedy, *Tarahumara*, pp. 10–26.

15. Smith, "Apache Plunder Trails," pp. 20–42; Smith, "Indians in American-Mexican Relations," pp. 34–64; Smith, "The Scalp Hunt in Chihuahua," pp. 117–40.

16. I have synthesized the information on the *presidios* from Moorhead, *The Presidio*, pp. 1–113.

17. García Conde, "Ensayo estadístico," p. 283; Escudero, *Noticias estadísticas*, p. 82.

18. Chihuahua, Secretarío del Despacho, *Memoria, 1830*, p. 19.

19. See Smith's articles in note 15.

20. The classification of Conservatives and Liberals remains one of the most controversial debates of nineteenth-century Mexican political history. See Powell, "Priests and Peasants," pp. 296–98; Chevalier, "Conservateurs et Liberaux," pp. 456–74; and Hale, *Mexican Liberalism*.

21. Smith, "The Comanche Sun," pp. 25–62; Smith, "Poor Mexico," pp. 78–105; Smith, "The Scalphunter in the Borderlands," pp. 5–22; Smith, "The Scalp Hunt in Chihuahua," p. 133; Jordán, *Crónica*, pp. 247–49; McGaw, *Savage Scene*.

22. Almada, *Diccionario*, pp. 575–77; Lister and Lister, *Storehouse*, p. 161; Bartlett, *Personal Narratives*, 2:344; *La Coalición*, 10 May 1859, pp. 1–2; *El Republicano*, 25 March 1865, p. 1; *POC*, 29 December 1885, pp. 2–3, 2 November 1929, p. 8, 7 November 1885, p. 3, 10 January 1909, pp. 18–19, and 25 October 1906, p. 23; *La Nueva Era*, 25 November 1906, p. 2; Almada, *La revolución*, 1:58–9; Chihuahua, *Anuario*, 1905–9.

23. Almada, *Resumen de la historia*, p. 218.

24. Almada, *Diccionario*, pp. 538–40; Almada, *Gobernadores*, pp. 122–49; Almada, *General Angel Trías*; Bartlett, *Personal Narratives*, 2:417–27. For the younger Trías: Almada, *Diccionario*, pp. 240–41; Almada, *Gobernadores*, pp. 363–73.

25. Almada, *Diccionario*, pp. 550–51; Almada, *Gobernadores*, pp. 7–10 and 172–78; *POC*, 27 October 1888, p. 3.

26. Almada, *Diccionario*, pp. 116–18; Almada, *Gobernadores*, pp. 179–84; Bartlett, *Personal Narratives*, 2:427; *Chihuahua Enterprise*, 15 April 1883, p. 69; *La República*, 11 October 1872, p. 4; *El Chihuahuense*, 14 July 1863, p. 4; *La Alianza de la Frontera*, 17 October 1861; Almada, *Juárez y Terrazas*, pp. 143–62; Santleben, *Texas Pioneer*, p. 103; *POC*, 26 December 1885, pp. 2–3, 27 May 1909, p. 7; *EPMT*, 12 May 1910, p. 9; AGNRR, 260/14.

27. Almada, *Diccionario*, p. 371; Almada, *Gobernadores*, pp. 195–203.

28. Almada, *Diccionario*, pp. 351–52; Almada, *Gobernadores*, pp. 204–18.

29. Voss, *On the Periphery*.

CHAPTER 2

1. I have synthesized the narrative from Almada, *Resumen de la historia*, pp. 247–361; Fuentes Mares, *Luis Terrazas*; Almada, *Juárez y Terrazas*; and Almada, *Gobernadores*, pp. 195–434.

2. González Flores, *Chihuahua*, p. 149; Beezley, "Opportunity," pp. 30–40.

3. *La República*, 9 October 1868, 12 April 1874. *Semanario Oficial*, 20 February 1876. *POC*, 26 May 1878, p. 4. L. H. Scott, U.S. Consul, Chihuahua City, to William H. Seward, Secretary of State, 19 September 1879; Scott to Assistant Secretary of State, 13 November 1879; George L. McManus to Secretary of State, 3 February 1860, all in NARG 59. *Alianza de la Frontera*, 9 March 1861, p. 2. *La República*, 26 February 1869, p. 3. *Semanario Oficial*, Alcance, 25 January 1876. Joaquín Terrazas, *Memorias*, pp. 71–82. Scott to Second Assistant Secretary of State, 22 October 1880, NARG 59. See also *POC*, 25 March 1882, p. 3, 25 November 1882, p. 3, 24 February 1883, p. 3, and 5 June 1886, p. 3; *EPDT*, 24 September 1892, p. 1.

4. Santleben, *Texas Pioneer*, p. 167. Henry Cuniffe, U.S. Consul, to Seward, 1 October 1863 and 10 October 1864; Reuben W. Creel, U.S. Consul, Chihuahua City, to Secretary of State, 14 July 1865; Charles Moye, U.S. Consul, Chihuahua City, to Secretary of State, 16 November 1867; W. H. Brown, U.S. Consul, Chihuahua City, to Second Assistant Secretary of State, 1 October 1871 and 9 March 1872; J. C. Huston, U.S. Consul, Chihuahua City, to Second Assistant Secretary of State, 4 October 1873; Scott to Second Assistant Secretary of State, 20 July 1879, all in NARG 59.

5. *POC*, 26 May 1878, pp. 2–3, 5 May 1878, p. 2, 19 May 1878, pp. 2, 4, and 9 February 1879, p. 2.

6. Fuentes Mares, *Luis Terrazas*, pp. 5–9, 168–69.

7. Almada, *Diccionario*, pp. 522–23, 526; Almada, *Gobernadores*, pp. 451–53; *Boletín Comercial*, 15 April 1908, p. 1.

8. Almada, *Gobernadores*, pp. 437–47; Almada, *Diccionario*, p. 124; Creel Cobián, *Enrique Creel*; Helguera, *Enrique Creel*.

9. Federico Sisniega to R. G. Dun and Co., Torreón, Coahuila, 25 June 1904, part 2, reel 8, STP; Sisniega to R. G. Dun and Co., 18 July 1906, part 2, reel 10, STP; *El Correo*, 16 April 1906, p. 1.

10. Almada, *Juárez y Terrazas*, p. 337; Almada, *Diccionario*, p. 323; Márquez Montiel, *Hombres célebres*, pp. 146–47; *Revista de Chihuahua*, 1895.

11. Almada, *Juárez y Terrazas*, p. 337; Almada, *Diccionario*, p. 255; *Chihuahua Enterprise*, 15 April 1883, p. 69; *Nueva Era*, 3 February 1911, p. 1; *POC*, 26 December 1891, p. 2, 10 January 1909, pp. 18–19, 29 December 1885, pp. 2–3; *Semanario Oficial*, 15 January 1876.

12. Almada, *Diccionario*, pp. 554–55, 351; Almada, *Juárez y Terrazas*, p. 337; Fuentes Mares, *Luis Terrazas*, p. 281; *POC*, 24 January 1907, p. 17.

13. *EPMT*, 16 January 1914, p. 2, 17 December 1913, p. 1; González Ramírez, *La revolución social*, 1:328; Almada, *Diccionario*, pp. 128–29; *POC*, 27 January 1907, p. 8, 16 January 1910, p. 21; *El Siglo XX*, 10 August 1904, p. 4; *La Nueva Era*, 11 January 1903, p. 5; *Mexican Herald*, 21 January 1896, p. 7; *El Correo*, 3 May 1906, p. 4.

14. Almada, *Diccionario*, p. 314.

15. *POC*, 23 June 1883, p. 4, 12 July 1906, p. 16, 15 July 1906, p. 16, 12 January 1908, p. 16, 31 May 1924, p. 2; AGNRR 225/35, documents dated from 18 October 1916 to 30 April 1919; Martín Falomir to Francisco Valdes, 16 August 1910, part 2, reel 14, STP; Statement of Martín Falomir, 12 November 1910, part 2, reel 14, STP; AGNRR, 217/7, dated 20 June 1917.

16. Almada, *Juárez y Terrazas*, p. 338; Almada, *Diccionario*, p. 349; Márquez Montiel, *Hombres célebres*, p. 96; Santleben, *Texas Pioneer*, p. 299; Hall, "Colonel James Reiley's Missions," p. 234; *POC*, 24 April 1886, p. 4, 5 October 1929, p. 8, and 26 December 1885, pp. 2–3.

17. Almada, *Diccionario*, p. 122, and *Gobernadores*, pp. 435–36.

18. *BSCEH* 1, no. 11 (15 April 1939): 384; Almada, *Diccionario*, pp. 43–44; *El Correo*, 3 November 1904, p. 1, 7 March 1904, p. 1, and 17 March 1905, p. 1; *La Nueva Era*, 16 March 1885 and 19 June 1885; Almada, *La revolución*, 1:29; González Flores, *Chihuahua*, p. 150; enclosure of letter of Martín Falomir to Enrique C. Creel, 22 December 1910, STP.

19. Almada, *Diccionario*, pp. 351, 354; Almada, *Gobernadores*, pp. 170–71.

20. Almada, *Juárez y Terrazas*, pp. 72–73, 123–27, 171; Reuben W. Creel to Secretary of State, 10 December 1863, 2 March 1864, 4 May 1864, 7 June 1864, and 17 June 1864, NARG 59; *Alianza de la Frontera*, 3 May 1864.

21. Sinkin, "Modernization and Reform in Mexico," pp. 211–23.

22. The relationship between Juárez and Terrazas is a matter of hot controversy between Fuentes Mares and Almada. See Almada, *Juárez y Terrazas*, pp. 222–25, and Fuentes Mares, *Luis Terrazas*, pp. 103–10.

23. Reuben W. Creel to Brigadier James H. Carleton, 18 September 1864; Creel to Secretary of State, 20 July 1865; Creel to Seward, 30 March 1866, 2 March 1866, 28 February 1866, and 7 June 1864; Cuniffe to Seward, 2 February 1866, 12 January 1866, and 17 June 1864, all in NARG 59.

24. Almada, *Gobernantes*, pp. 60–63; Almada, *Juárez y Terrazas*, pp. 143–62; T. H. Smith to F. McManus, 30 October 1863, NARG 59.

25. Reuben W. Creel to Secretary of State, 10 December 1863; Moye to Secretary of State, 18 July 1870, NARG 59.

26. Cosío Villegas, *La república restaurada*: *La vida política*, pp. 735–36. *AGPD*, vol. 10, p. 112. J. R. Robinson to William H. Brown, 31 January 1872; William H. Brown to Second Assistant Secretary of State, 10 February 1872, 14 February 1872, 10 June 1872, 27 June 1872, 16 July 1872, 18 July 1872, 31 July 1872, and 31 August 1872; Pierson, U.S. Consul, Paso del Norte, to Second Assistant Secretary of State, 15 March 1872 and 2 September 1872, all in NARG 59.

27. Porfirio Díaz to Luis Terrazas, 12 October 1872, *AGPD*, vol. 10, p. 162. Díaz to Terrazas, 21 October 1872, *AGPD*, vol. 10, pp. 174–75. Pierson to Second Assistant Secretary of State, 2 September 1872, 24 September 1874; Brown to Second Assistant Secretary of State, 14 September 1872, both in NARG 59.

28. J. C. Huston, U.S. Consul, Chihuahua City, to Second Assistant Secretary of State, 2 June 1876; F. McManus and Son and H. Nordwald to John W. Foster, U.S. Minister to Mexico, 5 March 1871; Scott to Foster, 8 March 1871, all in NARG 59. *POC*, 9 February 1879, p. 2.

29. Scott to Second Assistant Secretary of State, 12 September 1879 and 18 September 1879, NARG 59.

30. *BSCEH* 1, no. 4 (15 August 1938): 130.

31. Scott to Steward, 31 October 1879; Scott to Newton, 28 November 1879, both in NARG 59.

32. Womack, *Zapata*, pp. 14–17; DeHart, "Pacification of the Yaquis," pp. 74–77; Haden, "The Federalist"; Bryan, "Mexican Politics in Transition"; Cosío Villegas, *El Porfiriato*: *La vida política interior*, 2:54–124.

33. Haden, "The Federalist."

34. Almada, *Gobernadores*, pp. 385–94; Beezley, "Opportunity," pp. 34–35.

35. Almada, *Diccionario*, pp. 557, 90–91; Chihuahua, Gobernador, *Mensaje del Gobernador*,

1888; POC, 17 May 1906, p. 21; and Chihuahua, *Anuarios*, 1905–9; Almada, *Gobernadores*, pp. 408–15; *POC*, 23 December 1882, p. 3, 20 January 1883, p. 2, 6 January 1883, p. 2, 20 April 1887, p. 4, 19 July 1884, p. 3.

36. Almada, *Diccionario*, pp. 94–95; Almada, *Gobernadores*, pp. 290–95, 333–37, 381–84; *EMJ* 88 (13 November 1909): 1002; *SAJ*, 10 July 1909, p. 36; *POC*, 26 September 1909, p. 28, and 11 November 1882, p. 1; AGNRR 274/60, document dated 11 March 1919.

37. Almada, *Diccionario*, pp. 316–17; Almada, *Gobernadores*, pp. 403–7.

38. Almada, *Gobernadores*, p. 382.

39. Chihuahua, Gobernador, *Mensaje del Gobernador, 1888; POC*, 29 October 1892, p. 1.

40. Mills, *Forty Years*, pp. 182–88; Almada, *Gobernadores*, pp. 338–42; Charles W. Kindrick, U.S. Consul, Ciudad Juárez, to David J. Hill, Assistant Secretary of State, 9 December 1898, NARG 59; Almada, *Juárez y Terrazas*, p. 338; *El Siglo XX*, 10 August 1904, p. 4; *POC*, 5 August 1882, p. 3, 24 February 1883, p. 4; *La República*, 11 April 1870, p. 4; AGNRR 211/58, document dated 24 March 1917; *POC*, 11 October 1906, p. 17, 18 January 1866, p. 2; *El Boletín*, 3 April 1866, p. 1; *Mexican Herald*, 18 January 1896, p. 7; Max Weber to H. R. Wood, 14 August 1898, Weber Collection, copy book, roll 2.

41. Mills, *Forty Years*, p. 188; *El Correo*, 27 February 1902, p. 2.

42. Almada, *Diccionario*, p. 73; *POC*, 17 February 1878, p. 4; *Mexican Financier*, 28 December 1889, p. 320; *El Correo*, 4 September 1906, p. 1; *Mexican Investor*, 9 September 1905, p. 10; *Mexican Herald*, 8 May 1908, p. 11; *POC*, 19 December 1909, p. 30.

43. Almada, *Diccionario*, pp. 424–25; Almada, *Juárez y Terrazas*, p. 337; *Mexican Herald*, 6 September 1908, p. 2; *POC*, 26 December 1885, pp. 2–3, 5 October 1887, p. 2.

44. Almada, *Diccionario*, p. 445; *Semanario Oficial*, 12 January 1877, p. 2, and 31 March 1876, p. 2; "Mineral de Uruáchic," *Revista Chihuahuense*, 30 April 1909, pp. 1–3; *El Centinela*, 27 November 1855, p. 2; *POC*, 14 October 1882, p. 2, 26 December 1885, pp. 2–3, 26 August 1885, pp. 2–3, 21 January 1888, p. 2, 11 June 1887, p. 4, 5 September 1907, p. 40, 23 January 1908, p. 13, and 7 July 1910, p. 24; *La Nueva Era*, 3 March 1866, pp. 2–4; *El Boletín*, 8 September 1866, pp. 1–2, and 15 December 1866, p. 3; Southworth, *Directory of Mines*, p. 77.

45. Southworth, *Directory of Mines*, p. 68; Almada, *Diccionario*, pp. 67, 387; AGNRR 211/78, documents dated 14 December 1914 to 22 January 1919; *Mexican Herald*, 6 February 1908, p. 11, 15 September 1907, p. 11, 19 February 1896, p. 2, and 23 November 1907, p. 11; *Mexican Financier*, 20 July 1899, pp. 392–93, 19 January 1889, p. 392, and 2 July 1887, pp. 222–23; Hamilton, *Border States*, pp. 149–51; *Chihuahua Enterprise*, 15 December 1882, p. 9; *EMJ* 47 (5 January 1889): 5, and 85 (4 April 1908): 692; *POC*, 28 May 1887, p. 3, 23 March 1889, p. 2, 6 May 1882, pp. 2–3, 20 July 1887, p. 3, 20 November 1886, p. 3, 3 September 1887, p. 2, and 2 August 1906, p. 9; *El Centinela*, 23 October 1855, p. 14; *El Boletín*, 8 September 1866, pp. 1–2; *La República*, 8 August 1868, p. 4, and 13 August 1869, p. 2; *La Guardia Nacional*, 12 July 1877, p. 2.

46. Almada, *Diccionario*, pp. 574, 127; Chávez M., "Hombres de la Revolución," pp. 304, 68; *El Correo*, 20 January 1908, p. 4; Meyer, *Pascual Orozco*, pp. 17 and 19.

47. See chapter 3.

48. Almada, *La revolución*, 1:87.

49. *El Correo*, 24 May 1903, p. 2.

50. Chihuahua, Gobernador, *Memoria, 1892–1896*, pp. 175–81.

51. Beezley, "Opportunity," pp. 36–39; Almada, *La revolución*, 1:98; Cosío Villegas, *El Porfiriato: La vida política interior*, 2:58–64.

52. Cosío Villegas, *El Porfiriato: La vida política interior*, 2:58–64; *POC*, 21 February 1887, p. 2, 2 July 1887, p. 3, and 30 July 1887, p. 2.

53. Almada, *Tomochi. POC*, 26 November 1892 and 2 September 1892. *BSCEH* 1, no. 7 (December 1938): 230; 1, no. 8 (15 January 1939): 214; and 2, no. 2 (15 July 1939): 71. Beezley, "Opportunity," p. 36. Jordán, *Crónica*, pp. 242–57. Almada, *Resumen de la historia*, pp. 350–51.

54. Almada, *Resumen de la historia*, p. 356.

55. Almada, *Gobernadores*, pp. 426–34; Almada, *Diccionario*, pp. 21–22.

56. Cosío Villegas, *El Porfiriato: La vida política interior*, 2:458–60.

57. "Mexican Revolution from Publication of the Plan de San Luis Potosí, February 6, 1910, to Madero's Entry into Mexico City, June 7, 1911," monograph no. 4, to be found in U.S., National Archives, Record Group 76, Records of the United States and Mexican Claims Commission, Suitland, Maryland, pp. 37–38.

58. Cosío Villegas, *El Porfiriato: La vida política interior*, 2:458–60; Beezley, "Opportunity," p. 38.

59. Jacobs, "Rancheros of Guerrero," pp. 79–81; Acuña, *Sonoran Strongman*; Meyers, "Interest Group Conflict," pp. 295–303; Richmond, "Factional Political Strife," pp. 49–51.

60. Meyers, "Interest Group Conflict," pp. 50–191.

61. Voss, "Porfirian Sonora"; DeHart, "Pacification of the Yaquis," pp. 75–81; Luna, *Ramón Corral.*

CHAPTER 3

1. Cortes Conde, *The First Stages of Modernization*, pp. 1–10, 57–77, 115–58; Cardoso and Faletto, *Dependency and Development*; Smith, *Politics and Beef*, pp. 57–81; Mamalakis and Reynolds, *Chilean Economy.*

2. Kilby, "Hunting the Heffalump," in Kilby, *Entrepreneurship and Economic Development*, p. 13; Lipset, "Values, Education, and Entrepreneurship," in Lipset and Solari, *Elites in Latin America*, pp. 3–60; Morner, "The Spanish American Hacienda," pp. 203–7.

3. Coatsworth, "Obstacles to Economic Growth," p. 87; see also Halperin-Donghi, *The Aftermath of Revolution*, and Oppenheimer, "National Capital and National Development."

4. Saragoza, "The Formation of a Mexican Elite," pp. 74–132; Wells, "Henequén and Yucatán," pp. 81–148; Meyers, "Interest Group Politics," pp. 50–143.

5. Coatsworth, "Obstacles to Economic Growth," p. 92.

6. Ibid., pp. 91–94.

7. Costeloe, *Church Wealth in Mexico*, pp. 14–18.

8. Coatsworth, "Obstacles to Economic Growth," p. 99.

9. *CR, 1885–1886*, 1:897, 901; *Mexican Financier*, 14 December 1889, p. 272; Dusenberry, "The Mexican Agricultural Society," pp. 394–95.

10. *Bankers' Magazine* 80 (January–June 1910): 793; *Revista de Chihuahua*, February 1895, p. 23; Hall, "Colonel James Reiley's Missions," p. 234.

11. *POC*, 18 October 1906, p. 13; Chihuahua, Gobernador, *Memoria, 1892–1896*, p. 55; Chihuahua (Ciudad), Ayuntamiento, *Informe, 1907*, p. 5.

12. Federico Sisniega to Ernesto Madero, 25 September 1900, part 2, reel 7, STP.

13. Almada, *La revolución*, 1:60–63; see also Chihuahua, *Anuarios.*

14. F. H. Howard to Secretary of State, 26 June 1908, numerical files, 14164/2, NARG 59; *Mexican Herald*, 19 August 1907, p. 11.

15. Max Weber to Max Miller, 6 September 1904, copy book, roll 4, Weber Collection.

16. See Table 3-2.

17. Meyers, "Interest Group Conflict," pp. 259, 197–99.

18. See *El Correo*, 1909–10, and *POC*, 1909–10.

19. Saragoza, "The Formation of a Mexican Elite," pp. 121–30; Meyers, "Interest Group Conflict," pp. 200–201.

20. This is based on an estimated family size of 3.5, which probably understates the number of residents on the family's *haciendas*. There are also sometimes large discrepancies in or disagreements over the estimates of the *haciendas'* populations. For example, various estimates of the number of residents on the Hacienda de Encinillas range from 1,000 to 2,000.

21. Fuentes Mares, *Luis Terrazas*, p. 171; Almada, *Juárez y Terrazas*, p. 350; Federico Sisniega to the Administración Central del Banco Nacional de México, 19 August 1908, part 2, reel 10, STP; U.S., Department of Commerce and Labor, Bureau of Manufactures, *Monthly Trade and Consular Reports*, no. 305, February 1906; Chihuahua, *Anuario*, *1909*, pp. 142–43, 146, *1907*, pp. 54–57, *1906*, pp. 140–43.

22. *Mexican Herald*, 18 June 1906, p. 3; *El Correo*, 19 January 1907, p. 1; Martín Falomir to Enrique C. Creel, 19 January 1911, part 2, reel 14, STP; *Mexican Investor*, 6 August 1904, p. 6; Compañía Eléctrica y de Ferrocarriles de Chihuahua, S.A., *Concesiones*, pp. 31–35; *La Nueva Era*, 29 November 1906, p. 2; *El Correo*, 16 January 1899, p. 1; Max Weber to Britton Davis, 10 March 1900, copy book, roll 2, Weber Collection.

23. There are several important sources for information on the landholding of the Terrazas family: Chihuahua, *Anuarios*, *1905–1909*; Fuentes Mares, *Luis Terrazas*, pp. 169, 279–83; Almada, *La revolución*, 1:58–60; Creel Cobián, *Enrique Creel*; "Relación de las calificaciones que reportan las fincas rústicas intervenidas que a continuación se expresan ubicadas en la municipalidad de Chihuahua," file 267/76, AGNG; file 806-T-1, 1921–22, AGNRP; *POC*, 27 January 1907, p. 8; and two documents from the papers of the Creel family, "Negocios de Enrique C. Creel" and "The General Terrazas Estate." I am greatly indebted to Sr. Eduardo Creel of Mexico City and Harold D. Sims for giving me copies of these.

24. The Galeana properties, owned by General Terrazas, encompassed the *haciendas* of La Carbonera, El Carmen, La Nariz, San Isidro, San Diego, San Lorenzo, San Luis, San Miguel de Bavícora, San Pedro, Santa María, and Tapiecitas, covering 1.4 million acres. They contained the state's largest cattle-raising area, grazing more than two hundred thousand head. This land was fertile, beautiful, and well watered. Together these *haciendas* had more than 17,000 acres under irrigated cultivation, producing wheat, maize, and sugar beet. They also included some of the state's best timberland.

   Luis Terrazas also owned the second tract north of Ciudad Chihuahua, which consisted of the *haciendas* Aguanueva, Encinillas, Gallego, Las Hormigas, Hinojeño, Quinta Carolina, Sacramento, San Felipe, El Sauz, and El Torreón, stretching over more than 1.7 million acres. More than one hundred thousand cattle grazed these lands.

   The general's third tract comprised the *haciendas* San Isidro, San Ignacio, San Felipe, and San Dionisio, extending over 500,000 acres, much of it in the Valle de Allende in Jiménez District, a fertile fruit-producing area. Perhaps fifty thousand cattle grazed on these properties.

   The fourth group of properties, in Camargo District, included 515,000 acres owned by Enrique Creel and the 247,000-acre Hacienda de Gallina owned by Alberto Terrazas. The fifth section, Creel's 1,235,000-acre Hacienda de Orientales, was desert. In addition, family members owned other land throughout the state.

   Informe de Toribio G. Galindo, Presidente Municipal de Casas Grandes, 6 February 1918, AGNG, file 247/17; map of the Mexican Northwestern Railway, box 9, Mexico Northwestern Railway Papers, JMC.

25. *Mexican Investor*, 27 October 1910, pp. 12–13, 1 April 1905, p. 19, and 2 September 1905, p. 10; *El Correo*, 23 April 1902, p. 2.

26. Almada, *La revolución*, 1:59–60; *La Nueva Era*, 25 November 1906, p. 2; *POC*, 25 October 1906, p. 23, 2 November 1929, p. 8, 11 July 1885, p. 3, and 29 December 1885, pp. 2–3.

27. *POC*, 23 June 1883, p. 4, 12 July 1906, p. 16, and 15 July 1906, p. 16; statement of Martín Falomir, 12 November 1910, part 2, reel 14, and statement of property of Martín Falomir, 26 August 1908, letterbook, part 2, reel 13, STP; Almada, *La revolución*, 1:59.

28. Almada, *La revolución*, 1:60; *El Siglo XX*, 17 August 1904, p. 4; *POC*, 19 January 1908, p. 24; *Mexican Herald*, 27 March 1909, p. 5; *El Correo*, 12 August 1904, p. 1; Juan N. Amador to Paul Fleming, 10 March 1914, 312.114, F 62/A3, NARG 59, decimal file.

29. Almada, *Juárez y Terrazas*, p. 332, accuses Terrazas of using his public position and power to acquire the *haciendas* Aguanueva and El Carmen. There were evidently hard feelings about the sale of Aguanueva. See Max Weber to E. Ketelsen and B. Degeteau, 5 March 1898, copy book, roll 1, Weber Collection. While governor, Luis Terrazas was in a position to influence land values by the way he stationed state troops under his command to fight the Apaches. The following provide a good description of the Apache onslaught: Henry Cuniffe, U.S. Consul, Paso del Norte, to Seward, 1 October 1863; Reuben Creel, U.S. Consul, Chihuahua City, to Secretary of State, 14 July 1864; Charles Moye, U.S. Consul, Chihuahua City, to Secretary of State, 16 November 1869; W. H. Brown, U.S. Consul, Chihuahua City, to Secretary of State, 1 October 1871 and 9 March 1872, all in NARG 59.

30. Martínez del Río eventually returned to Mexico and conducted a long, drawn-out litigation which ultimately forced Terrazas to pay for two large parcels illegally included in the 1866 sale.

    Almada, *Juárez y Terrazas*, pp. 323–27, 649–90, 668; Bazant, *Alienation of Church Wealth*, p. 54; *POC*, 14 March 1885, p. 3; *El Correo*, 1 September 1906, p. 1, and 1 January 1906, p. 1.

31. *El Correo*, 24 May 1903, p. 2; *POC*, 9 April 1908, p. 32; Fuentes Mares, *Luis Terrazas*, p. 283.

32. Chihuahua, Gobernador, *Mensaje del Gobernador, 1888*; *POC*, 26 June 1885, cited in Almada, *Juárez y Terrazas*, p. 340. México, Ministerio de Fomento, Colonización e Industria, *Memoria, de 1905 a 1907*, pp. 125, 129; Carlos Haerter to Senator Albert B. Fall, in U.S., Congress, Senate, Committee on Foreign Relations, *Revolutions in Mexico*, p. 645.

33. *POC*, 12 April 1924, pp. 12–14, and 18 December 1886, p. 4.

34. *POC*, 12 April 1924, pp. 12–14.

35. *El Correo*, 24 July 1909, p. 1.

36. *POC*, 21 May 1883, pp. 3–4.

37. *POC*, 2 February 1884, p. 4.

38. *El Correo*, 14 March 1904, p. 1; *Mexican Herald*, 13 August 1906, p. 3; "Catastro de propiedad raíz de la Ciudad de Chihuahua," in Chihuahua, Gobernador, *Mensaje del Gobernador, 1888*; "Relación de las propiedades intervenidas que existen actualmente bajo el control de la Administración de Bienes Intervenidos en el estado de Chihuahua," 31 March 1919, box 88, item 32, AGNG.

39. *El Correo*, 2 March 1909, p. 1; map, box 11, item 154, Papers of the American Board of Commissioners for Foreign Missionaries, ABC 18.2.

40. Lister and Lister, *Storehouse*, pp. 156–61; Fuentes Mares, *Luis Terrazas*, pp. 12, 244.

41. Katz, "Labor Conditions," pp. 31–38; Clark, "Mexican Labor in the United States," p. 473; *CR*, *1899*, p. 431, *1900*, p. 556, *1901*, p. 468, *1903*, p. 122, *1905*, p. 269.
42. Santleben, *Texas Pioneer*, pp. 146–47.
43. Jacques Levy, *Cesar Chávez*, p. 7.
44. Woods, "Cattleman," p. 38.
45. Report of R. M. Burke, U.S. Consul, Chihuahua City, 20 July 1896, *U.S. Consular Reports*, no. 193 (October 1896), p. 265; Katz, "Labor Conditions," p. 34.
46. Katz, "Labor Conditions," p. 35.
47. "Memorándum al Señor Presidente de la República sobre las contribuciones de los Bienes Intervenidos en el estado de Chihuahua," 5 March 1919, AGNG 270/1.
48. Katz, "Labor Conditions," pp. 45–46.
49. Chihuahua, *Anuario*, 1905, p. 72, *1906*, pp. 216–17, *1907*, p. 129, *1908*, p. 171, *1909*, p. 210.
50. *POC*, 12 April 1924, pp. 12–14; Womack, *Zapata*, p. 47.
51. Teodisio Duarte Morelos, "Memorias de un precursor de la Revolución de 1910," manuscript in the possession of Ing. Benjamín Herrera Vargas of Ciudad Juárez, cited in Estrada, "Liderazgo," p. 72.
52. Interview of Richard M. Estrada with Mrs. Nelle Spilsbury Hatch, El Paso, Texas, cited in Estrada, "Liderazgo," p. 74.
53. Duarte Morelos, "Memorias," cited in Estrada, "Liderazgo," pp. 73–74.
54. Ibid.
55. *El Correo*, 15 July 1911, p. 4.
56. Chihuahua, *Anuario*, *1909*, pp. 112, 114.
57. *El Correo*, 10 October 1911, p. 4.
58. Memorandum to Ministerio de Agricultura y Fomento, 21 October 1921, AGNRP, 818-C-49; Katz, "Agrarian Changes," and "Labor Conditions," pp. 32–33; *POC*, 19 April 1924, pp. 5–7.
59. Bush, *Gringo Doctor*, p. 106; Woods, "Cattleman," p. 40.
60. Katz, "Labor Conditions," p. 46; Uriostegui Miranda, ed., *Testimonios del proceso revolucionario de México*, pp. 81–135.
61. *Bankers' Magazine* 78 (March 1909): 395.
62. *Mexican Financier*, 18 January 1896, pp. 415–16; Sims, "Los Terrazas," pp. 391–94.
63. *Bankers' Magazine* 80 (January–June 1910): 793. The Banco Mexicano, founded by Luis Terrazas, Félix Francisco Maceyra, Antonio Asúnsolo, and Miguel Salas in 1878, merged with the Banco Minero in order to save it during the depression of 1891–95; its capital and assets declined from 1888 to 1895. *Mexican Financier*, 19 January 1889, p. 399, 11 January 1896, p. 399; *POC*, 10 March 1878, p. 1.
64. *Mexican Financier*, 18 January 1896, p. 415; Walter U. Falla, "A Study of Economic Development Banking in Mexico during the Victorian Age, 1857–1910 (M.A. thesis, University of California, 1965), p. 374; *Revista de Chihuahua*, January 1896, pp. 378–79; Banco Minero, Consejo de Administración, *Informes*, 1908, pp. 9, 13; *Mexican Herald*, 5 January 1909, p. 9, 28 June 1908, p. 5, and 16 April 1906, p. 10; "Negocios de Enrique Creel"; *Mexican Investor*, 2 January 1904, p. 32; Southworth, *Directorio oficial bancario*, pp. 362–63. By 1907 the Banco Minero had seven branch offices in Ciudad Juárez, Camargo, Jiménez, Hidalgo del Parral, Hermosillo in Sonora, and Gómez Palacio in Durango. The bank was so profitable that in 1908, despite the loss of three hundred thousand pesos in a robbery, it earned six hundred thousand pesos. According to Enrique Creel his 200,000-peso investment in 1882 was worth more than 2.3 million when the Revolution broke out in 1910.

65. *El Correo*, 13 August 1903, p. 1, 8 January 1904, p. 2, 8 March 1904, p. 2. *CR*, *1904*, pp. 502–3. *Bankers' Magazine* 78 (March 1909): 395; 76 (March 1908): 409. See also the correspondence in part 2, reel 11, STP.

66. Muñoz A. to Silvestre Terrazas, 3 April 1907, part 2, reel 14, and Martín Falomir to Enrique Creel, 31 December 1910, part 2, reel 14, STP; *El Correo*, 17 March 1905, p. 1; *Mexican Herald*, 6 November 1895, p. 5.

67. Federico Sisniega to the Central Administration of the Banco Nacional de México, 21 November 1909, part 2, reel 11, STP.

68. *El Correo*, 28 December 1907, p. 1; *Mexican Herald*, 28 June 1910, p. 6; *Mexican Yearbook*, *1911*, p. 136, *1912*, p. 63.

69. *Mexican Herald*, 22 January 1906, p. 7. The family, through the Banco Minero, also owned the Guaranty National Bank of El Paso, Texas. Established in 1902, it was plagued by inept management and eventually was forced into liquidation. Walter M. Brodie to Enrique C. Creel, 5 November 1910, and E. N. Schwabe, Cashier, Guaranty Trust, to W. E. D. Stokes, 28 December 1910, part 2, reel 2, STP; Business and Personal Correspondence, Weber Collection, has extensive documentation of the ill-fated bank.

70. *El Correo*, 10 March 1904, p. 2. *Bankers' Magazine*, 80 (January–June 1910): 488; 77 (October 1908): 525–29.

71. *Bankers' Magazine* 77 (October 1908): 537–41. Creel's other banking interests consisted of considerable stock in the Banco Oriental de México, membership on the board of the Banco de Guanajuato, the presidency of the Compañía de los Almacenes Generales de Depósito de México y Veracruz, and the honorary presidency of the Mexican Trust Company. In 1899 he was president of the national bankers' association. He also headed or served on several important commissions that dealt with national monetary policies and represented Mexico at international conferences in the United States and Europe. Creel Cobián, *Enrique Creel*, pp. 305–6; *Mexican Herald*, 5 May 1907, p. 6.

72. Sims, "Los Terrazas," pp. 391–94; Fernando Rosenzweig, et al, *El Porfiriato: La vida económica*, 2 pts., vol. 7 of the *Historia Moderna de México*, ed. Cosío Villegas, 1:802; *Mexican Financier*, 1 August 1885, p. 287; Dueñes, *Bancos*, pp. 81–82.

73. Almada, *Juárez y Terrazas*, pp. 343–58; *POC*, 18 October 1906, p. 13. As early as the first administration of Colonel Miguel Ahumada, governor from 1892 to 1902, the state borrowed from the family's banks. In 1896, loans of $15,000 and $25,000 to the Banco Minero and Banco Nacional, respectively, made up more than half the state's debt. Under the successive governorships of Luis Terrazas (1903–4) and Enrique C. Creel (1904–10), the state undertook a massive program of public works financed by heavy borrowing from Terrazas-controlled banks. In both 1908 and 1909 loans from family banks accounted for 50 percent of the state's public debt. The Banco Minero also lent heavily to local municipalities: Ciudad Chihuahua, for example, owed the bank 395,000 pesos in 1907. Chihuahua, Gobernador, *Memoria*, *1892–1896*, p. 55; Chihuahua, *Anuario*, *1908*, p. 167, *1909*, p. 205; Chihuahua (Ciudad), Ayuntamiento, *Informe*, *1907*, p. 5.

74. Federico Sisniega to Rodríguez Hermanos y Cía., 30 May 1902, part 2, reel 7; Sisniega to F. Pimentel y Fagoaga, 3 May 1902 and 3 June 1903, part 2, reel 7; Sisniega to S. de Sisniega, Durango, 4 May 1909, part 2, reel 11; Martín Falomir to Enrique C. Creel, 5 January 1911, part 2, reel 14, all in STP.

75. Federico Sisniega to Sra. María B. Vda. de Asúnsolo, 10 April 1901, part 2, reel 7, and Falomir to Creel, 24 October 1910, part 2, reel 14, STP; *POC*, 25 February 1909, pp. 18–19; *El Correo*, 9 November 1905, p. 1. *Mexican Financier*, 18 January 1896, p. 415.

76. Rosenzweig, *La vida económica*, 2:853–54.

77. Saragoza, "The Formation of a Mexican Elite."

78. Shepherd, *The Silver Magnet*, pp. 254, 140; *Mexican Financier*, 22 October 1892, p. 111, 8 December 1894, p. 277.

79. *Mexican Financier*, 18 January 1896, 415.

80. *El Correo*, 7 October 1909, p. 1, and 8 October 1909, pp. 1, 4.

81. Sandels, "Silvestre Terrazas," pp. 136–54, is the best account of the Banco Minero affair; Bush, *Gringo Doctor*, p. 165; *El Correo*, 19 October 1908, p. 1, and 1 January 1910, p. 1.

82. Fuentes Mares, *Luis Terrazas*, p. 168 (n. 11); Almada, *Juárez y Terrazas*, p. 346; Sims, "Los Terrazas," p. 395; *New York Times*, 19 February 1901, p. 10, and 26 February 1901, p. 1; *El Correo*, 3 September 1902, p. 1; Federico Sisniega to Enrique C. Creel, 2 July 1904, part 2, reel 8, STP; *Mexican Herald*, 29 July 1908, p. 1, 30 July 1908, p. 2, and 27 September 1908, p. 1; *POC*, 12 November 1905, p. 15, 5 February 1911, p. 23; Martín Falomir to Enrique C. Creel, 1 May 1911, part 2, reel 14, STP.

83. *El Correo*, 23 April 1902, p. 2.

84. Fuentes Mares, *Luis Terrazas*, p. 171; Almada, *Juárez y Terrazas*, p. 350; Federico Sisniega to the Administración Central del Banco Nacional de México, 19 August 1908, part 2, reel 10, STP; U.S., Department of Commerce and Labor, Bureau of Manufactures, *Monthly Consular and Trade Reports*, no. 305 (February 1906); Chihuahua, *Anuario*, *1909*, pp. 142–43, *1907*, pp. 54–57, *1906*, pp. 140–43.

85. *El Correo*, 10 January 1906, p. 1, 28 January 1902, p. 3; Vicente Requera to Silvestre Terrazas, 15 February 1904, STP; Report of R. M. Burke, U.S. Consul, Chihuahua City, October 1896, U.S., Department of Commerce and Labor, Bureau of Manufactures, *Monthly Consular and Trade Reports*, no. 193 (October 1896), pp. 264–65; *AERM*, *1899*, pp. 70–71, *1898*, pp. 52–53.

86. Fuentes Mares, *Luis Terrazas*, p. 171; *Chihuahua Enterprise*, 15 January 1883, p. 25; González Navarro, *Las huelgas*, pp. 238–40, 244–45; *POC*, 12 July 1890, p. 3; *AERM*, *1893*; Federico Sisniega to Juan Terrazas, 20 July 1902, part 2, reel 7, STP.

87. González Navarro, *Las huelgas*, pp. 240–43; *Revista de Chihuahua*, 18 May 1896, p. 130; *El Correo*, 25 April 1902, p. 1; *Mexican Herald*, 28 November 1895, p. 7; *AERM*, *1893*; Federico Sisniega to Seratín Legarreta, Presidente Municipal, 4 July 1904, part 2, reel 8, STP; Chihuahua, *Anuario*, *1907*, pp. 142–43. Federico Sisniega to Juan Terrazas, 20 July 1902, part 2, reel 7, STP.

88. Federico Sisniega to Antonio Teresa, 29 September 1903, and Sisniega to Teresa, 20 July 1904, part 2, reel 8, STP; *Mexican Herald*, 22 November 1909, p. 3; Chihuahua, *Anuario*, *1909*, pp. 135–55.

89. *EMJ* 72 (November 1901): 698; *Mexican Herald*, 21 May 1896, p. 8, 12 March 1896, p. 2, 31 October 1905, p. 7, 15 October 1906, p. 11, 25 August 1907, p. 11, and 30 August 1907, p. 11; *Mexican Financier*, 7 December 1895, p. 265, and 27 August 1891, p. 541; Chihuahua, *Anuario*, *1907*, pp. 54–55.

90. *El Correo*, 9 June 1908, p. 1, 21 May 1903, p. 1, 11 October 1904, p. 1, 13 February 1905, p. 1, 17 June 1905, p. 1, 7 May 1908, p. 1; *Mexican Herald*, 4 November 1906, p. 10, 7 May 1906, p. 11, 9 February 1906, p. 3.

91. *El Correo*, 1 September 1904, p. 4, 13 December 1904, p. 1, 24 August 1904, p. 4, 15 November 1904, p. 1, 5 August 1902, p. 3, 9 March 1904, p. 1, and 5 December 1909, p. 1; Federico Sisniega to M. Wagener, 31 October 1910, part 2, reel 7, STP; Chihuahua, *Anuario*, *1907*, pp. 85–87.

92. *Boletín Comercial*, 15 July 1908, pp. 246–47, 15 December 1909, p. 1; *Mexican Herald*, 6 November 1908, p. 5; *POC*, 17 November 1910, p. 30.

93. *Boletín Comercial*, 1 September 1908, advertisements; *El Correo*, 21 October 1903, p. 1, 10 February 1903, p. 3, and 4 November 1910, p. 1; Meyers, "Interest Group

Conflict," pp. 198–212, describes the serious dispute between the Terrazas and the Maderos over the operation of the Compañía Jabonera.

94. *AERM, 1900*, pp. 201–3; Minutes of the Stockholders Meeting, Compañía Ferrocarril Mineral de Chihuahua, 27 March 1899; Max Weber to Solon Humphries, 7 April 1897, copy book, roll 1, Weber Collection; Grant Schley to Henry M. Sage, 12 May 1903, and Schley to Simpson Thatcher, Executor, 11 May 1903, box 8, JMC; Rosenzweig, et al., *La vida económica*, 1:582–83, 586; Almada, *Juárez y Terrazas*, pp. 346–47; *Poor's Manual of Industrials, 1910*, pp. 1584–85, *1912*, p. 2118; *Mexican Yearbook, 1908*, p. 397; Pletcher, *Rails, Mines*, p. 270; *Bankers' Magazine* 79 (July–December 1909): 258–59; *El Correo*, 13 May 1902, p. 4.

95. Creel Cobián, *Enrique Creel*, p. 352; *El Correo*, 29 March 1910, p. 2.

96. In 1906, Luis Terrazas and others won a concession to build a dam on the Río San Pedro near Rosales in Camargo. The clan had another concession to construct a dam in Santa Rosalía on the Río Conchos. The latter they sold to a Canadian company. *POC*, 10 August 1884, p. 3; *El Correo*, 1 August 1903, p. 1, and 13 December 1907, p. 1; *Mexican Herald*, 10 December 1895, p. 1, 16 February 1906, p. 7, 30 March 1909; *BSCEH* 2, no. 2 (15 July 1939): 71, and 2, no. 6, p. 224; *EMJ* 87 (13 February 1909): 384; Federico Sisniega to Hugo Marquand, 29 July 1909, part 2, reel 11, STP; *SAJ*, 13 February 1909, p. 178, and 23 April 1908, p. 468.

97. *Revista de Chihuahua*, July 1896, p. 194; Lister and Lister, *Storehouse*, p. 181; Chihuahua, *Anuario, 1909*, p. 122; *Boletín Comercial*, 15 July 1908, p. 5; *El Correo*, 6 November 1906, p. 2, advertisements.

98. *El Siglo XX*, 8 June 1904, p. 3; *El Correo*, 6 November 1906, p. 1, 5 January 1907, p. 1, 1 January 1899, p. 4, 19 December 1906, p. 1, 4 November 1905, p. 1, 3 June 1910, p. 4, and 11 September 1910, p. 6.

99. *POC*, 9 February 1887, p. 1; *La Nueva Era*, 26 April 1900, p. 5, and 9 January 1908, p. 4; Federico Sisniega to Fernando Pimentel, 30 April 1903, part 2, reel 7, and Sisniega to Amilien Lacaud, 3 September 1904 and 29 July 1904, part 2, reel 8, all in STP; *Revista Internacional*, 12 March 1904, p. 3; *El Chihuahuense*, 24 November 1904; *El Correo*, 7 March 1904, p. 1, 9 August 1903, p. 1. The Terrazas themselves made major claims against the fire insurance company, for from 1902 to 1908 almost all of their food processing and manufacturing plants suffered tremendous fire damage. *El Correo*, 19 October 1908, p. 1; *El Siglo XX*, 3 May 1905, p. 1.

100. *EPT*, 22 January 1909, p. 5; *EPMT*, 31 October 1909, sect. 2, p. 1, 7 November 1909, p. 6, 11 December 1909, p. 3, and 19 December 1909, p. 3; *Mexican Herald*, 1 December 1909, p. 1; Martín Falomir to Lic. Guillermo Porras, Secretario de Gobierno, 7 November 1910, part 2, reel 14, STP; Almada, *Abraham González*, p. 185.

101. Enrique C. Creel to William Heimke, 14 September 1896, part 2, reel 17; Juan A. Creel to H. L. Hollins, President of the International Company, 4 and 9 May, and Hollins' reply, part 2, reel 17, all in STP. *El Correo*, 12 September 1905, p. 1. *Mexican Herald*, 15 June 1908, p. 11, and 15 September 1908, p. 8. Griggs, *Mines*, p. 336.

102. *El Correo*, 9 February 1905, p. 1 and 1 March 1906, p. 1, 25 January 1905, p. 1; *Mexican Herald*, 22 April 1907, p. 11 and 17 June 1907, p. 11.

103. Griggs, *Mines*, p. 337; *Mexican Investor*, 27 October 1910, pp. 12–13; C. M. Leonard to Assistant Secretary of State, 3 September 1908, NARG 59, numerical files, 11770/5; *EMJ* 86 (31 October 1908): 852; *Mexican Herald*, 19 April 1908, p. 5, 23 November 1908, p. 1; *El Correo*, 19 March 1903, p. 3, 14 February 1902, p. 4; Creel Cobián, *Enrique Creel*, p. 337; *EMJ* 78 (1 March 1902): 332; *MMJ* 6 (August 1908): 33.

104. Chihuahua, Gobernador, *Memoria, 1892–1896*, p. 337; *Mexican Financier*, 27 June

1896, p. 329; *Mexican Herald*, 22 June 1896, p. 7; *EMJ* 77 (3 March 1904): 371; Wasserman, "Foreign Investment," pp. 3–21.

105. *El Correo*, 1 July 1911, p. 1, and 25 September 1911, p. 1.

106. *El Correo*, 5 July 1911, p. 1, 7 July 1911, p. 1, and 16 July 1911, p. 3. Workers at the Terrazas textile factories also struck in July. At La Paz they objected to pay of 2 to 6.50 pesos per week. At La Concordia they demanded a ten-hour day, 25 percent salary increase, workmen's injury compensation, a guarantee of $1.25 a day under any circumstances, an increase in women's pay from 50 to 70 centavos, and a 10-centavo raise for children. At Río Florido they complained bitterly against the German manager who fired some of their fellow workers without just cause.

107. *AERM*, *1893*; Chihuahua, *Anuario*, *1907*, pp. 56–57.

108. Anderson, *Outcasts*, pp. 94–95, 341.

109. *EMJ* 72 (30 November 1901): 692.

110. *Chihuahua Enterprise*, 15 January 1883, p. 25; *El Correo*, 1 December 1903, p. 1, 14 January 1902, p. 1; Federico Sisniega to Serafín Legarreta, 14 July 1904, part 2, reel 8, STP.

111. *El Correo*, 25 April 1902, p. 1.

112. Wells, "Henequén and Yucatán," pp. 100–122.

113. Saragoza, "The Formation of an Elite," pp. 267–69.

114. Voss, "Porfirian Sonora," pp. 48–53.

115. Meyers, "Interest Group Conflict," pp. 294–309; Cumberland, *Mexican Revolution*, p. 30.

116. Knight, "Nationalism," p. 73; Ceceña, *Órbita*, pp. 81–84.

117. Mathew, "Imperialism of Free Trade," pp. 568–74; Cortes Conde, *First Stages*, pp. 10–28.

118. Mamalakis and Reynolds, *Chilean Economy*; Smith, *Politics and Beef*, pp. 57–81.

119. Smith, *Politics and Beef*, pp. 32–47. The Argentine cattle-raising sector was divided into breeders and fatteners.

120. Furtado, *The Economic Growth of Brazil*, pp. 193–213.

CHAPTER 4

1. Rock, *Politics in Argentina*; Cardoso and Faletto, *Dependency and Development*, pp. 82–112.

2. Rosenzweig, "Las exportaciones mexicanas," pp. 537–51; Coatsworth, "Obstacles to Economic Growth," p. 100.

3. Cardoso and Faletto, *Dependency and Development*, p. 77. The expanding export sector produced rapid economic growth, which in turn produced "dysfunction." See Olson, "Rapid Economic Growth as a De-stabilizing Force," pp. 529–52; Davis, "Toward a Theory of Revolution," pp. 5–18. Davis argues that rapid growth followed by a sharp downturn creates a revolutionary potential (the "j" curve). The depression of 1907 was the downturn in Chihuahua.

4. *CR*, *1902*, pp. 500–503. See also the reports from the consuls of the U.S. during early 1911 in the U.S. State Department, NARG 59, decimal files, 1910–29. For example, Alexander V. Nye, U.S. Consul, Nogales, to Department of State, 18 March 1911, NARG 59, decimal files, 812.00/1006.

5. Ibid., Hanna, U.S. Consul, Monterrey, 19 March 1911, NARG 59, decimal files, 812.995/995; Freeman, U.S. Consul, Durango, 19 March 1911, 812.00/992.

6. Womack, *Zapata*, pp. 42–48; Waterbury, "Non-Revolutionary Peasants," pp. 410–42; Salamini, *Agrarian Radicalism*, pp. 4–14; DeHart, "Pacification of the Yaquis," pp. 72–93; Estrada, "Liderazgo."

7. Katz, "Peasants in the Mexican Revolution"; Knight, "Peasant and Caudillo"; Katz, *The Secret War*, pp. 12–15; see also Wolf, *Peasant Wars*.

8. Furtado, *Economic Development of Latin America*, pp. 29–32; Lewis, *America's Stake*; Walter LaFeber, *The New Empire* (Ithaca: Cornell University Press, 1963).

9. Spence, *Mining Engineers*, p. 288.

10. *CR, 1902*, 1:500–503; *Mexican Herald*, 10 August 1907, p. 5. The $50 million estimate was for the consular district of Chihuahua City, which included only the southern half of the state.

11. Moorhead, *Royal Road*; A. B. Clarke, *Travels in Mexico and California* (Boston: 1852), p. 51, cited in Dumke, "Across Mexico in '49," p. 38.

12. W. W. Mills, U.S. Consul, Chihuahua City, to David J. Hill, Assistant Secretary of State, 10 August 1899, NARG 59.

13. Santleben, *Texas Pioneer*, p. 299; Charles Moye, U.S. Consul, Chihuahua City, to Secretary of State, 20 September 1870, NARG 59. Carlos (Charles) Moye began the Chihuahua Woolen works and Cassimere Manufactory, a textile business, in 1860. Initially, Moye had at least two partners, Antonio Asúnsolo and José María S. Terrazas. Later Luis Terrazas, Enrique Müller, Carlos Zuloaga, Emilio Ketelsen, and Canuto Elías entered the business. *Chihuahua Enterprise*, 15 January 1883, p. 25.

14. Voss, "Porfirian Sonora," pp. 4–5.

15. *Revista de Chihuahua*, March 1896, p. 62.

16. J. C. Huston, U.S. Consul, Chihuahua City, 4 October 1873, NARG 59.

17. Business was so bad that the United States consulate in Ciudad Chihuahua was closed from 1874 to 1877. *El Monitor Constitucional,* 21 March 1877, cited in Ryan, "Selected Aspects," pp. 49, 52; Pierson, U.S. Consul, Chihuahua City, to Department of State, 21 July 1874, NARG 59; Pletcher, "México, campo de inversiones," pp. 564–65.

18. The favorable climate continued until 1907. A. R. Townsend, "Some Suggestions for Travel in Northern Mexico," *EMJ* 77 (25 February 1904): 315–17; James W. Malcolmson, "Mining in Mexico," *EMJ* 77 (7 January 1904): 21–22.

19. *EMJ* 31 (7 May 1881): 320; Frederick A. Ober, *Mexican Resources*, p. 37.

20. *Revista de Chihuahua*, March 1896, p. 62; *Chihuahua Enterprise*, 15 April 1883, p. 65, and 15 December 1882, p. 16; George Wilson, "Mexico as a Field for Miners," *EMJ* 34 (29 July 1882): 55; *EMJ* 36 (8 September 1883): 155; *EMJ* 36 (29 December 1883): 401; *Mexican Financier*, 29 December 1883, p. 199, and 12 September 1885, p. 375.

21. *Mexican Financier*, 14 December 1889, p. 272, 14 November 1885, p. 108, and 5 December 1888, p. 157; *Stock Exchange Intelligence, 1901*, pp. 1282, 1295; Chihuahua, Gobernador, *Mensaje del Gobernador, 1888*; *The Two Republics*, 16 October 1886, cited in Ryan, "Selected Aspects," p. 354; U.S., Department of State, Bureau of Foreign Commerce, *Reports of the Consular Officers of the United States: Emigration and Immigration*, p. 642.

22. *Chihuahua Enterprise*, 15 January 1884, p. 7; *Mexican Financier*, 14 December 1889, p. 272, and 5 December 1888, p. 157; Robert R. Stormer, "British Investment in Mexico" (M.A. thesis, University of Chicago, 1949), p. 22; Chihuahua, Gobernador, *Mensaje del Gobernador, 1888*.

23. *Mexican Financier*, 7 March 1885, pp. 356–57, 11 July 1885, p. 227, and 17 October 1885, p. 37; U.S., Department of State, *Report from the Consuls*, no. 89 (December 1887).

24. *Mexican Herald*, 6 November 1910, p. 2; *Mexican Financier*, 5 January 1890, p. 421,

14 June 1890, p. 311, 7 March 1885, pp. 356–57, 17 October 1885, p. 37, 9 February 1889, p. 464, and 20 April 1889, pp. 82–83; Bett, *Central Banking in Mexico*, p. 6.

25. "The Mining Industry in Mexico, 1894," *EMJ* 53 (9 January 1892): 87; *Mexican Financier*, 4 November 1893, p. 167; *Bankers' Magazine* 66 (January–June 1906): 16. In spite of adverse economic conditions, several foreign mining entrepreneurs were well established by 1892: the MacDonald Brothers, Roland Anderson, Walter M. Brodie, A. Bronnimann, William Dailey, Britton Davis (the manager of Corralitos), William Dale, and A. P. Bronn. See *POC*, 1890–92. *EMJ* 56 (1 July 1893): 16, and 60 (12 October 1895): 356.

26. Pletcher, "American Capital and Technology," p. 159; O'Connor, *Guggenheims*, p. 88.

27. S. E. Gill, "Mineral District of Hidalgo de Parral," *EMJ* 63 (22 May 1897): 509.

28. *Mexican Financier*, 27 May 1893, p. 229, 27 April 1895, p. 133; U.S., Department of State, *Report from the Consuls*, no. 152, p. 93; Dusenberry, "Agricultural Society," p. 394; Charles W. Kindrick, U.S. Consul, Paso del Norte, to Day, 12 January 1898, NARG 59; Matías Romero, *Geographical and Statistical Notes on Mexico*, p. 56.

29. *El Correo*, 19 May 1903, p. 2; Robert T. Hill, "The Santa Eulalia District, Mexico," *EMJ* 76 (1 August 1903): 158–60; J. W. Malcolmson, "Mexico," *EMJ* 79 (5 January 1905): 33–36.

30. *Mexican Investor*, 9 January 1904, p. 3, and 17 September 1904, pp. 6–8.

31. *Mexican Herald*, 5 May 1907, p. 4, 21 October 1907, p. 5, 10 February 1908, p. 4, 11 May 1908, p. 11, 17 February 1906, p. 4, and 8 February 1907, p. 4; Pletcher, "American Capital and Technology," p. 121; *El Correo*, 9 February 1904, p. 2; Kindrick to Day, 25 January 1898, NARG 59; Lister and Lister, *Storehouse*, p. 176; G. A. Burr and Louis S. Cates, "Minas Nuevas, Parral, Mexico," *EMJ* 75 (14 March 1903): 404–5, and continuation (21 March 1903): 440.

32. *EMJ* 75 (7 February 1903): 216, and (21 February 1903): 308; *EMJ* 72 (12 October 1901): 456.

33. *Bankers' Magazine* 79 (July–December 1909): 256; U.S., Department of Commerce and Labor, *Monthly Consular and Trade Report*, no. 312 (September 1906), p. 91; Pletcher, "American Capital and Technology," p. 162.

34. U.S., Department of Commerce and Labor, *Monthly Consular and Trade Report*, no. 203 (November 1905), p. 47; *El Correo*, 27 November 1906, p. 1, and 4 January 1907, p. 1; *Mexican Herald*, 10 July 1907, p. 5; *Mexican Investor*, 12 January 1907, p. 8.

35. *EMJ* 76 (5 September 1903): 366; 80 (21 October 1905): 756; and 81 (10 February 1906): 299. O'Connor, *Guggenheims*, p. 329. *Nueva Era*, 19 November 1905, pp. 1–2. Report of the San Francisco del Oro Company, 15 November 1903, box 2, file folder 60A; James A. Hyslop to Ernesto Madero, President, Compañía Metalúrgica de Torreón, 15 April 1904 and Hyslop to Crawford Cook, British Mexican Mines, 6 October 1904, box 3, both in James E. Hyslop Collection.

36. Parral was the hardest hit. By the fall of 1904, only three companies were shipping ore there. Hundreds were unemployed. *Mexican Herald*, 10 December 1905, p. 1, 16 June 1907, p. 6, 5 November 1907, p. 11; *El Correo*, 14 June 1905, p. 1, 1 June 1907, p. 1, and 14 September 1907, p. 1; *SAJ*, 1 June 1907, p. 616; American Smelting and Refining Company, *Annual Report, 1907*, p. 8; Bernstein, *Mexican Mining*, p. 33.

37. *Mexican Herald*, 16 June 1907, p. 6, 23 September 1907, p. 11, and 14 June 1908, p. 11; *El Correo*, 15 October 1907, p. 1; A. Van Zwaluwenberg, "Mexico," *EMJ* 85 (4 January 1908): 68–69.

38. *Mexican Herald*, 7 November 1907, p. 10, 18 December 1907, p. 11, 13 December 1907, p. 11, and 18 March 1908, p. 11; *EMJ* 84 (28 December 1907): 1237.

39. *El Correo*, 28 October 1907, p. 1, and 15 October 1907, p. 1; *Mexican Herald*, 4 November 1907, p. 2; Sandels, "Silvestre Terrazas," p. 163; Hyslop to San Francisco del Oro

Company, 20 May 1907 (?), box 2, file folder 60B, Hyslop Collection.

40. *MMJ* 6 (June 1908): 30; *Mexican Herald*, 6 February 1908, p. 11; Franklin Wheaton Smith, "Present Condition of Mining in Mexico," *EMJ* 86 (3 October 1908): 655–56; *EMJ* 89 (8 January 1910): 117.

41. *Mexican Herald*, 17 October 1908, p. 1, 5 September 1907, p. 4, and 10 September 1907, p. 4; *El Correo*, 2 June 1906, p. 1, 27 July 1906, p. 1, 7 August 1906, p. 1, 23 April 1908, p. 1, and 25 April 1908, p. 1; Ryan, "Selected Aspects," pp. 332–33.

42. *EMJ* 88 (3 July 1909): 36, and (17 July 1909): 142. *EMJ* 90 (6 August 1910): 265. A. P. Rogers, "Recent Mining Developments in Chihuahua," *EMJ* 88 (2 October 1909): 681–82. W. H. Seamon, "Mining Operations in the State of Chihuahua," *EMJ* 90 (1 October 1910): 654–56. *MMJ* 7 (October 1909): 39; 8 (January 1910): 17; and 8 (October 1910): 33. *SAJ*, 23 July 1910, p. 89. "Mining in Chihuahua," *EMJ* 91 (7 January 1911): 71–72.

43. Rogers, "Recent Mining," p. 681.

44. Thomas Kirby, "Mining in Mexico in 1910," *EMJ* 91 (7 January 1911): 65; *EMJ* 90 (1 October 1910): 679; U.S., Department of Commerce and Labor, *Monthly Consular and Trade Report*, no. 355 (10 April 1910), p. 156, and no. 351 (December 1909), pp. 208–9.

45. Voss, "Porfirian Sonora," pp. 54–55.

46. *CR, 1902*, pp. 500–503.

47. Compiled from Griggs, *Mines*, pp. 324–49.

48. Chihuahua, *Anuarios, 1905–1909*; Griggs, *Mines*; Southworth, *Directory*.

49. Voss, "Porfirian Sonora," p. 19.

50. *Mexican Herald*, 2 January 1907, p. 10, 7 February 1907, p. 11, 19 June 1907, p. 11, 29 August 1909, p. 3; *SAJ*, 25 September 1909, p. 344; deed attached to letter of Max Weber to W. J. Cox, 25 July 1902, copy book, roll 3, Weber Collection; *EPMT*, 1 April 1914, p. 4.

51. *El Correo*, 16 June 1903, p. 2, and 3 August 1908, p. 1; *Mexican Herald*, 4 September 1906, p. 10, 5 July 1907, p. 11, 16 July 1907, p. 10, 18 September 1908, p. 11, and 9 March 1909; *SAJ*, 9 October 1909, p. 399, 23 July 1910, p. 89, 23 April 1910, p. 456, 20 November 1909, p. 575, and 9 October 1909, p. 401; Leon J. Keena, U.S. Consul, Chihuahua, to Secretary of State, 2 December 1909, numerical files, case 14164/8, NARG 59.

52. Rosenzweig, *La vida económica*, 2:1107–8.

53. AGNRP, 818-C-49.

54. DeHart, "Pacification of the Yaquis," pp. 76–77.

55. Meyers, "Politics and Vested Rights," p. 60.

56. *CR, 1902*, p. 503. Huston, U.S. Consul, Chihuahua, to Uhl, 10 January 1894, NARG 59.

57. Ponce de León, *Directorio*, pp. 64–65; Huston to Uhl, 10 January 1894, NARG 59; *Revista de Chihuahua*, March 1896, p. 62; M. Weber to J. A. Walker, 25 August 1898, copy book, roll 1, Weber Collection; confidential statement on Ketelsen and Degeteau, roll 10, Weber Collection; Weber to Max Nauman, 16 August 1902, copy book, roll 3, Weber Collection; *El Correo*, 24 February 1904, p. 4; testimony of William N. Fink, U.S., Congress, Senate, *Revolutions in Mexico, 1913*, p. 693. Foreign merchants often had extensive social and business relations with Chihuahuan society. They lived in the state and married into the local elite. Martín Falomir to Krakauer, Zork, Moye, 5 January 1911, part 2, reel 14, STP; *EMJ* 92 (25 November 1911): 1060; *El Correo*, 22 October 1904, p. 1, 10 June 1904, p. 1, and 20 November 1908, p. 1.

58. Voss, "Porfirian Sonora."

CHAPTER 5

1. Cosío Villegas, *El Porfiriato: La vida política*, 1:255–798 and 2:393–626; Coerver, *The Porfirian Interregnum*, pp. 60–123.

2. Voss, "Porfirian Sonora"; DeHart, "Pacification of the Yaquis," pp. 73–81; Haden, "The Federalist."

3. Lister and Lister, *Storehouse*, p. 118.

4. Bartlett, *Personal Narratives*, 2:346, 425–26.

5. Diffendriffer, U.S. Consul, Paso del Norte, to Marcy, 7 October 1856, NARG 59.

6. *Boletín Militar*, 1 July 1876, p. 3. Frederick S. Dunn, *The Diplomatic Protection of Americans in Mexico*, vol. 2 of *Mexico in International Finance and Diplomacy*, pp. 138, 144. John W. Foster, U.S. Minister to Mexico, to Secretary of State Evarts, 6 October 1877, *FR 1878*, p. 528. Solomon Schutz, Commercial Agent at El Paso, to Department of State, 5 May 1877, NARG 59; Foster, *Memoirs*, p. 142. Reuben Creel, U.S. Consul, Chihuahua City, to Secretary of State, 14 July 1865; J. R. Robinson to William H. Brown, 31 January 1872; and L. H. Scott to Secretary of State, 23 July 1877, 9 July 1877, and 7 November 1879, all in NARG 59.

7. Lloyd C. Baker to Secretary of State, 7 May 1871, NARG 59.

8. Lyon, U.S. Consul, Paso del Norte, to Secretary of State, 5 October 1871, NARG 59. F. MacManus and F. MacManus to John W. Foster, 5 March 1877, NARG 59. Foster, *Memoirs*, pp. 119, 142.

9. Eugene O. Fetchet, U.S. Consul, Paso del Norte, to Second Assistant Secretary of State William Hunter, 13 May 1884, NARG 59.

10. *Mexican Herald*, 11 January 1896, p. 7. The other American Díaz trusted was railroad tycoon Collis Huntington. Shepherd, *Silver Magnet*, pp. 213–17; Ryan, "Selected Aspects," p. 296; Southworth, *Directory*, p. 68; *POC*, 5 July 1890, p. 2; J. M. Wilkinson to J. R. Robinson, 3 August 1887, vol. 3, George F. Crane Collection.

11. Hoyt, *Guggenheims*, pp. 80–81; O'Connor, *Guggenheims*, pp. 92, 116; Hammond, *Autobiography*, pp. 506, 508.

12. *EMJ* 80 (22 July 1905): 131, and (7 October 1905): 658. ASARCO reportedly offered $4.5 million for the smelter, but the Maderos wanted $5 million. *Mexican Herald*, 11 February 1906, p. 7, 2 March 1908, p. 11, 12 February 1908, p. 11, 11 December 1908, p. 10, 15 August 1907, p. 11; *El Correo*, 16 June 1905, p. 1. The Maderos had a large stake in Chihuahuan mining. Ranking among the state's top ten producers, they owned one of its most important mines, the San Diego. *EMJ* 78 (8 September 1904): 403. Creel had owned a concession for a smelter in Ciudad Chihuahua as early as 1896. Chihuahua, Gobernador, *Memoria, 1892–1896*, p. 337; Hoyt, *Guggenheims*, p. 159; *Mexican Financier*, 27 June 1896, p. 329; *Mexican Investor*, 1 July 1905, p. 16, and 18 November 1905, p. 3; *EMJ* 80 (11 November 1905): 900; Lister and Lister, *Storehouse*, p. 181; Almada, *La revolución*, 1:73. The land was the Haciendas de Tabalaopa and Avalos.

13. Pletcher, "American Capital and Technology," p. 172; *El Correo*, 25 January 1905, p. 1, 1 March 1906, p. 1, and 9 February 1905, p. 1; *Mexican Herald*, 16 July 1907, p. 11, 7 March 1906, p. 5, and 11 March 1907, p. 11.

14. Swanberg, *Citizen Hearst*, p. 207; Winkler, *Hearst*, p. 34; Older, *Hearst*, p. 65; Almada, *La revolución*, 1:79. Follansbee planned to build a racetrack in Ciudad Juárez. *Mexican Herald*, 12 March 1908, p. 10, and 26 March 1908, p. 5.

15. W. W. Mills, U.S. Consul, Chihuahua City, to Robert Bacon, Assistant Secretary of State, 1 January 1906; Mills to Francis B. Loomis, Assistant Secretary of State, 7 April 1905; James I. Long to W. W. Mills, 15 April 1905, all in NARG 59.

16. *POC*, 10 May 1884, p. 4, 7 June 1884, p. 4, 27 February 1886, p. 3, 12 April 1890, pp. 3–4; *Mexican Herald*, 21 January 1896, p. 7; *El Correo*, 28 November 1909, p. 3.

17. E. M. Wilkinson to J. R. Robinson, 16 August 1887, vol. 3, Crane Collection; Report on Santa Eulalia, 1917, p. 21, box 3, Hyslop Collection.

18. *Mexican Financier*, 1 August 1885, p. 285, and 24 October 1891; *EPDT*, 25 September 1891, p. 7; *POC*, 1 June 1889, p. 3, and 18 September 1886, p. 4; Smith, *Horace Tabor*, pp. 291–96.

19. *Mexican Herald*, 23 August 1907, p. 11, 30 October 1907, p. 4, 10 December 1907, p. 11, and 23 February 1908, p. 15; *El Correo*, 5 March 1907, p. 1; *EMJ* 84 (21 December 1907): 1191, and 85 (7 March 1908): 526; Luther T. Ellsworth, U.S. Consul, Chihuahua City, to Assistant Secretary of State, 20 July 1907, numerical files, 7808, NARG 59.

20. *Mexican Investor*, 23 January 1904; *EMJ* 77 (7 January 1904): 21.

21. Bernstein, *Mexican Mining*, pp. 78–83; *Mexican Herald*, 9 August 1908, p. 2, 2 August 1908, p. 2, 12 August 1908, p. 2, and 15 October 1908, p. 1.

22. Lewis A. Martin, U.S. Consul, Chihuahua City, to Secretary of State, 5 February 1909, numerical files, 14059/3–5, NARG 59.

23. *EMJ* 79 (18 May 1905): 952.

24. Lewis Morgan and Hubert Blackart to Enrique C. Creel, 2 December 1896, and Creel to Gran Fundición Central Mexicana, Aguascalientes, 7 July 1897, part 2, reel 17, STP; *EMJ* 72 (30 November 1901): 698; 84 (5 October 1907): 656; and 86 (8 August 1908): 278.

25. *Mexican Herald*, 14 October 1905, p. 3, and 14 April 1908, p. 1. *MMJ* 6 (January 1908): 25. *EMJ* 81 (26 May 1906): 1020; 85 (4 April 1908): 692; 86 (21 November 1908): 1031; 89 (30 April 1910): 939; 92 (9 December 1911): 1153. *Mexican Investor*, 15 December 1906, p. 11. *El Correo*, 20 November 1902, p. 2. *Mexican Herald*, 28 October 1896, p. 2.

26. Almada, *Juárez y Terrazas*, p. 662; undated document discussing the Callahan interests, part 2, reel 7, STP; *El Correo*, 12 November 1904, p. 1, 18 January 1905, p. 1, 14 August 1905, p. 1, and 3 December 1904, p. 1; Federico Sisniega to José Varea, 14 May 1910, part 2, reel 11, STP.

27. Grant Schley to C. L. Graves, General Manager, 27 August 1903, and Secretary of the Company to Lic. Ricardo del Río, 30 November 1903, Mexico Northwestern Railway Papers, box 8, JMC.

28. Report of W. W. Mills, U.S. Consul, Chihuahua City, 24 October 1900 in *CR, 1900*, p. 656; report of C. W. Kindrick, U.S. Consul, Ciudad Juárez, 5 November 1900, in *CR, 1900*, pp. 362–63.

29. Lister and Lister, *Storehouse*, p. 182; *Mexican Herald*, 28 November 1895, p. 7, 21 May 1896, p. 8, 10 February 1908, p. 2, and 19 April 1908, p. 5; *El Correo*, 19 September 1906, p. 1; Griggs, *Mines*, pp. 336, 340; *Mexican Financier*, 22 August 1891, p. 541.

30. Walter M. Brodie to Enrique C. Creel, 5 November 1910; E. N. Schwabe, Cashier of Guaranty Trust, to W. E. D. Stokes, 28 December 1910; Schwabe to Juan A. Creel, 29 December 1910; two undated documents among the above correspondence concerning the affairs of the bank, all in part 2, reel 2, STP. Max Weber to Enrique C. Creel, 23 October 1913, roll 8, Weber Collection. Minutes of a Meeting of the Stockholders of the Guaranty Trust and Banking Company, 7 March 1911, roll 7, Weber Collection. Enclosure to letter of Martín Falomir to Enrique Creel, 12 December 1910, part 2, reel 14, STP.

31. *El Correo*, 24 October 1903, p. 1, 25 August 1903, p. 1, 20 January 1903, p. 1, 31 July 1902, p. 3, 5 February 1903, p. 2; *Chihuahua Mail*, 3 December 1883, p. 4; Southworth, *Directory*, p. 68.

32. Voss, "Porfirian Sonora," pp. 19–20.

33. Cockcroft, *Precursors*, p. 17.

34. Katz, *The Secret War*, p. 60.

35. Saragoza, "Elite Formation," p. 9.

36. Meyers, "Interest Group Conflict," pp. 430–52.

37. Saragoza, "Elite Formation," pp. 10–12, and "The Formation of an Elite," pp. 121–32; Meyers, "Interest Group Conflict."

38. Knight, "Nationalism," p. 73; Ceceña, *La órbita*, p. 82; *El Correo*, 16 March 1904, p. 3.

39. *El Correo*, 10 March 1904, p. 2; Dueñes, *Los bancos*, pp. 119, 122, 124.

40. *Bankers' Magazine* 77 (October 1908): 537–41.

41. *El Correo*, 28 December 1907, p. 1; *Mexican Herald*, 28 June 1910, p. 6.

42. *EMJ* 76 (17 December 1903): 918; 81 (3 March 1906): 429–30; 73 (22 March 1902): 428, and (12 April 1902): 528; 78 (14 November 1904): 950.

CHAPTER 6

1. Chihuahua, *Anuario*, *1905*, p. 38, and *1906*, p. 139.

2. Chihuahua, *Anuario*, *1906*, pp. 144–60. There were 820 small industrial and artisan shops in Chihuahua in 1906. The *Anuario* furnishes the founding dates for 710. The percentages in the text are calculated from the 710.

3. Chihuahua, *Anuario*, *1905*, p. 75; *1906*, p. 216; *1907*, p. 129; *1908*, p. 171; and *1909*, p. 210. There are numerous problems with the data on *ranchos*. First, *rancho* is never defined in the *Anuarios* and, as a result, this category may not accurately indicate the number of small landholders or *rancheros*. *Hacendados* owned *ranchos*. (The Terrazas owned the Rancho de Avalos.) In addition, there are some significant discrepancies in the data. The most glaring is for the Mina district in 1905. The *Anuario* states that there were 330 ranches in the district in 1905, but in succeeding years only 93, 93, 36, and 35. If we eliminate 250 to 300 of the 1905 total from the total for the state, there is a steady growth of the number of *ranchos* from 1905 to 1908.

   The question of how to categorize small landowners is still open to debate. Should they be considered peasants or middle class? As we will see in chapter 7, class was a complicated matter, indeed. Some observers have labeled these small holders peasant-bourgeoisie. Others call them peasant-workers (or peasant proletariat). The key point is that many small landowners also engaged in other occupations. In the circumstances of early twentieth-century Chihuahua their very status "in between" made them a very volatile group.

4. *EMJ* 90 (1 October 1910): 177.

5. Mexico, Secretaría de Economía, *Estadísticas sociales del Porfiriato*, pp. 16–19.

6. SHMM, *Estadísticas económicas*, p. 54.

7. Mexico, Secretaría de Economía, *Estadísticas sociales*, pp. 43, 45, 48, 50, 122–23.

8. Ibid., p. 34.

9. *CR, 1871*, p. 897. *CR*, 1897–1908, provides ample evidence of the widespread commercial activities of foreigners in Chihuahua.

10. *Mexican Financier*, 19 May 1888, p. 172; Hamilton, *Border States*, pp. 136–37.

11. U.S., Department of Commerce and Labor, Bureau of Manufactures, *Monthly Consular and Trade Reports*, no. 303 (December 1905), p. 165.

12. U.S., Department of Commerce, *Daily Consular and Trade Reports*, 23 January 1911, p. 278.

13. Louis M. Buford, "Mormon Colonists in Mexico," in U.S., Department of Commerce and Labor, Bureau of Manufactures, *Monthly Consular and Trade Reports*, no. 190 (July 1896), p. 409; *Mexican Herald*, 7 August 1896, p. 2, and 5 September 1907, p. 4; Hardy,

"Cultural Encystment," pp. 445–48; Johnson, *Colonia Díaz*, p. 126. Later, Chinese originally imported to work on the railroads competed strongly as small vegetable farmers.

14. *EMJ* 72 (12 October 1901): 456.

15. *El Correo*, 28 December 1907, p. 1.

16. Chihuahua, Gobernador, *Informe, 1 de junio de 1908*, p. 4.

17 *Mexican Herald*, 13 December 1907, p. 11; *EPDT*, 13 May 1892, p. 2; report on Chihuahua by James Malcolmson, box 2, p. 8, Hyslop Collection; *EPMT*, 30 August 1909, p. 1.

18. Lavis, "Chihuahua and Pacific," pp. 242–43; Pletcher, "American Capital and Technology," p. 114; Caraveo, "Memorias," p. 2. My thanks to Richard Estrada for uncovering this manuscript and providing me a copy. Affidavit of Niels Larsen, U.S., Senate, *Revolutions in Mexico*, pp. 330–31.

19. *Mexican Herald*, 6 July 1907, p. 4, 27 February 1908, p. 4, 9 February 1905, p. 7, 18 December 1907, p. 5, 18 November 1908, p. 5, and 5 November 1909, p. 4; *EPMT*, 2 December 1909, sect. 2, p. 1, and 8 December 1909, p. 8; Chihuahua, Gobernador, *Informe, 1 de junio de 1908*, p. 21; report of Ignacio Irigoyen, 17 October 1906, roll 607, Archivo del Ayuntamiento de Ciudad Chihuahua.

20. *MMJ* 8 (August 1909): 12; Manahan, "Mining and Milling," p. 24; *El Correo*, 11 December 1909, p. 4.

21. Testimony of Bagge, U.S., Senate, Committee on Foreign Relations, *Investigation of Mexican Affairs*, p. 1429; Christiansen, "Pascual Orozco," p. 97.

22. Beezley, *Abraham González*, pp. 13–31; Almada, *Abraham González*, pp. 15–31.

23. Meyer, *Pascual Orozco*, pp. 15–18.

24. *POC*, 7 June 1906, p. 30; *El Correo*, 14 July 1909, p. 1; *La Nueva Era*, 10 May 1900, p. 2; *El Padre Padilla*, 27 May 1911, p. 2; Almada, *Diccionario*, p. 215.

25. *POC*, 23 November 1905, p. 13; Almada, *Diccionario*, p. 249.

26. *La Nueva Era*, 18 July 1909, p. 4, 11 January 1906, p. 3, 10 December 1908, p. 4; *El Correo*, 18 August 1903, p. 2.

27. Beezley, "State Reform," pp. 524–38. It is indicative of the attitude of these men toward private property and of their own ambitions that at least seven members of Anti-reelectionist clubs claimed municipal lands under the provisions of the law of 1905: Ildefonso Manjarrez, Aniceto Flores, Francisco Jiménez, Tomás Gameros, Juan Ortega, and José Velarde. Chihuahua, *Anuario, 1908*, pp. 47–103, *1909*, pp. 79–90.

28. *CR, 1909*, p. 521.

29. *El Correo*, 18 September 1909, p. 1, and 23 January 1910, p. 5; *POC*, 25 July 1909, p. 22; Chihuahua, *Anuario, 1909*, pp. 135–55. The figures for 1909 do not include Rayón and Guerrero districts. Consequently, I have excluded their figures for 1905 and 1906 from the comparative calculations.

30. *El Correo*, 27 June 1911, p. 1; *La Nueva Era*, 17 January 1911, p. 4, and 18 July 1909, p. 4.

31. *Revista Chihuahuense*, 15 January 1911, p. 18; Chihuahua, *Anuario, 1906*, p. 94, and *1909*, pp. 93–94, 97.

32. *El Correo*, 16 May 1909, p. 1, 6 April 1909, p. 1, and 28 October 1910, p. 1; Chihuahua, *Anuario, 1906*, p. 148.

33. *El Defensor del Pueblo*, 27 September 1911; Beezley, *Abraham González*, p. 95.

34. Chihuahua, *Anuario, 1906*, p. 146.

35. *La Nueva Era*, 2 February 1908, p. 1; *El Correo*, 30 January 1908, p. 1, 11 February 1910, p. 1, 17 June 1907, p. 1, and 13 August 1910, p. 1.

36. *La Nueva Era*, 5 December 1909, p. 1; *El Correo*, 6 August 1906, p. 4, 21 September 1910, p. 1, 16 May 1909, p. 1, 26 August 1909, p. 4, 10 May 1909, p. 1, 1 January 1899, p. 1, 4 January 1904, p. 2, and 9 June 1910, p. 4.

37. *El Padre Padilla*, 27 May 1911, p. 2; Ponce de León and Alcocer, *Directorio*, pp. 68, 30; Chihuahua, *Anuario*, *1905*, p. 41; *POC*, 27 January 1907, pp. 12–13; Chihuahua, *Anuario*, *1909*, p. 124; *El Correo*, 16 July 1909, p. 1.

38. Chihuahua, *Anuario*, *1907*, pp. 145, 148, 165–73, *1908*, p. 56; *POC*, 25 April 1907, p. 18, 20 June 1909, p. 31, 6 October 1910, p. 20, 24 June 1906, p. 17, and 11 July 1906, p. 11; *MMJ* 16 (January 1913): 42.

39. *CR*, *1907*, p. 104, *1909*, p. 523.

40. Gottschalk to Assistant Secretary of State, 6 August 1907, numerical files, case no. 8057, NARG 59.

41. *El Correo*, 30 September 1909, p. 4, 7 October 1909, p. 1, and 8 October 1909, p. 1.

42. Sandels, "Silvestre Terrazas," pp. 134–36 and throughout.

43. SHMM, *Estadísticas económicas*, p. 54.

44. Mexico, Secretaría de Economía, *Estadísticas sociales*, pp. 18–19.

45. See, for example, the revolutionaries discussed by Ruiz, *The Great Rebellion*, pp. 216–38; Knight, "Nationalism," pp. 113–17.

46. Jacobs, "Rancheros," pp. 76–88. Knight, "Peasant and Caudillo," pp. 28–33.

47. Knight, "Nationalism," pp. 113–14; Ruiz, *The Great Rebellion*, pp. 216–38; Katz, "Pancho Villa," pp. 27–28.

C H A P T E R   7

1. Smith, "Fantasy," pp. 43–45. In Chihuahua, as in other parts of Mexico, the villages held their own until the 1870s and sometimes were actually able to reclaim land stolen from them. Coatsworth, "Railroads and Land," pp. 51–55. In 1866 the Indians of Tomochi and Arizeachic in western Chihuahua were so bold as to seek to acquire *terrenos baldíos*. *El Boletín*, 8 December 1866, p. 1.

2. *Semanario Oficial*, 27 March 1874, p. 1; *POC*, 14 January 1882 and 17 February 1883, p. 1; *Mexican Financier*, 10 January 1891, pp. 365–66.

3. *Mexican Financier*, 28 September 1889, p. 7.

4. Whetten, *Rural Mexico*, pp. 98–99; Wistano Luis Orozco, *Legislación y jurisprudencia sobre terrenos baldíos* (México: 1895), 2:800–801.

5. Whetten, *Rural Mexico*, pp. 97, 86–89. Another series of laws passed beginning in 1888, regarding water rights, further undermined the position of small landholders and landholding villages. The federal government gradually got control over most rivers and streams by extending the definition of what was navigable and acquired the authority to grant large-scale concessions for the use of the nation's precious water. Since the land was worthless without a water supply, these concessions, given exclusively to influential *hacendados* and companies, gave the elite life-and-death power over *rancheros* and villages. Phipps, *Some Aspects*, p. 115.

6. *Mexican Financier*, 20 June 1885, p. 184, and 13 February 1892, p. 492; González Navarro, *El Porfiriato: La vida social*, p. 188; AGNRP, 818-C-49.

7. *POC*, 12 April 1924, pp. 12–14.

8. *POC*, 8 September 1883, p. 3, and 4 October 1884, p. 1.

9. *POC*, 2 February 1884, p. 4.

10. Almada, *Tomochi*.

11. *AERM*, *1902*, p. 300; *Mexican Herald*, 28 January 1906, p. 11.

12. W. W. Mills, U.S. Consul, Chihuahua City, to Assistant Secretary of State, 30 June 1906, NARG 59. Rents were so high in the capital in 1903 that American Protestant missionaries had to move their headquarters from downtown to the outskirts of the city. Report for

1903–1904, Chihuahua and Out-stations, 48–128, p. 5, Papers of the American Board of
Commissioners for Foreign Missionaries.

13. *El Correo*, 30 May 1905, p. 4, 26 May 1905, p. 1, 2 May 1905, p. 1, 8 May 1905, p. 4,
15 May 1905, p. 1; *POC*, 23 November 1905, p. 12, 30 November 1905, pp. 5–6, 7
December 1905, pp. 9–10.
14. *Mexican Herald*, 11 May 1905, p. 11, and 10 February 1908, p. 4.
15. Womack, *Zapata*, pp. 37–66; Chihuahua, *Ley sobre medida y engenación de terrenos
municipales*, 1905.
16. "Un amigo de la verdad: Enrique C. Creel, el hombre y el estadista," (n.p., n.d.), p. 11.
17. *POC*, 15 February 1930, p. 8; Mexico, Departamento Agrario, Dirección de Terrenos
Nacionales Diversos, Expediente 37 x 5, Junta Directiva de los Vecinos de Cuchillo Parado
to Secretario de Fomento, 10 January 1903, cited in Katz, "Peasants in the Mexican Revolution," pp. 89–120.
18. *El Correo*, 24 July 1909, p. 1, and 1 July 1909, p. 1.
19. Chihuahua, *Anuario, 1908*, pp. 47–103, *1909*, pp. 83–90; Mexico, Departamento
Agrario, Dirección de Terrenos Nacionales Diversos, Expediente 75–1407, Porfirio Talamantes, as representative of the inhabitants of Janos, to President Díaz, 22 August 1908,
cited in Katz, "Peasants in the Mexican Revolution," p. 99.
20. *El Correo*, 18 May 1909, p. 2, and 8 June 1909, p. 1; Chávez M., "Hombres," p. 268.
21. Reply of Governor Terrazas to the complaint of the citizens of Bachíniva, Distrito Guerrero, Flores Magón Correspondence, file no. 3B, STP; *El Correo*, 20 April 1910, p. 4,
14 June 1910, p. 4, 17 March 1910, p. 1, and 30 October 1910, p. 3; *POC*, 21 April
1907, pp. 28–29.
22. *POC*, 4 October 1906, pp. 21–23, and 9 April 1908, p. 36.
23. Mendoza, *Chihuahua revolucionario*, pp. 22–23.
24. Report of W. W. Mills, U.S. Consul, Chihuahua City, 1 October 1903, in *CR, 1903*,
p. 122; Report of James I. Long, U.S. Consular Agent, Parral, *CR, 1908*, p. 150.
25. According to the *Anuarios* there were forty-five adjudications in the region during the
fifteen months before the riot.
26. *POC*, 30 December 1906, pp. 4–6, 23 July 1908, p. 4.
27. *El Correo*, 25 April 1907, p. 1, 24 March 1910, p. 4, 12 June 1906, p. 1, and 2 March
1909, p. 1.
28. *El Correo*, 6 June 1910, p. 1, 7 June 1910, p. 1, 8 June 1910, p. 1, and 22 July 1910,
p. 4; *POC*, 13 August 1908, p. 17. Villa ordered Benton executed on 16 February 1914,
for attempting to kill him. The shooting set off an international incident between the
United States and the Carranza government. Cumberland, *The Constitutionalist Years*,
pp. 282–87.
29. *POC*, 20 September 1908, p. 15, 4 March 1909, p. 23, 13 January 1910, pp. 24–25,
and 17 February 1910, pp. 15–18.
30. *POC*, 14 October 1908, p. 5, and 15 March 1909, p. 23; *El Correo*, 30 October 1907,
p. 1, 26 October 1907, p. 1, and 28 November 1908, p. 1; Chihuahua, Gobernador,
Informe, 1 de junio de 1907, pp. 29–30, and *1 de junio de 1908*, pp. 35–37. The law
was passed 25 February 1905 and changed in September 1906 to limit the number of
claims per person to three, one of each type (agricultural, pastoral, *fundo legal*).
31. *EPT*, 25 January 1909, p. 2; *POC*, 23 February 1908, p. 13.
32. *POC*, 29 October 1908, p. 12, 12 December 1909, pp. 23, 38, 26 November 1908,
p. 31, 10 September 1908, p. 37, 16 December 1909, p. 2, and 26 October 1905, p. 2.
33. Schmidt, *Chihuahua*, pp. 23–24.
34. *CR, 1877*, pp. 716, 727, *1879*, 1:427; Louis H. Scott, U.S. Consul, Chihuahua City, to

Second Assistant Secretary of State, 10 July 1879, NARG 59; Beezley, "Opportunity," p. 33.

35. *Mexican Financier*, 6 September 1884, p. 327; *POC*, 4 December 1910, p. 4; SHMM, *Estadísticas económicas*, pp. 156–63.

36. Almada, *La revolución*, 1:96–106.

37. U.S., Department of State, *Reports from the Consuls of the United States*, no. 153, p. 200, and no. 166, p. 423; SHMM, *Estadísticas económicas*, pp. 156–63.

38. Almada, *La revolución*, 1:96–106; *POC*, 24 April 1886, supplement, and 1 May 1886, p. 3, discuss the uprising in Cusihuiriachic. There was a riot in Casas Grandes in early 1889. *POC*, 9 March 1889, p. 1; *POC*, 4 June 1892, p. 2, discusses the protest at Ascensión. For rebel activities in 1893 and 1894 see Huston to Department of State, 30 November 1893; Huston to Josiah Quincy, Assistant Secretary of State, 7 and 12 December 1893; Huston to Uhl, 24 January 1894 and 30 March 1894, all in NARG 59. See also *Revista de Chihuahua*, February 1895, p. 24; *EPT* of 16, 22, 25, 26, 28, 29, 30 November 1893. For Palomas see *Mexican Herald*, 16 October 1896, p. 1, 17 September 1896, p. 1; Buford to Rockhill, 9 September 1896, NARG 59. Enrique C. Creel to Ramón Corral, Vice-President of Mexico, 17 October 1906, Flores Magón Correspondence, file 7A, STP.

39. SHMM, *Estadísticas económicas*, pp. 156–63.

40. Katz, *The Secret War*, pp. 14–16; Estrada, "Liderazgo."

41. Katz, "Peasants in the Mexican Revolution"; Turner, *Barbarous Mexico*, pp. 3–26; Friedrich, *Agrarian Revolt*, p. 44.

42. Katz, "Peasants in the Mexican Revolution"; DeHart, "Pacification of the Yaquis," p. 92.

43. Katz, "Peasants in the Mexican Revolution"; Womack, *Zapata*.

44. Jacobs, "The Rancheros of Guerrero."

45. Waterbury, "Non-revolutionary Peasants."

46. Wolf, "On Peasant Rebellions," pp. 264–74; Buve, "Peasant Movements," pp. 112–52; Knight, "Peasant and Caudillo," pp. 19–37.

CHAPTER 8

1. West, *Parral Mining District*, pp. 47–56, 72–74; Katz, "Labor Conditions," pp. 1–47; Katz, *La servidumbre agraria*.

2. Escudero, *Noticias estadísticas*, pp. 115–16, 20; García Conde, "Ensayo estadístico," p. 299; Rondé, "Voyage," p. 151; Chevalier, "North Mexican Hacienda," pp. 94–109; Katz, "Labor Conditions," p. 31.

3. L. H. Scott, U.S. Consul, Chihuahua City, to Second Assistant Secretary of State, 30 September 1879 and 13 November 1879, NARG 59. These contain a report written by a Frenchman in 1864. *La República*, 28 August 1868, p. 4.

4. Charles Moye, U.S. Consul, Chihuahua City, to Secretary of State William H. Seward, 3 June 1867, NARG 59.

5. Moye to Seward, 8 April 1867, NARG 59.

6. *Semanario Oficial*, 30 July 1875, pp. 2–3.

7. *POC*, 10 March 1878, p. 3, and 15 September 1878, p. 4.

8. U.S., Department of State, "Labor in North America: Mexico," in *Reports of the Consuls of the United States*, no. 67 (September 1886), p. 117; *Mexican Financier*, 13 February 1892, p. 493; *POC*, 30 August 1884, p. 4, 6 November 1886, p. 2, 24 September 1892,

p. 1; U.S., Department of State, Bureau of Statistics, *Special Consular Reports: Money and Prices in Foreign Countries*, v. 13, pt. 1, pp. 111–50.

9. SHMM, *Estadísticas económicas*, p. 45.

10. Levy, *Cesar Chávez*, p. 7; Duarte Morelos, "Memorias," cited in Estrada, "Liderazgo," pp. 72–74; *POC*, 15 November 1884, p. 3.

11. *EMJ* 37 (12 April 1884): 282.

12. *Chihuahua Enterprise*, 14 January 1884, p. 7.

13. U.S., Department of State, *Reports from the Consuls of the United States*, no. 105 (May 1889), p. 4; *EMJ* 40 (28 November 1885): 375.

14. Almada, *Resumen*, pp. 329–30.

15. Mexico, Secretaría de Fomento, Colonización e Industria, *Informes y documentos relativos a comercio interior y exterior, agricultura, minería e industrias*, no. 22 (April 1887), pp. 62–66, 53, 105–8.

16. Ryan, "Selected Aspects," p. 321; *POC*, 15 November 1884, p. 3; interview of Mrs. Nelle Spilsbury Hatch by Richard Estrada, cited in Estrada, "Liderazgo," pp. 73–74.

17. U.S., Department of State, "Labor in North America: Mexico," pp. 122–60.

18. Ibid., p. 153.

19. "Informe del Gobernador," in *POC*, 4 June 1893, p. 2, and 24 September 1892, p. 1; *BSAM* 20, no. 33 (8 September 1896): 515; report of R. M. Burke, U.S. Consul, Chihuahua City, in *CR*, *1897*, p. 493; *Mexican Herald*, 9 March 1896, p. 2; reports of W. W. Mills, U.S. Consul, Chihuahua City, 18 August 1898 in *CR*, *1898*, p. 566, and *1900*, p. 555.

20. Report of R. M. Burke, U.S. Consul, Chihuahua City, 20 July 1896, in U.S., *Consular Reports*, no. 193 (October 1896), p. 265; Katz, "Labor Conditions," p. 34.

21. U.S., Department of State, *Money and Prices*, pp. 138–50; Nava, "Jornales y jornaleros," p. 70.

22. Shepherd, *Silver Magnet*, p. 250; M. Weber to Vermehren, 21 June 1902, roll 3, Weber Collection; reports of W. W. Mills, U.S. Consul, Chihuahua City, 17 October 1901, in *CR*, *1901*, p. 468, 23 October 1902 in *CR*, *1902*, p. 505, and 24 October 1900 in *CR*, *1900*, p. 555.

23. Clark, "Mexican Labor," pp. 466–522.

24. E. A. H. Tays, "Present Labor Conditions in Mexico," *EMJ* 84 (5 October 1907): 621–24.

25. Report of Thomas D. Edwards, U.S. Consul, Ciudad Juárez, in *CR*, *1907*, p. 105; Edwards to Assistant Secretary of State, 28 August 1908, numerical files, 13911/83–84, NARG 59.

26. Alden B. Case to Rev. James L. Barton, Ciudad Guerrero, 25 June 1906, vol. 9, item 21, Papers of the American Board of Commissioners for Foreign Missionaries.

27. Clark, "Mexican Labor," p. 520; *Mexican Herald*, 16 July 1906, p. 11.

28. *Mexican Herald*, 4 April 1906, p. 2; *El Correo*, 21 February 1907, p. 1.

29. Clark, "Mexican Labor," p. 466 and throughout.

30. Ibid., p. 470.

31. *Mexican Herald*, 8 July 1907; *EMJ* 83 (2 February 1907): 223.

32. *EMJ* 83 (2 February 1907): 223.

33. *Mexican Herald*, 9 August 1908, p. 4.

34. *Mexican Herald*, 15 January 1906, p. 7.

35. Despite some inconsistencies in the data, it appears that the average minimum daily wage for agricultural workers remained at fifty centavos through 1907.

36. Katz, "Labor Conditions," p. 34.

37. Memorandum to Ministerio de Agricultura y Fomento, 21 October 1921, AGNRP, 818-

C-49; Katz, "Agrarian Changes in Northern Mexico"; Katz, "Labor Conditions," pp. 32–33; Dobie, "Babicora."

38. Memorandum to Ministerio de Agricultura y Fomento, 21 October 1921, AGNRP, 818-C-49.

39. Informe de José Muñoz, Jefe Político del Distrito de Benito Juárez, in *POC*, 17 May 1908, pp. 11–12. Letter to General Ignacio C. Enríquez, Governor of Chihuahua, 24 January 1922, box 11, Mexican Northwestern Railway Papers, JMC.

40. Buve, "Peasant Movements," pp. 10, 123–24. See also Robert E. Johnson, *Peasant and Proletarian: The Working Class of Moscow in the Late Nineteenth Century* (New Brunswick: Rutgers University Press, 1979), pp. 31–50, for a similar phenomenon in Russia before the Revolution.

41. All of the qualitative data point to unprecedented high wages. The calculations of SHMM, *Estadísticas económicas*, concur. The Chihuahua *Anuarios* indicate a slight (less than 5 percent) drop in the average minimum wage from 1904 to 1906. But that does not reflect the fact that most miners received above the minimum in the state.

42. *El Correo*, 10 September 1906, p. 2.

43. Chihuahua, *Anuario, 1907*, p. 136. According to the testimony of George A. Laird in U.S., Senate, *Revolutions in Mexico*, p. 16, 975 of 1,000 employees at Candelaria were Mexican.

44. James Hyslop to Hugh Rose, Superintendent, Minas Tecolotes, 23 February 1906, Hyslop Collection.

45. Lewis A. Martin, U.S. Consul, Chihuahua City, to Assistant Secretary of State, 31 October 1908, numerical files, case no. 15600/16, NARG 59; Chihuahua, *Anuario, 1905*, p. 102, *1906*, p. 234, *1907*, p. 142, *1908*, pp. 184–87, *1909*, p. 221.

46. *El Correo*, 4 January 1907, p. 1, claims that 35 mines operated in Santa Eulalia, while the *Anuario* lists 14. Santa Eulalia reportedly had 300 *tiendas de raya*, a clear indication that there were more mines actively worked, at least part of the year, than the *Anuarios* show. *El Correo*, 27 February 1907, p. 1.

47. Ryan, "Selected Aspects," p. 309.

48. Testimony of William J. McGarrack, in U.S., Senate, *Investigation of Mexican Affairs*, pp. 866–67.

49. Cited in Ryan, "Selected Aspects," p. 262.

50. *Mexican Investor*, 17 September 1904, p. 8.

51. The wages are calculated from the Chihuahua, *Anuarios, 1905–1909*.

52. Nava, "Jornales y jornaleros," p. 70.

53. See reports from U.S. consuls in Acapulco, Hermosillo, Durango, Ciudad Juárez, and Chihuahua City in numerical file, case no. 13911, NARG 59.

54. Anderson, *Outcasts*, p. 70; González Navarro, *El Porfiriato: La vida social*, pp. 34–53.

55. Almada, *Resumen*, p. 329.

56. *El Minero* (Batopilas), 16 June 1895, p. 3, and 23 June 1895, p. 1; Shepherd, *Silver Magnet*, p. 218.

57. Chihuahua, *Anuario, 1907*, p. 177; Anderson, *Outcasts*, pp. 90–91.

58. *La Nueva Era*, 13 May 1900, p. 1; Anderson, *Outcasts*, p. 91; Chihuahua, *Anuario, 1907*, p. 177.

59. *Mexican Herald*, 1 September 1896, p. 2.

60. Ryan, "Selected Aspects," p. 333.

61. Anson W. Burchard, Second Vice-President and Comptroller, to A. C. Bernard, 28 April 1902, Greene Day Book, JMC.

62. *El Correo*, 27 February 1907.

63. *POC*, 20 September 1908, p. 4; *El Correo*, 2 December 1905, p. 1. Employers, particu-

larly in the more isolated camps, claimed that they operated the company stores for the benefit of the miners, and they actually kept the prices of staples lower than they otherwise would have been. Other employers claimed that the *boleto* system was the only way they could keep the native miner from squandering his pay and leaving his family hungry. In truth, workers did not fare well at the hands of either the company stores or merchants in neighboring towns and villages. For example, in 1900 merchants in Parral complained bitterly that the system of paying workers every fifteen days (*quincenal*) put them at a disadvantage in competition with the company stores. Two years later these same businessmen had through their speculations pushed up the prices of staples alarmingly. Obviously, the company stores did not have a monopoly on high prices, nor were they the only enterprises that cheated the workers. *Mexican Herald*, 11 May 1896, p. 8; Shepherd, *Silver Magnet*, pp. 246–47; Anson W. Burchard, Vice-President and Comptroller, to A. C. Bernard, 28 April 1902, Greene Day Book, JMC; Ryan, "Selected Aspects," p. 321; *La Nueva Era*, 5 July 1900, p. 1; *El Correo*, 3 July 1902, p. 2, and 16 July 1902, p. 1.

64. *El Correo*, 20 March 1908, p. 1, and 25 May 1908, p. 1.
65. *El Correo*, 27 July 1906, p. 1, 1 August 1906, p. 1, and 31 July 1906, p. 1.
66. Enrique C. Creel to Porfirio Díaz, 14 July 1906, in General Porfirio Díaz Collection, 31:8128, cited in Anderson, *Outcasts*, p. 120.
67. *El Correo*, 4 August 1906, p. 4.
68. *Mexican Herald*, 2 March 1907, p. 4, and 3 August 1907, p. 1; *El Correo*, 16 March 1907, p. 1, 5 September 1907, p. 4, and 10 September 1907, p. 4.
69. Anderson, *Outcasts*, p. 122.
70. *El Correo*, 28 February 1907, p. 1.
71. Anderson, *Outcasts*, pp. 231–33.
72. *El Correo*, 31 July 1906, p. 1.
73. Ibid.; *El Correo*, 3 July 1907, p. 1, 5 July 1907, p. 1, and 9 July 1907, p. 1.
74. *El Correo*, 10 December 1906, p. 1.
75. *El Correo*, 15 October 1907, p. 1, and 28 October 1907, p. 1; *Mexican Herald*, 4 November 1907, p. 2.
76. *El Correo*, 21 October 1907, p. 1; *Mexican Herald*, 4 November 1907, p. 2.
77. *Mexican Herald*, 7 November 1907, p. 10, and 18 December 1907, p. 11.
78. *Mexican Herald*, 13 December 1907, p. 11.
79. *EMJ*, 84 (28 December 1907): 1237; A. Van Zwaluwenberg, "Mexico," *EMJ* 85 (4 January 1908): 68–69; *Mexican Herald*, 14 June 1908, p. 11, and 21 March 1908, p. 11.
80. *Mexican Herald*, 16 September 1906, p. 4, 2 March 1907, p. 3, 25 November 1907, p. 11, 6 January 1908, p. 1, 13 January 1908, p. 1, 23 January 1908, p. 5, 27 August 1908, p. 3, and 24 January 1908, p. 3; *El Correo*, 19 February 1907, p. 1, and 1 March 1910, p. 1; *EPMT*, 5 March 1910, p. 5, and 1 April 1910, p. 8.
81. Chihuahua, *Anuario*, *1907*, pp. 136–40, *1908*, pp. 181–83, *1909*, pp. 219–20; *Mexican Herald*, 8 January 1908, p. 11, 28 January 1908, p. 11, 7 November 1907, p. 11, 15 November 1907, p. 11, 18 December 1908, p. 11; *El Correo*, 1 June 1908, p. 1.
82. SHMM, *Estadísticas económicas*, pp. 159, 163; *Mexican Herald*, 7 July 1908, p. 5, 8 August 1908, p. 8, and 11 August 1908, p. 5. Because of these shortages, the state government urged municipalities to purchase staples and sell them at cost. *EPMT*, 29 October 1909, in numerical files, case no. 12754/40-41, NARG 59; *SAJ*, 2 January 1909, p. 2; *Mexican Herald*, 8 August 1907, p. 5.
83. *Mexican Herald*, 3 August 1907, p. 1.
84. Anderson, *Outcasts*, pp. 214–15; *El Correo*, 23 April 1908, p. 1.
85. *EMJ* 87 (6 March 1909): 505.

86. *El Correo*, 22 April 1909, p. 1, 5 October 1909, p. 1; Anderson, *Outcasts*, p. 228.
87. Testimony of George Laird, Manager of the Candelaria Mining Company, U.S., Senate, *Revolutions in Mexico*, p. 16.
88. *Mexican Herald*, 18 August 1909, p. 8.
89. *El Correo*, 18 October 1910, p. 3, 4 November 1909, p. 1, 12 December 1909, p. 1, and 23 January 1910, p. 1.
90. *El Correo*, 8 March 1910, p. 1.
91. *El Correo*, 17 July 1910, p. 1.
92. *EPMT*, 22 February 1909, p. 3.
93. *El Correo*, 5 January 1910, p. 1.
94. *EPMT*, 7 September 1910, p. 8; *El Correo*, 15 September 1910, p. 2.
95. *Mexican Herald*, 14 August 1910, sect. 2, p. 2; *EMJ* 90 (6 August 1910): 262; Report of C. M. Leonard, U.S. Vice-consul, Chihuahua City, 3 February 1911, in U.S., Department of State, *Daily Consular and Trade Reports, 1911*, p. 457; report on wages in Parral compiled by the Engineers' Association of the Parral District, January and August 1910, Hyslop Collection.
96. *Mexican Herald*, 25 April 1910, p. 9.
97. *La Nueva Era*, 1 September 1910, p. 1.
98. *El Correo*, 18 January 1910, pp. 2 and 4.
99. *El Correo*, 27 October 1909, p. 1, 9 March 1910, p. 1, and 28 October 1910, p. 1.
100. Sandels, "Silvestre Terrazas," p. 175; Christiansen, "Pascual Orozco," p. 99.
101. F. Portillo to Alberto Terrazas, 19 December 1910, cited in Sandels, "Silvestre Terrazas," p. 205.
102. Juan Hernández to Díaz, 16 December 1910, Colección General Porfirio Díaz, 35:20646, 35:20634, cited in Anderson, *Outcasts*, p. 287.
103. Estrada, "Border Revolution," pp. 78–79; *EPMT*, 24 April 1911.
104. *El Correo*, 20 June 1911, p. 2, 26 June 1911, p. 4, and 15 July 1911, p. 4.
105. *El Correo*, 24 June 1911, p. 1, and 16 July 1911, pp. 2–3.
106. Almada, *Abraham González*, p. 60.
107. *El Correo*, 5 July 1911, p. 1; *EMJ* 92 (22 July 1911): 180.
108. Anderson, *Outcasts*, pp. 273–97.
109. Cumberland, *Genesis*, pp. 14–15; Coatsworth, "Anotaciones," pp. 167–87.
110. See, for example, Lewis A. Martin, U.S. Consul, Chihuahua City, to Assistant Secretary of State, 31 October 1908, numerical file, case no. 15600/6, and Thomas D. Edwards, U.S. Consul, Ciudad Juárez, to Department of State, 28 August 1908, numerical file, case no. 13911/83–84, both in NARG 59.

CHAPTER 9

1. Helguera, *Enrique Creel*, p. 60. *El Correo*, 30 August 1904, p. 1. *BSCEH*, 1, no. 8 (15 January 1939): 272; 1, no. 10 (15 March 1939): 344. Almada, *Gobernadores*, pp. 441–42. POC, 14 December 1905, pp. 4–5. *Mexican Herald*, 23 October 1907, p. 5, and 2 November 1906, p. 3. Chihuahua, Gobernador, *Informe, 16 de septiembre de 1904*, p. 16.
2. Helguera, *Enrique Creel*, pp. 61, 82–83, 120–57; Almada, *Gobernadores*, pp. 441–42; *Bankers' Magazine* 74 (January–June 1907): 589.
3. Chihuahua, Gobernador, *Informe, 16 de septiembre de 1903*, pp. 11–12; *1 de junio de 1905*, pp. 22, 25; *1 de junio de 1906*, pp. 34–39. *MMJ* (October 1908): 12. Chihuahua, *Anuarios, 1905–1909*.

4. *Mexican Herald*, 24 September 1906, p. 1, 2 November 1906, p. 3, 30 December 1906, p. 3, 18 November 1907, p. 5; Helguera, *Enrique Creel*, pp. 182–92.

5. *Mexican Herald*, 25 October 1906, p. 3, 2 November 1906, p. 3, 23 October 1907, p. 5; *Bankers' Magazine* 79 (January 1909): 85–86.

6. *Mexican Herald*, 5 November 1906, p. 3; Chihuahua, Gobernador, *Informe, 1 de junio de 1907*, p. 6, and *16 de septiembre de 1908*, p. 5. Creel's crusade for temperance, however, never interfered with the family's business interests, for the Terrazas still owned a large, profitable brewery. Several retail and wholesale houses owned by family members specialized in imported wines and liquors. Their priorities were clearly indicated by the examples provided by "El Cosmopolita," a saloon and gambling spot operated by Mauricio Asam, who was married to the daughter of Francisco Molinar, a cousin of Luis Terrazas, and two other nightclubs owned by Juan Ramonfaur, who married a niece of the general. The harsh laws that restricted the sale of alcoholic beverages were ignored by the proprietors, and drinking went on at all hours. Roque López to Jesús Martínez Carrión, 30 December 1903, STP.

7. *BSCEH* 1, no. 8 (15 January 1939): 272.

8. Report of Leo J. Keena, U.S. Consul, Chihuahua City, *CR, 1909*, p. 522.

9. Anderson, *Outcasts*, pp. 210, 117–18.

10. Almada, *Gobernantes*, pp. 82–97.

11. Almada, *La revolución*, 1:27–36; Almada, *Gobernantes*, pp. 116–18.

12. *El Correo*, 31 May 1907, p. 1.

13. Almada, *La revolución*, 1:27–36; *POC*, 3 March 1894, p. 1; Chihuahua, *Anuario, 1907*, p. 181.

14. Chihuahua, *Anuario, 1907*, pp. 181–82; Almada, *Diccionario*, pp. 322–23.

15. *El Correo*, 8 June 1908, p. 1. Silvestre made the same charges in 1909. *El Correo*, 8 June 1909, p. 1.

16. *El Correo*, 10 December 1909, p. 1.

17. *POC*, for 1908–10. In early 1910 the legislature nullified elections in Galeana, the very backyard of the Terrazas. *POC*, 17 February 1910, p. 8.

18. This debate began in *El Correo* on 9 June 1906 and continued through September.

19. *El Correo*, 16 March 1907, p. 1, and 23 March 1907, p. 1.

20. *El Correo*, 2 March 1907, p. 1, 30 March 1907, p. 1, 27 July 1907, p. 1; *POC*, 28 July 1888, p. 1; *La Guardia Nacional*, 12 July 1877, p. 2.

21. *El Correo*, 2 March 1907, p. 1, and 30 March 1907, p. 1.

22. Sandels, "Silvestre Terrazas," pp. 136–54, presents a detailed account of the Banco Minero Affair. Bush, *Gringo Doctor*, p. 165.

23. *El Correo*, 20 May 1908, p. 1, and 10 April 1908, p. 1.

24. *El Correo*, 25 November 1905, p. 1, and 4 February 1907, p. 1; Chihuahua, *Ley reglamentaria para la organización de los distritos*.

25. See, for example, *El Correo*, 25 August 1906, p. 1, and 26 May 1908, p. 1.

26. *El Correo*, 26 April 1907, p. 1, 24 April 1909, p. 1, and 27 November 1910, p. 1.

27. *El Correo*, 18 June 1910, p. 1, 24 June 1910, p. 1, 17 July 1910, p. 1, 30 July 1910, p. 1, 13 October 1910, p. 2, 19 October 1910, p. 1, 9 November 1910, p. 2, and 16 November 1910, p. 3.

28. *El Correo*, 19 February 1909, p. 1, 26 February 1909, p. 2, 7 April 1909, p. 1, 29 April 1909, p. 1, 19 May 1909, p. 1, 1 October 1909, p. 1, 2 December 1909, p. 1; Almada, *La revolución*, 1:177.

29. *El Correo*, 19 May 1910, p. 1, and 23 November 1910, p. 1.

30. *El Correo*, 5 February 1909, p. 1, and 1 July 1910, p. 4.

31. Meyer, *Pascual Orozco*, pp. 14–15; Antonio Alderete and others to Governor Luis Terra-

zas, 18 August 1903, Flores Magón Correspondence, folder 3B, STP; *El Correo*, 27 November 1909, p. 4, and 11 August 1909, pp. 2–3.

32. *El Correo*, 3 August 1909, p. 1.
33. *El Correo*, 28 January 1908, p. 1, and 29 January 1908, p. 2.
34. Meyer, *Pascual Orozco*, pp. 14–15.
35. *El Correo*, 19 October 1908, p. 1, and 1 January 1910, p. 1.
36. *El Correo*, 3 August 1910, p. 1, 10 August 1910, p. 1, 14 May 1909, p. 1, 5 October 1910, p. 3, 2 September 1910, p. 2, 30 May 1909, p. 1, 23 November 1908, p. 2, 12 October 1904, p. 1, 5 March 1909, p. 1, 11 August 1909, p. 2, and 14 August 1909, p. 2; Meyer, *Pascual Orozco*, p. 17; Chihuahua, Gobernador, *Informe, 16 de septiembre de 1904*, p. 13.
37. *El Correo*, 14 May 1909, p. 1.
38. *El Correo*, 26 February 1903, p. 3, 27 August 1910, p. 2, 10 August 1910, p. 1; *POC*, 21 September 1911, p. 2; Beezley, "State Reform," p. 535.
39. *Mexican Herald*, 5 November 1907, p. 5, 11 November 1907, p. 5, and 4 November 1907, p. 5; *El Correo*, 19 May 1909, p. 1, 1 October 1909, p. 1, and 14 January 1910, p. 1.
40. *El Correo*, 4 November 1909, p. 1, 7 May 1909, p. 1, and 9 May 1909, p. 1; Sandels, "Silvestre Terrazas," pp. 134–36.
41. Almada, *Juárez y Terrazas*, p. 464; Chihuahua, *Anuario, 1908*, p. 167.
42. Almada, *La revolución*, 1:81; Sandels, "Silvestre Terrazas," pp. 164–65.
43. Ibid.; Chihuahua, *Ley de hacienda municipal*.
44. *El Correo*, 5 September 1908, pp. 5–6.
45. *El Correo*, 20 December 1908.
46. Bush, *Gringo Doctor*, pp. 165–66.
47. *El Correo*, 10 March 1909, p. 1.
48. *POC*, 4 April 1909, pp. 2–3; *El Correo*, 30 March 1909, p. 1, 31 March 1909, p. 1, and 2 April 1909, p. 1; *EPT*, 1 April 1909, p. 1; Meyer, *Pascual Orozco*, p. 14.

CHAPTER 10

1. Cumberland, *Genesis*, pp. 47–48.
2. Ibid., pp. 10–11.
3. Bryan, "Bernardo Reyes"; Cumberland, *Genesis*, pp. 66–67.
4. Cumberland, *Genesis*, p. 75.
5. Quoted from letter of Madero to Limantour, 18 November 1909, published in *La Opinión*, 18 February 1934, p. 2, cited in Cumberland, *Genesis*, p. 87.
6. Cumberland, *Genesis*, p. 111.
7. Ibid., p. 94; Almada, *La revolución*, 1:153; Beezley, *Abraham González*, pp. 21–24.
8. Beezley, *Abraham González*, pp. 28–29; *El Correo*, 17 February 1910.
9. *El Correo*, 7 July 1910, p. 1.
10. Raat, *Revoltosos*, pp. 175–202. *El Correo* throughout the years 1909 and 1910 documents these abuses. At the Dolores Mines officials threatened to fire workers who joined Anti-reelectionist clubs. *El Correo*, 17 October 1909, p. 1. For examples of local repression of the Anti-reelectionists see *El Correo*, 3 July, 8 July, and 10 July 1910 for Parral; 14 December 1909, for Iturbide; 30 July 1910 for Villa López.
11. Beezley, *Abraham González*, p. 25. The Club issued a public salute to Díaz on the occasion of his meeting with United States President Taft. *El Correo*, 5 October 1909.

12. Raat, *Revoltosos*, gives an excellent account of the *magonistas*, pp. 13–62. See also Cockcroft, *Precursors*, pp. 148–53.
13. Raat, *Revoltosos*, pp. 92–123; Cockcroft, *Precursors*, pp. 148–53.
14. Raat, *Revoltosos*, p. 36.
15. *El Correo*, 8 March 1910, and 7 July 1910; Meyers, "Interest Group Conflict," pp. 266–67.
16. Cumberland, *Genesis*, pp. 70–71. For biographical material on Madero see also Beezley, "Madero," pp. 1–23; Ruiz, *The Great Rebellion*, 139–52; Ross, *Madero*.
17. Cumberland, *Genesis*, pp. 55–69.
18. Ibid., pp. 32–33.
19. Ruiz, *The Great Rebellion*, pp. 154–55; Deeds, "José María Maytorena," pp. 21–40, 125–48.
20. Rock, *Politics in Argentina*.
21. Katz, "Pancho Villa," pp. 27–28; Katz, *The Secret War*, pp. 37–40; Knight, "Peasant and Caudillo," p. 32; Beezley, "Madero."
22. Katz, "Pancho Villa," pp. 28–29.
23. Estrada, "Liderazgo"; Katz, *The Secret War*, p. 18; Aguilar Camín, *La frontera nomada*, pp. 127–63.
24. Aguilar Camín, *La frontera nomada*; Meyers, "Interest Group Conflict," pp. 345–49.
25. Vanderwood, "Response to Revolt," pp. 551–79; Katz, *The Secret War*, pp. 27–29.
26. Voss, "Porfirian Sonora"; Womack, *Zapata*, pp. 15–19.
27. The *científicos* themselves were split over the matter of Díaz's ouster. Bulnes, for example, believed Díaz was the nation, but Limantour was willing to sacrifice the old man for peace. See Iturribarria, "Limantour y la caída de Porfirio Díaz," pp. 243–81.
28. Ruiz, *The Great Rebellion*, pp. 153–66.
29. Vanderwood, "Response to Revolt," especially 575–79; Ruiz, *The Great Rebellion*, pp. 40–43.
30. Raat, *Revoltosos*, pp. 175–99.
31. Almada, *Gobernantes*, pp. 23–24.
32. Vanderwood, "Response to Revolt," p. 569.
33. Cumberland, *Genesis*, pp. 124–25.
34. Meyer, *Pascual Orozco*, pp. 19–20.
35. Vanderwood, "Response to Revolt," pp. 576–79; Perry, *Juárez and Díaz*.

CHAPTER II

1. Voss, "Porfirian Sonora."
2. Haden, "The Federalist"; Langston, "Coahuilan Politics."
3. Pacheco was sent to Chihuahua, Torres to Sonora, Cervantes to Coahuila, and Reyes to Nuevo León.
4. Saragoza, "The Formation of a Mexican Elite."
5. Jacobs, *Ranchero Revolt*, pp. 2–28.
6. Wells, "Henequén and Yucatán"; Joseph, *Revolution from Without*, pp. 71–89.
7. Vanderwood, "Response to Revolt."
8. Hansen, *Politics of Mexican Development*, pp. 13–28.
9. Womack, *Zapata*, pp. 46–47.
10. DeHart, "Yaquis," p. 93.
11. Buve, "Peasant Movements," p. 126.

12. DeHart, "Yaquis," pp. 78–81; Buve, "Peasant Movements," pp. 112–30; Wolf, *Peasant Wars*, pp. 27–28.

13. Waterbury, "Non-Revolutionary Peasants."

14. Joseph, *Revolution from Without*, pp. 82–89.

15. Anderson, *Outcasts*, pp. 137–71, 110–16.

16. DeHart, "Yaquis," p. 77.

17. Buve, "Peasant Movements," pp. 123–28.

18. DeHart, "Yaquis," p. 93.

19. Estrada, "Linderazgo."

20. Katz, "Pancho Villa," pp. 27–28.

21. Ross, *Madero*, p. 51.

22. See Frank, *Capitalism and Underdevelopment*, and Cardoso and Faletto, *Dependency and Development*, for the clearest statements of dependency theory. The literature on dependency is enormous. See Bath and James, "Dependency Analysis," for an extensive bibliography.

23. Cardoso and Faletto, *Dependency and Development*, pp. 54–76; Loveman, *Chile*, pp. 210–12; Smith, *Argentina*, pp. 1–12.

24. Rock, *Argentine Politics*; Loveman, *Chile*, pp. 213–55.

25. The leading statement of this discredited school is Thomas C. Cochran, "Cultural Factors in Economic Growth," *Journal of Economic History* 20 (1960): 515–30. See also Morner, "Haciendas," pp. 192–94, 203–7, and 208–12.

26. Rippy, *British Investments*; see especially the various monographs and articles of D. C. M. Platt.

27. Saragoza, "Formation."

28. Wells, "Henequén and Yucatán"; Diane Roazen and Fred Carstensen, "International Harvester, Molina y Compañía, and the Henequén Market: A Comment, *LARR*, forthcoming.

29. The Mexico City elite were also, as we have seen, adept at peddling their influence to foreigners, but unlike the Terrazas, they did not engage in entrepreneurial activities.

30. Oppenheimer, "National Capital," and Marchant, "Mauá the Banker."

31. Sonoran *hacendados* were especially desperate after the Yaqui deportations began.

32. Meyers, "Vested Rights."

33. Turner, *Barbarous Mexico*.

34. The literature on revolution is, of course, enormous. There have been several excellent attempts to organize and discuss the most recent studies: Aya, "Theories of Revolution Reconsidered"; Goldstone, "Theories of Revolution"; Himmelstein and Kimmel, "States and Revolutions"; Skocpol, "Explaining Revolutions"; Johnson, *Revolutionary Charge*, pp. 169–94. The best early effort is Stone, *The English Revolution*, pp. 3–25.

35. The exceptions are Wolf, *Peasant Wars*; Goldfrank, "Theories of Revolution" and "World System"; Skocpol, *States and Social Revolutions*, pp. 286–92.

36. Richmond, "Factional Political Strife."

37. Joseph, *Revolution from Without*, pp. 82–89.

38. Voss, "Porfirian Sonora," and Meyers, "Interest Group Conflict."

39. Critics include: Skocpol, "Explaining Revolutions," pp. 156–65; Aya, "Theories of Revolution Reconsidered," pp. 52–55. Proponents: Johnson, *Revolutionary Change*; M. Olson, "Rapid Growth"; and Davis, "Toward a Theory of Revolution."

40. The role of peasants in revolution is much debated; see, for example, Marx, *The Eighteenth Brumaire*, pp. 123–29; Wolf, *Peasant Wars*; Moore, *The Origins of Dictatorship and Democracy*; Paige, *Agrarian Revolution*; Scott, *The Moral Economy of the Peasant*; Skocpol, *States and Social Revolutions*.

41. Wolf, *Peasant Wars*, argues that it was the middle peasants that brought the Revolution. Katz, "Peasants," has identified three types of revolutionary peasants: residents of free villages, tribal communities, and small landowners or *rancheros*.

42. The degree to which peasant communities are isolated is a matter of considerable debate. It is clear that all three revolutionary peasant groups identified by Katz were not isolated. But the key, as Scott, "Hegemony and Peasantry," points out, is the internal coherence and organization of the peasant community.

43. Theories of revolution are, of course, only as good as the evidence which supports them. And it is in gathering evidence that historians sometimes contribute far more than social theorists think possible. Rather than dismiss the psychological aspects of why men rebel as unprovable, we should perhaps dig deeper for more evidence. Certainly, it is possible in men's own words and deeds to determine why they are willing to die.

E P I L O G U E

1. Fuentes Mares, *Luis Terrazas*, pp. 256–57.
2. Almada, *Gobernadores*, pp. 451–53.
3. Creel Cobián, *Enrique C. Creel*.
4. Woods, "The World's Greatest Cattleman," p. 86.
5. AGNRP, file folder 818-C-49, contains correspondence and documents pertinent to the expropriation of Terrazas landholdings. The government of Venustiano Carranza returned most of the land of other branches of the family from 1916 to 1919.
6. Mark Wasserman, "Persistent Oligarchs: Vestiges of the Porfirian Elite in Revolutionary Chihuahua, Mexico, 1920–1935," paper presented to the Sixth Conference of Mexican and United States Historians, Chicago, Illinois, September, 1981. Chihuahua, Secretaría del Gobierno, Sección Estadística, *Chihuahua, 1934* (Chihuahua: n.p., 1934), pp. 16, 181; Aguilar M., *México: riqueza y miseria*, p. 71; *POC*, 15 February 1930, p. 16.

Selected Bibliography

A R C H I V E S ,   C O L L E C T I O N S ,   A N D   P A P E R S

Austin, Texas
  University of Texas
        Nettie Lee Benson Collection
        Archivo del Ferrocarril Noroeste de México
Berkeley, California
  University of California
        Bancroft Library
          Silvestre Terrazas Collection
            Correspondence and Papers
Cambridge, Massachusetts
  Harvard University
        Baker Library
          George F. Crane Collection
        Houghton Library
          Papers of the American Board of Commissioners for Foreign Missionaries
Ciudad Chihuahua, Chihuahua
  Library of Francisco R. Almada
El Paso, Texas
  El Paso Public Library
  University of Texas
        Roland Anderson Collection
        Ian A. Benton Papers
        Carrizal Collection
        Ciudad Chihuahua
        Archivo del Ayuntamiento
        James Hyslop Collection
        John H. McNeely Collection
          Mexico Northwestern Railway Papers
        Max R. Weber III Collection
Mexico City
  Archivo General de la Nación

Selected Bibliography

Ramo de Gobernación
  Revolución
Ramo de Estado Mayor Presidencial, Obregón-Calles
Washington, D.C.
  United States National Archives
    Record Group 59. General Records of the Department of State
      Consular Despatches
        Paso del Norte (Ciudad Juárez after 1897), Mexico, 1850–1906
        Chihuahua City, Mexico, 1850–1906
      Decimal Files, 1910–29
      Minor File, 1906–10
      Numerical Files, 1906–10
    Record Group 76. Records of the United States and Mexican Claims Commission.

PRINTED DOCUMENTS

Carreño, A. M., ed. *Archivo del General Porfirio Díaz: Memorias y Documentos*. 30 vols. Mexico: N.p., 1947–61.

Chihuahua (Ciudad), Mexico. Ayuntamiento. *Informe sobre la administración municipal de la Ciudad de Chihuahua en el año de 1907*. Chihuahua: Imprenta del Gobierno, 1908.

Chihuahua, Mexico. *Constitución política del Estado de Chihuahua y leyes orgánicas relativas*. Chihuahua: Imprenta del Gobierno, 1888.

———. Gobernador. *Informe leído por el Gobernador en la apertura de sesiones ordinarias del Congreso Constitucional*. 1900, 1902, 1903, 1904, 1905, 1906, 1907, 1908. Chihuahua: Imprenta del Gobierno, 1900–1908.

———. Gobernador. *Memoria de la administración pública del Estado de Chihuahua, 1892–1896, presentada a la legislatura por el Gobernador Coronel Miguel Ahumada*. Chihuahua: Imprenta del Gobierno, 1896.

———. Gobernador. *Mensaje del Gobernador*. Chihuahua: N.p., 1888.

———. Gobernadores. *Informes que los Gobernadores del Estado de Chihuahua han presentado ante el Congreso del mismo, desde el año 1849 hasta el de 1906*. Chihuahua: Imprenta del Gobierno, 1910.

———. *Ley de hacienda del estado con sus adiciones y reformas*. Chihuahua: Imprenta del Gobierno, 1906, 1912.

———. *Ley de hacienda municipal*. Chihuahua: Imprenta del Gobierno, 1904.

———. *Ley reglamentaria para la organización de los distritos del estado*. Chihuahua: Imprenta del Gobierno, 1904.

———. *Ley reglamentaria para la organización de los municipalidades del Estado de Chihuahua*. Chihuahua: Imprenta del Gobierno, 1912.

———. *Ley sobre medida y engenación de terreños municipales con sus adiciones, reformas y demas disposiciones expedidas*. Chihuahua: Imprenta del Gobierno, 1910.

Chihuahua. Secretario del Despacho. *Memoria presentada al honorable Congreso tercero constitucional del Estado de Chihuahua, 1830*. Chihuahua: Imprenta del Gobierno, 1830.

———. Secretaría del Gobierno. Sección Estadística. *Anuario estadístico del Estado de Chihuahua, 1905, 1906, 1907, 1908, 1909*. Chihuahua: Imprenta del Gobierno, 1906, 1908, 1909, 1910, 1913.

Great Britain. Foreign Office. *Diplomatic and Consular Reports on Trade and Finance*. Ann. ser. no. 637. *Mexico. Finances of Mexico and System of Land Tenure in That Country*. London: His Majesty's Stationery Office, 1890.

Selected Bibliography

————. Foreign Office. Board of Trade. *Diplomatic and Consular Reports*. Ann. ser. nos. 3888, 4287, and 4498. *Mexico. Report for the Year 1906, 1908, and 1909 on the Trade of Mexico*. London: His Majesty's Stationery Office, 1907, 1909, and 1910.

Mexico. Ministerio de Fomento. Dirección General de Estadística. *Censo General de la República Mexicana. Censo del Estado de Chihuahua, 1895, 1900*. Mexico: Oficina Tip. de la Secretaría de Fomento, 1898, 1904.

————. *Anuario estadístico de la República Mexicana*. 1893–1907. Mexico: Oficina Tip. de la Secretaría de Fomento, 1894–1908.

————. Secretaría de Economía. Dirección General de Estadística. *Estadísticas sociales del Porfiriato, 1877–1910*. Mexico: N.p., 1956.

————. Secretaría de Fomento. Dirección General de Estadística. *Noticia del movimiento de sociedades mineras y mercantiles habido en la oficina del Registro Público de la Propriedad y del comercio durante los años de 1886 a 1910*. Mexico: Imprenta y Fototipia de la Secretaría de Fomento, 1911.

————. Secretaría de Fomento, Colonización, e Industria. *Informes y documentos relativos a comercio interior y exterior, agricultura, mineria, e industrias*. Numbers 22 (April 1887), 69 (March 1891), 70 (April 1891), and 72 (June 1891). Mexico: Oficina Tip. de la Secretaría de Fomento, 1887, 1891.

————. Ministerio de Fomento, Colonización e Industria. *Memoria presentada al Congreso de la Unión corresponde a los años transcurridos de 1892 a 1896*. Mexico: Oficina Tip. de la Secretaría de Fomento, 1897.

————. Ministerio de Fomento, Colonización e Industria. *Memoria presentada al Congreso de la Unión corresponde a los años transcurridos de l de enero de 1905 a 30 de junio de 1907*. Mexico: Imprenta y Fototipia de la Secretaría de Fomento, 1909.

United States. Congress. Senate. Committee on Foreign Relations. *Investigation of Mexican Affairs. Hearings* before a subcommittee of the Committee on Foreign Relations, Senate on S. Res. 106, 66th Cong., 2d sess., 1919 (Fall Committee). Washington, D.C.: Government Printing Office.

————. Congress. Senate. Committee on Foreign Relations. *Revolutions in Mexico*. Hearing before a subcommittee of the Committee on Foreign Relations, Senate, 62d Cong., 2d sess., 1913. Washington, D.C.: Government Printing Office.

————. Department of Commerce and Labor. Bureau of Manufactures. *Commercial Relations of the United States with Foreign Countries during the Years 1904, 1905, 1906, 1907, 1908, and 1909*. Washington, D.C.: Government Printing Office, 1905, 1906, 1907, 1908, 1909, and 1911.

————. Department of Commerce and Labor. Bureau of Manufactures. *Daily Consular and Trade Reports*. Washington, D.C.: Government Printing Office, 1911–13.

————. Department of Commerce and Labor. Bureau of Manufactures. *Monthly Consular and Trade Reports*. Washington, D.C.: Government Printing Office.

————. Department of Commerce and Labor. Bureau of Statistics. *Commercial Relations of the United States with Foreign Countries during the Year 1903*. Washington, D.C.: Government Printing Office, 1904.

————. Department of State. *Commercial Relations of the United States with Foreign Countries during the Years 1885 and 1886*. Washington, D.C.: Government Printing Office, 1887.

————. Department of State. *Report on the Commercial Relations of the United States with Foreign Countries for the Year 1876, 1877, and 1879*. Washington, D.C.: Government Printing Office, 1877, 1878, and 1880.

————. Department of State. *Reports of the Consuls of the United States*. Washington, D.C.: Government Printing Office.

——. Department of State. *United States Consular Reports: Labor in America, Asia, Africa, Australia, and Polynesia.* Washington, D.C.: Government Printing Office, 1887.

——. Department of State. Bureau of Foreign Commerce. *Commercial Relations of the United States with Foreign Countries during the Years 1896 and 1897, 1898, 1899, 1900, 1901, 1902.* Washington, D.C.: Government Printing Office, 1898, 1899, 1900, 1901, 1902, 1903.

——. Department of State. Bureau of Foreign Commerce. *Reports of the Consular Officers of the United States. Emigration and Immigration.* Washington, D.C.: Government Printing Office, 1887.

——. Department of State. Bureau of Statistics. *Commercial Relations of the United States with Foreign Countries during the Years 1895 and 1896.* Washington, D.C.: Government Printing Office, 1897.

——. Department of State. Bureau of Statistics. *Special Consular Reports. Money and Prices in Foreign Countries.* Washington, D.C.: Government Printing Office, 1896.

N E W S P A P E R S

Boletín Comercial. Organ of the Cámara Nacional de Comercio de Chihuahua. Ciudad Chihuahua. 1908–9.

Chihuahua Enterprise. Ciudad Chihuahua. 1882–84.

Chihuahua Mail. Ciudad Chihuahua. 1882–83.

El Chihuahuense. Ciudad Chihuahua. 1884, 1889, 1904.

El Ciudadano. 1892.

El Clarín del Norte. El Paso. 1905–7.

El Correo de Chihuahua. Ciudad Chihuahua. 1898–99, 1902–12.

El Defensor. 1894–95.

Diario Chihuahuense. Chihuahua. 1900.

Los Dos Americas. 1898.

El Paso Daily Times. El Paso, Texas. 1885–1908.

El Paso Morning Times. El Paso, Texas. 1908–11.

El Financiero Mexicano/The Mexican Financier. Mexico City. 1883–97.

The Mexican Herald. Mexico City. 1896–1910.

The Mexican Investor. Mexico City. 1904–7.

El Minero. Batopilas, Chihuahua. 1895.

El Monitor. El Paso, Texas. 1897–1900.

La Nueva Era/New Era. Ciudad Juárez.

La Nueva Era. Hidalgo del Parral. 1900–1911.

El Padre Padilla. Chihuahua. 1910–11.

El Periódico Oficial del Estado de Chihuahua. Chihuahua. 1853–1912. (This newspaper was published under various names during this period. The following are cited in the notes: *Alianza de la Frontera, Boletín Militar, El Boletín, El Centinela, La Guardia Nacional, La República, El Republicano,* and *Semanario Oficial.*) See Charles R. McClure, *Guide to the Microfilm Collection of the Periódico Oficial del Estado de Chihuahua* for a complete listing.

Regeneración. 1900, 1910.

Revista Internacional. Ciudad Juárez. 1904–5.

El Siglo XX. Chihuahua. 1904–5.

The South American Journal and Brazil and River Plate Mail. London. 1898–1911.

El Telégrafo de Chihuahua. Chihuahua. 1911.

Selected Bibliography

The Two Republics. Mexico City. 1881–1900.
La Voz de la Frontera. Chihuahua. 1911.

P E R I O D I C A L S

The Bankers' Magazine. New York. 1880–1911.
Boletín de la Sociedad Agrícola Mexicana. Mexico City. 1880, 1894–96.
Boletín de la Sociedad Chihuahuense de Estudios Históricos. Ciudad Chihuahua. 1938–70.
The Engineering and Mining Journal. New York. 1880–1911.
The Mexican Mining Journal. 1908–11.
The Mining Magazine. London. 1909–11.
Moody's Magazine. New York. 1905–11.
Moody's Manual of Corporation Securities. New York. 1901–5.
Moody's Manual of Railroads and Corporation Securities. New York. 1906–11.
Revista Católica de Chihuahua. Chihuahua. 1896–1901.
Revista Chihuahuense. Chihuahua. 1909.
Revista de Chihuahua. Chihuahua. 1895–97.
Stock Exchange Intelligence. London. 1900–1902.

C O M P A N Y   R E P O R T S

American Smelting and Refining Company. *Annual Report.* 1904–11.
Banco Comercial de Chihuahua. *Estatutos.* Chihuahua: Imprenta de S. Terrazas, 1899.
Banco Minero de Chihuahua. *Estatutos.* Mexico: Tip. Bouligny & Schmidt Sucs., 1898.
Banco Minero de Chihuahua. Consejo de Administración. *Informes del Consejo de Administración y Comisario a la Asamblea General de Acionistas de 28 de marzo de 1908.* Chihuahua: Imp. del Norte, 1908.
Compañía Eléctrica y de Ferrocarriles de Chihuahua, S.A. *Concesiones y franquicias.* Chihuahua: El Norte, 1908.
Compañía Minera de Naica. Consejo de Administración. *Informe que rinde el Consejo de Administración de la Compañía Minera de Naica, S.A. a la asamblea ordinaria celebrada el 30 de junio de 1909.* San Pedro, Coahuila: Talleres Tip. Las Amazonas, 1909.
Mexico North Western Railway Company. *Directors' Report and Accounts. First Annual Report.* 1910.
Toomer, Fletcher. *Report on the Parral and Durango Railway Company's Properties and the Hidalgo Mining Company's Properties.* Parral, Mexico. London: Waterlow Bros. and Layton, 1905.

D I R E C T O R I E S

Griggs, Jorge. *Mines of Chihuahua, 1907: History, Geology, Statistics, Mining Companies Directory.* N.p., n.d.
Ponce de León, José María. *Chihuahua y sus distritos: datos geográficos, estadísticos del estado de Chihuahua.* 3d ed. Chihuahua: Imp. de Simón Alarcón, n.d.
————, and Alcocer, Pedro, Jr. *Directorio industrial, mercantil, agrícola, y oficial del estado de Chihuahua, año de 1907.* Chihuahua: Imprenta El Chihuahuense, M. A. Gómez, 1907.

Selected Bibliography

Southworth, John R. *Directorio oficial bancario de México—Bankers' Official Directory of Mexico*. Mexico: Compañía Directorio Bancario de México, 1906, 1909.
————. *The Official Directory of Mines and Estates of Mexico*. Mexico: John R. Southworth, 1910.

S T A T I S T I C A L   S O U R C E S

El Colegio de México. Seminario de Historia Moderna de México. *Estadísticas económicas del Porfiriato: Fuerza de trabajo y actividad económica por sectores*. Mexico: El Colegio de México, n.d.
Escudero, J. A. de. *Noticias estadísticas del estado de Chihuahua*. Mexico: Oficina del Puente de Palacio y Flamencoa, 1834.
García Conde, Pedro. "Ensayo estadístico del estado de Chihuahua." *Boletín de la Sociedad Mexicana Geografía y Estadística* 5 (1857): 166–320.
The Mexican Yearbook. 1908, 1909, 1911, 1914. London: McCorquodale & Co., 1908, 1909, 1911, 1914.
La República Mexicana: Chihuahua, reseña geografía y estadística. Mexico: Libreria Vda. de C. Bouret, 1909.

M E M O I R S

Bartlett, John Russell. *Personal Narratives of Explorations and Incidents in Texas, New Mexico, California, Sonora, and Chihuahua, connected with the United States and Mexican Boundary Commission during the Years 1850, '51, '52, and '53*. New York: Appleton, 1856.
Caraveo, Marcelo. "Memorias del General Marcelo Caraveo." Unpub. ms., 1930. Copy in John H. McNeely Collection, University of Texas at El Paso.
Case, Alden Buell. *Thirty Years with the Mexicans*. New York: Revell, 1917.
Fall, Albert. *Memoirs*. Ed. David H. Stratton. Southwest Studies Monograph no. 11. El Paso: Texas Western College Press, 1965.
Foster, John W. *Diplomatic Memoirs*. Vol. 1. Boston: Houghton Mifflin, 1909.
Hamilton, Leonidas. *Border States of Mexico: Sonora, Sinaloa, Chihuahua, and Durango*. 2d ed., rev. and enl. San Francisco: n.p., 1881.
Hammond, John Hays. *The Autobiography of John Hays Hammond*. 2 vols. New York: Farrar and Rinehart, 1935.
Harris, Theodore D., ed. *Negro Frontiersman: The Western Memoirs of Henry O. Flipper*. El Paso: Texas Western College Press, 1963.
Johnson, Annie R. *Heartbeats of Colonia Díaz*. Mesa, Ariz.: Annie R. Johnson, 1972.
Jones, Daniel W. *Forty Years among the Indians*. Los Angeles: Westernlore Press, 1962.
Gressley, Gene M., ed. *Bostonians and Bullion: The Journal of Robert Livermore, 1892–1915*. Lincoln: University of Nebraska Press, 1968.
Mills, William Wallace. *Forty Years at El Paso*. Intro. and notes by Rex W. Strickland. El Paso: Carl Hertzog, 1962.
Parker, Morris B. *Mules, Mines and Me in Mexico, 1895–1932*. Ed. James M. Day. Tucson: University of Arizona Press, 1979.
Rickard, T. A. *Journey of Observation*. San Francisco: Dewey Publishing Co., 1907.
Ronde, M. "Voyage dans l'état de Chihuahua, 1849–1852." Barker Collection, University of Texas at Austin.

Santleben, August. *A Texas Pioneer: Early Staging and Overland Freighting Days on the Frontiers of Texas and Mexico*. New York: Neal Publishing, 1910.

Shepherd, Grant. *The Silver Magnet: Fifty Years in a Mexican Silver Mine*. New York: Dutton, 1938.

Terrazas, Joaquín. *Memorias del Sr. Coronel Joaquín Terrazas*. Ciudad Juárez: Imp. de El Agricultor Mexicano, 1905.

Uriostegui Miranda, Píndaro. *Testimonios del proceso revolucionario de México*. Mexico: Talleres de Argrin, 1970.

Wagner, Henry R. *Bullion to Books: Fifty Years of Business and Pleasure*. Los Angeles: Zamorano Club, 1942.

B O O K S

Acuña, Rudolfo F. *Sonoran Strongman: Ignacio Pesqueira and His Times*. Tucson: University of Arizona Press, 1974.

Aguilar, Alonso, and Carmona, Fernando. *México: Riqueza y miseria*. Mexico: Editorial Nuestro Tiempo, 1976.

Aguilar Camín, Hector. *La Frontera nomada: Sonora y la Revolución Mexicana*. Mexico: Siglo Veintiuno Editores, 1977.

Almada, Francisco R. *Apuntes históricos de la región de Chínipas*. Chihuahua: n.p., 1937.

———. *Apuntes históricos del municipio de Madera*. Chihuahua: n.p., 1946.

———. *Diccionario de historia, geografía, y biografía Chihuahuenses*. 2d ed. Chihuahua: Universidad de Chihuahua, Departamento de Investigaciones Sociales, Sección de Historia, n.d.

———. *El Ferrocarril de Chihuahua al Pacífico*. Mexico: n.p., n.d.

———. *Geografía del estado de Chihuahua*. Chihuahua: n.p., n.d.

———. *Gobernadores del estado de Chihuahua*. Mexico: Imprenta de la Cámara de Diputados, 1950.

———. *Gobernantes de Chihuahua*. Chihuahua: Talleres Gráficos de Gobierno del Estado, 1929.

———. *La imprenta y el periodismo en Chihuahua*. Mexico: Gobierno del Estado de Chihuahua, 1943.

———. *La intervención francesa y el imperio en el estado de Chihuahua*. Chihuahua: Ediciones Universidad Autónoma de Chihuahua, 1972.

———. *La Rebelión de Tomochi*. Chihuahua: Sociedad Chihuahuense de Estudios Históricos, 1938.

———. *Juárez y Terrazas: Aclaraciones históricas*. Mexico: Libros Mexicanos, 1958.

———. *Perfiles biográficos del General Angel Trías (p)*. *Cuadernos de Lectura Popular*. Series: La victoria de la República. Mexico: Secretaría de Educación Pública, Subsecretaría de Asuntos Culturales, 1967.

———. *Resumen geográfico del municipio de Jiménez*. Ciudad Juárez: Editorial El Labrador, n.d.

———. *Resumen de la historia del estado de Chihuahua*. Mexico: Libros Mexicanos, 1955.

———. *La revolución en el estado de Chihuahua*. 2 vols. Chihuahua: Biblioteca del Instituto Nacional de Estudios Históricos de la Revolución Mexicana, 1964.

———. *La revolución en el estado de Sonora*. Mexico: Biblioteca del Instituto Nacional de Estudios Históricos de la Revolución Mexicana, 1971.

———. *La ruta de Juárez*. Chihuahua: Universidad de Chihuahua, Departamento de Investigaciones, Sección de Historia, n.d.

————. *Vida, proceso, y muerte de Abraham González*. Mexico: Biblioteca del Instituto de Estudios Históricos de la Revolución Mexicana, 1967.

Anderson, Rodney D. *Outcasts in Their Own Land: Mexican Industrial Workers, 1906–1911*. DeKalb: Northern Illinois University Press, 1976.

Basurto, Jorge. *El proletariado industrial en México, 1850–1930*. Mexico: UNAM, 1975.

Bazant, Jan. *Alienation of Church Wealth in Mexico: Social and Economic Aspects of the Liberal Revolution, 1856–1875*. London: Cambridge University Press, 1971.

————. *A Concise History of Mexico*. New York: Cambridge University Press, 1977.

Beezley, William H. *Insurgent Governor: Abraham González and the Mexican Revolution in Chihuahua*. Lincoln: University of Nebraska Press, 1973.

Bernstein, Marvin. *The Mexican Mining Industry, 1890–1950*. New York: State University of New York Press, 1964.

Bett, Virgil M. *Central Banking in Mexico: Monetary Politics and Financial Crises, 1846–1940*. Ann Arbor: University of Michigan Bureau of Business Research, 1957.

Bottomore, T. B. *Elites and Society*. Baltimore: Penguin, 1966.

Brading, D. A., ed. *Caudillo and Peasant in the Mexican Revolution*. New York: Cambridge University Press, 1980.

————. *Miners and Merchants in Bourbon Mexico, 1763–1810*. New York: Cambridge University Press, 1971.

Bush, I. J. *Gringo Doctor*. Caldwell, Id.: Caxton Printers, 1939.

Calzadíaz Barrera, Alberto. *Dos gigantes: Sonora y Chihuahua*. Hermosillo, Sonora: Escritores Asociados del Norte, 1964.

Cardoso, F. H., and Faletto, Enzo. *Dependency and Development in Latin America*. Berkeley: University of California Press, 1979.

Ceceña, José Luis. *México en la órbita imperial*. 7th ed. Mexico: Ediciones El Caballito, 1976.

Chávez, José Carlos. *Peleando en Tomochi*. Chihuahua: Sociedad Chihuahuense de Estudios Históricos, 1943.

Chávez M., Armando B. *Sesenta años de gobierno municipal: Jefes políticos del Distrito Bravos y presidentes del municipio de Juárez*. Mexico: n.p., 1959.

Coatsworth, John H. *Growth against Development: The Economic Impact of Railroads in Porfirian Mexico*. DeKalb: Northern Illinois University Press, 1981.

Cockcroft, James D. *Intellectual Precursors of the Mexican Revolution, 1900–1913*. Austin: University of Texas Press, 1968.

Coerver, Don M. *The Porfirian Interregnum: The Presidency of Manuel González of Mexico, 1880–1884*. Fort Worth: Texas Christian University Press, 1979.

Coolidge, Dane. *Old California Cowboys*. New York: Dutton, 1939.

Cortes Conde, Roberto. *The First Stages of Modernization in Spanish America*. New York: Harper Torchbooks, 1974.

Cosío Villegas, Daniel, ed. *Historia Moderna de México*. 9 vols. Mexico: Editorial Hermes, 1953–72.

Cossío, José L. *Como y por quienes se ha monopolizado la propiedad rústica en México?* Mexico: Tip. Mercantil, Jesús A. Laguna, 1911.

Costeloe, Michael. *Church Wealth in Mexico: A Case Study of the Juzgado de Capellanias in the Archbishopric of Mexico*. New York: Cambridge University Press, 1967.

Creel Cobián, Alejandro. *Enrique C. Creel: Apuntes para su biografía*. Mexico: Edición Familiar, 1974.

Creel, Enrique C. *El estado de Chihuahua: su historia, geografía y riquezas naturales*. Mexico: Tipo El Progreso, 1928.

Cumberland, Charles C. *Mexican Revolution: The Constitutionalist Years*. Austin: University of Texas Press, 1972.

————. *Mexican Revolution: Genesis under Madero*. Austin: University of Texas Press, 1952.

Díaz Díaz, Fernando. *Caudillos y caciques*. Mexico: El Colegio de México, 1972.

Dueñes, Heliodoro. *Los bancos y la revolución*. Mexico: Editorial Cultura, 1945.

Dunn, Robert W. *American Foreign Investments*. New York: Viking, 1926.

Frank, Andre G. *Capitalism and Underdevelopment in Latin America*. Rev. and enl. New York: Monthly Review Press, 1969.

Friedrich, Paul. *Agrarian Revolt in a Mexican Village*. Chicago: University of Chicago Press, 1977.

Fuentes Mares, José. *. . . Y México se refugió en el desierto: Luis Terrazas, su historia y destino*. Mexico: Editorial Jus, 1954.

Furtado, Celso. *Economic Development of Latin America*. New York: Cambridge University Press, 1970.

————. *The Economic Growth of Brazil*. Berkeley: University of California Press, 1968.

González, Luis, et al. *La economía mexicana en la época de Juárez*. Mexico: Secretaría de Industria y Comercio, 1972.

González Flores, Enrique. *Chihuahua de la independencia a la Revolución*. Mexico: Ediciones Botas, 1949.

González Navarro, Moises. *Anatomía del poder en México, 1848–1853*. Mexico: El Colegio de México, 1977.

————. *La colonización en México*. Mexico: n.p., 1960.

————. *Las huelgas textiles en el Porfiriato*. Puebla: Editorial José M. Cajica, Jr., 1970.

————. *Raza y tierra: La guerra de castas y el henequén*. Mexico: El Colegio de Mexico, 1970.

González Ramírez, Manuel. *La revolución social en México*. 3 vols. Mexico: Fundo de Cultura Económica, 1960, 1965, 1966.

González y González, Luis. *Invitación a la microhistoria*. Mexico: Sepsetentas, 1973.

Graham, Richard, and Smith, Peter H., eds. *New Approaches to Latin American History*. Austin: University of Texas Press, 1974.

Hale, Charles A. *Mexican Liberalism in the Age of Mora, 1821–1853*. New Haven: Yale University Press, 1968.

Halperin-Donghi, Tulio. *The Aftermath of Revolution in Latin America*. New York: Harper Torchbooks, 1973.

Hansen, Roger D. *The Politics of Mexican Development*. Baltimore: Johns Hopkins University Press, 1971.

Harris, Charles H., III. *A Mexican Family Empire: The Latifundio of the Sánchez Navarro Family, 1765–1867*. Austin: University of Texas Press, 1975.

Helguera, Alvaro de la. *Enrique Creel: Apuntes biográficos*. Madrid: Imprenta de Ambrosio Pérez Asensio, 1910.

Hoyt, Edwin P., Jr. *The Guggenheims and the American Dream*. New York: Funk and Wagnalls, 1967.

Jacobs, Ian. *Ranchero Revolt: The Mexican Revolution in Guerrero*. Austin: University of Texas Press, 1982.

Johnson, Chalmers. *Revolutionary Change*. 2d. ed. Stanford: Stanford University Press, 1982.

Johnson, Richard A. *The Mexican Revolution of Ayutla, 1854–1855*. Rock Island, Ill.: Augustana College, 1939.

Jordán, Fernando. *Crónica de un pais bárbaro*. Chihuahua: Centro Libro La Prensa, 1975.

Joseph, Gilbert M. *Revolution from Without. Yucatán, Mexico, and the United States, 1880–1924*. New York: Cambridge University Press, 1982.

Katz, Friedrich, ed. *La servidumbre agraria en México en la época porfiriana*. Mexico: Sepsetentas, 1976.

————. *The Secret War in Mexico: Europe, the United States and the Mexican Revolution*. Chicago: University of Chicago Press, 1981.

Kennedy, John G. *Tarahumara of the Sierra Madre*. Arlington Heights, Ill.: AHM Publishing, 1978.

Kern, Robert, ed. *The Caciques: Oligarchical Politics and the System of Caciquismo in the Luso-Hispanic World*. Albuquerque: University of New Mexico Press, 1973.

Kilby, Peter, ed. *Entrepreneurship and Economic Development*. New York: Free Press, 1971.

Levy, Jacques. *Cesar Chávez*. New York: Norton, 1975.

Lewis, Cleona. *America's Stake in International Investments*. Washington, D.C.: Brookings Institution, 1938.

Lipset, S. M., and Solari, A., eds. *Elites in Latin America*. New York: Oxford University Press, 1967.

Lister, Florence C., and Lister, Robert H. *Chihuahua: Storehouse of Storms*. Albuquerque: University of New Mexico Press, 1966.

Loveman, Brian. *Chile*. New York: Oxford University Press, 1979.

Luna, Jesús. *La carrera pública de Don Ramón Corral*. Mexico. Sepsetentas, 1975.

McBride, George McCutcheon. *The Land Systems of Mexico*. New York: American Geographical Society, 1923.

McGaw, William C. *Savage Scene: The Life and Times of James Kirker, Frontier King*. New York: Hastings House, 1972.

Mamalakis, Markos. *The Growth and Structure of the Chilean Economy: From Independence to Allende*. New Haven: Yale University Press, 1976.

————, and Reynolds, Clark W. *Essays on the Chilean Economy*. Homewood, Ill.: Irwin, 1965.

Marcosson, Issac F. *Metal Magic: The Story of the American Smelting and Refining Company*. New York: Farrar, Strauss, 1949.

Márquez Montiel, Joaquín. *Hombres célebres de Chihuahua*. Mexico: Editorial Jus, 1953.

Martínez, Oscar. *Border Boom Town: Ciudad Juárez since 1848*. Austin: University of Texas Press, 1978.

Marx, Karl. *The Eighteenth Brumaire of Louis Bonaparte*. New York: International Publishers, 1963.

Mendoza, Francisco. *Chihuahua revolucionario, opiniones y comentarios*. Ciudad Juárez: Imp. Fab. de Sillos Cama, 1921.

Meyer, Michael C. *Mexican Rebel: Pascual Orozco and the Mexican Revolution, 1910–1915*. Lincoln: University of Nebraska Press, 1967.

————, and Sherman, William L. *The Course of Mexican History*. New York: Oxford University Press, 1979.

Moore, Barrington. *Social Origins of Dictatorship and Democracy*. Boston: Beacon Press, 1966.

Moorhead, Max L. *New Mexico's Royal Road: Trade and Travel on the Chihuahua Trail*. Norman: University of Oklahoma Press, 1958.

————. *The Presidio: Bastion of the Spanish Borderlands*. Norman: University of Oklahoma Press, 1975.

Niblo, Stephen R., and Hannon, James L. *Precursores de la revolución agraria*. Mexico: Sepsetentas, 1976.

Ober, Frederick A. *Mexican Resources: A Guide to and through Mexico*. Boston: Estes and Lauriat, 1884.

O'Connor, Harvey. *The Guggenheims: The Making of an American Dynasty*. New York: Covici-Friede, 1937.

Selected Bibliography

Older, Mrs. Fremont. *William Randolph Hearst: American.* New York: Appleton-Century, 1936.

Ontiveros, Francisco P. de. *Toribio Ortega y la brigada González Ortega.* Chihuahua: n.p., 1914.

Parry, Geraint. *Political Elites.* New York: Praeger, 1969.

Perry, Laurens B. *Juárez and Díaz: Machine Politics in Mexico.* DeKalb: Northern Illinois University Press, 1978.

Phipps, Helen. *Some Aspects of the Agrarian Question in Mexico.* Austin: n.p., 1925.

Pletcher, David M. *Rails, Mines, and Progress: Seven American Promoters in Mexico, 1867–1911.* Ithaca: Cornell University Press, 1958.

Ponce de León, José María. *Resumen de la historia política de Chihuahua desde la época colonial hasta 1921.* Chihuahua: Imprenta Gutenberg, 1922.

Powell, T. G. *El liberalismo y el campesinado en el centro de México.* Mexico: Sepsetentas, 1974.

Putnam, Robert D. *The Comparative Study of Political Elites.* Englewood Cliffs, N.J.: Prentice-Hall, 1976.

Raat, W. Dirk. *Revoltosos: Mexico's Rebels in the United States.* College Station: Texas A&M University Press, 1981.

Reynolds, Clark W. *The Mexican Economy: Twentieth-Century Structure and Growth.* New Haven: Yale University Press, 1970.

Rippy, J. Fred. *British Investments in Latin America, 1822–1949.* New York: Archon, 1966.

Rocha Chávez, Ruben. *Tres siglos de historia, biografía de una ciudad: Parral.* Parral: n.p., 1976.

Rock, David. *Politics in Argentina, 1890–1930: The Rise and Fall of Radicalism.* New York: Cambridge University Press, 1975.

Romero, Matías. *Geographical and Statistical Notes on Mexico.* New York: Putnam, 1898.

Romney, Thomas C. *The Mormon Colonies in Mexico.* Salt Lake City: Deseret Book Company, 1938.

Ross, Stanley R. *Francisco I. Madero: Apostle of Mexican Democracy.* New York: Columbia University Press, 1955.

Ruiz, Ramón E. *The Great Rebellion: Mexico, 1905–1924.* New York: Norton, 1980.

———. *Labor and the Ambivalent Revolutionaries: Mexico, 1911–1923.* Baltimore: Johns Hopkins University Press, 1976.

Salamini, Heather F. *Agrarian Radicalism in Veracruz, 1920–1938.* Lincoln: University of Nebraska Press, 1971.

Schmidt, Robert H., Jr. *A Geographical Survey of Chihuahua.* Southwestern Studies Monograph no. 37. El Paso: Texas Western Press, 1973.

Scholes, Walter V. *Mexican Politics during the Juárez Regime, 1855–1872.* Columbia: University of Missouri Press, 1957.

Schryer, Frans J. *The Rancheros of Pisaflores.* Toronto: University of Toronto Press, 1980.

Skocpol, Theda. *States and Social Revolutions.* New York: Cambridge University Press, 1979.

Smith, Duane A. *Horace Tabor: His Life and Legend.* Boulder: Colorado Associated University Press, 1973.

Smith, Peter H. *Labyrinths of Power: Political Recruitment in Twentieth-Century Mexico.* Princeton: Princeton University Press, 1979.

———. *Politics and Beef in Argentina.* New York: Columbia University Press, 1969.

Sonnichsen, C. L. *Colonel Greene and the Copper Skyrocket.* Tucson: University of Arizona Press, 1974.

Spence, Clark C. *Mining Engineers and the American West: The Lace Boot Brigade, 1849–1933.* New Haven: Yale University Press, 1970.

Stone, Lawrence. *The Causes of the English Revolution*. New York: Harper Torchbooks, 1972.

Swanberg, W. A. *Citizen Hearst: A Biography of William Randolph Hearst*. New York: Scribner, 1961.

Tannenbaum, Frank. *The Mexican Agrarian Revolution*. Washington, D.C.: Brookings Institution, 1930.

Tischendorf, Alfred. *Great Britain and Mexico in the Era of Porfirio Díaz*. Durham: Duke University Press, 1961.

Turner, John Kenneth. *Barbarous Mexico*. Austin: University of Texas Press, 1966.

Voss, Stuart F. *On the Periphery of Nineteenth-Century Mexico: Sonora and Sinaloa, 1810–1877*. Tucson: University of Arizona Press, 1982.

Warman, Arturo. *We Come to Object: The Peasants of Morelos and the National State*. Baltimore: Johns Hopkins University Press, 1980.

West, Robert C. *The Mining Community of Northern New Spain: The Parral Mining District*. Ibero-Americana no. 30. Berkeley: University of California Press, 1949.

Whetten, Nathan L. *Rural Mexico*. Chicago: University of Chicago Press, 1948.

Williams, Gatenby, and Heath, Charles M. *William Guggenheim*. New York: Lone Voice Publishing, 1934.

Winkler, John K. *William Randolph Hearst: A New Appraisal*. New York: Hastings House, 1955.

Wolf, Eric R. *Peasants*. Englewood Cliffs, N.J.: Prentice-Hall, 1966.

———. *Peasant Wars of the Twentieth Century*. New York: Harper and Row, 1969.

Wolfskill, George, and Richmond, Douglas W. *Essays on the Mexican Revolution: Revisionist Views of the Leaders*. Austin: University of Texas Press, 1979.

Womack, John, Jr. *Zapata and the Mexican Revolution*. New York: Knopf, 1968.

ARTICLES

Acuña, Rudolph F. "Ignacio Pesqueira: Sonoran Caudillo." *Arizona and the West* 12 (Summer 1970): 139–72.

Almada, Francisco R. "La Batalla de Tabaloapa." *BSCEH* 1 (May 1939): 391–94.

———. "Los Apaches." *BSCEH* 2 (June 1939): 5–15.

———. "Votos para la fundación de Ciudad Chihuahua." *BSCEH* 2 (May 1940): 6–17.

Amador y Trías de Noreña, Teresa. "Algunas notas bibliográficas del General Angel Trías." *BSCEH* 3 (October–December 1940): 427–29, 440.

Anderson, Rodney. "Mexican Workers and the Politics of Revolution, 1906–1911." *HAHR* 54 (February 1974): 94–112.

Arellano Schetelig, Lorenzo. "Don Enrique C. Creel, el intelectual." *Boletín de la Sociedad Mexicana de Geografía y Estadística* 49 (1944): 283–92.

Aya, Rod. "Theories of Revolution Reconsidered: Contrasting Models of Collective Violence." *Theory and Society* 8 (1979): 39–99.

Bailey, David C. "Revisionism and Recent Historiography of the Mexican Revolution." *HAHR* 58 (February 1978): 62–78.

Balmori, Diana, and Oppenheimer, Robert. "Family Clusters: The Generational Nucleation of Families in Nineteenth-Century Argentina and Chile." *Comparative Studies in History and Society* 21 (1979): 231–61.

Bath, C. Richard, and James, Dilmus D. "Dependency Analysis in Latin America." *LARR* 11 (1976): 3–54.

Bazant, Jan. "Landlord, Labourer, and Tenant in San Luis Potosí, 1822–1910." In Kenneth

Selected Bibliography

Duncan and Ian Rutledge, eds., *Land and Labour in Latin America*. Cambridge: Cambridge University Press, 1977, pp. 59–83.

Beezley, William H. "Madero: The Unknown President and His Political Failure to Organize Rural Mexico." In George Wolfskill and Douglas W. Richmond, eds., *Essays on the Mexican Revolution*, pp. 1–24.

———. "Opportunity in Porfirian Mexico." *North Dakota Quarterly* 40 (Spring 1972): 30–40.

———. "State Reform during the Provisional Presidency: Chihuahua, 1911." *HAHR* 50 (August 1970): 524–38.

Bernstein, Harry. "Regionalism in the National History of Mexico." In Howard F. Cline, ed., *Latin American History: Essays on Its Study and Teaching, 1898–1965*. 2 vols. Austin: University of Texas Press, 1966, pp. 389–94.

Brand, Donald D. "The Early History of the Range Cattle Industry in Northern Mexico." *Agricultural History* 35 (July 1961): 132–39.

Brandt, Nancy. "Pancho Villa: The Making of a Modern Legend." *Americas* 21 (October 1964): 146–62.

Brayer, Herbert D. "The Cananea Incident." *NMHR* 13 (October 1938): 387–415.

Breymann, Walter N. "The Científicos: Critics of the Díaz Regime, 1903–1910." *Proceedings of the Arkansas Academy of Science* 7 (1955): 91–97.

———. "The Científicos and the Collapse of the Díaz Regime: A Study in the Origins of Mexican Revolutionary Sentiment." *Proceedings of the Arkansas Academy of Science* 8 (1955): 192–97.

Briones Martínez, Esteban. "Cuando se erigió en Ciudad la Villa 'Paso del Norte' tomando el nombre de 'Ciudad Juárez'?" *BSCEH* 4 (October 1942): 212–15.

Bryan, Anthony T. "Political Power in Porfirio Díaz's Mexico: A Review and Commentary." *Historian* 38 (August 1976): 648–68.

Buve, Raymond Th. J. "Patronaje en las zonas rurales de México." *Boletín de Estudios Latinoamericanos* 16 (June 1974): 3–15.

———. "Peasant Movements, Caudillos, and Land Reform during the Revolution (1910–1917) in Tlaxcala, Mexico." *Boletín de Estudios Latinoamericanos* 18 (June 1976): 112–52.

———. "Protestas de obreros y campesinos durante el Porfiriato." *Boletín de Estudios Latinoamericanos* 13 (December 1972): 1–19.

Cadenhead, Ivie E. "The American Socialists and the Mexican Revolution of 1910." *Southwestern Social Science Quarterly* 43 (September 1962): 103–17.

Cardoso, Fernando Henrique. "The Consumption of Dependency Theory in the United States." *LARR* 12 (1977): 7–24.

Carr, Barry. "Las peculiaridades del norte mexicano, 1880–1927: Ensayo de interpretación." *Historia Mexicana* 22 (January 1973): 320–46.

———. "Recent Regional Studies of the Mexican Revolution." *LARR* 15 (1980): 3–15.

Casavantes González, Alberto. "Arbol genealógico de la familia de Sr. Abraham González." *BSCEH* 11 (1964): 7–8.

Chávez, José Carlos. "Peleando en Tomochi como luchas los serranos Chihuahuenses: Fragmentos de las Memorias del General D. Francisco Castro." *BSCEH* 4 (1943): 314–29.

Chávez Franco, Ignacio. "Don Miguel Ahumada: In Memoriam." *BSCEH* 2 (1939): 158–61.

Chevalier, François. "Conservateurs et Liberaux au Mexique: Essai de sociologie et geographie politiques de l'independance a l'intervention française." *Cahiers d'Histoire Mondiale* 8 (1964): 457–74.

———. "Un Factor Decisivo de la Revolución Agraria de México: El Levantimiento de

Zapata, 1911–1919." *Cuadernos Americanos* (Mexico) 113 (1960): 165–87.
———. "The North Mexican Hacienda: Eighteenth and Nineteenth Centuries." In Archibald R. Lewis and Thomas F. McGann, eds., *The New World Looks at Its History*. Austin: University of Texas Press, 1963, pp. 95–107.
———. "Survivances seigneuriales et presages de la Revolution agraire dans le nord du Mexique." *Revue Historique* 222 (July 1959): 1–18.
Chilcote, Ronald H. "A Question of Dependency." *LARR* 13 (1978): 55–68.
Christiansen, Paige W. "Pascual Orozco: Chihuahuan Rebel." *NMHR* 36 (April 1961): 97–120.
Clark, Victor S. "Mexican Labor in the United States." *Bulletin of the Bureau of Labor* 17 (September 1908): 466–522.
Coatsworth, John H. "Anotaciones sobre la producción de alimentos durante el Porfiriato." *Historia Mexicana* 26 (1976): 167–87.
———. "Obstacles to Economic Growth in Nineteenth Century Mexico." *American Historical Review* 83 (February 1978): 80–100.
———. "Los origenes del autoritarianismo en México. *Foro Internacional* 16 (1975): 205–32.
———. "Railroads and the Concentration of Land Ownership in the Early *Porfiriato*." *HAHR* 54 (February 1974): 48–71.
Daniel, James M. "The Spanish Frontier in West Texas and Northern Mexico." *Southwestern Historical Quarterly* 71 (April 1968): 481–95.
Davis, James C. "Toward a Theory of Revolution." *American Sociological Review* 27 (February 1962): 5–18.
Deeds, Susan M. "José María Maytorena and the Mexican Revolution in Sonora." *Arizona and the West* 18 (Spring 1976): 21–40, and (Summer 1976): 125–48.
DeHart, Evelyn Hu. "Pacification of the Yaquis in the late *Porfiriato*: Development and Implication." *HAHR* 54 (February 1974): 72–93.
DeKalb, C. "Impressions of the Mexican Highlands." *Nation* 69 (21 December 1899): 464–66; 70 (25 January 1900): 68–69; and 70 (5 February 1900): 124–26.
DePalo, William A., Jr. "The Establishment of the Nueva Vizcaya Militia during the Administration of Teodoro de Croix, 1776–1783." *NMHR* 48 (July 1973): 223–50.
Dobie, J. Frank. "Babícora." *American Hereford Journal*, 1 Jan. 1954.
Dos Santos, Theotonio. "The Structure of Dependence." *American Economic Review* 40 (May 1970): 231–36.
Drake, Paul W. "Mexican Regionalism Reconsidered." *Journal of Inter-American Studies and World Affairs* 12 (July 1970): 401–15.
Dumke, Glenn S. "Across Mexico in '49." *Pacific Historical Review* 18 (February 1949): 33–44.
Dusenberry, William H. "The Mexican Agricultural Society, 1879–1914." *Americas* 12 (January 1952): 385–98.
Eckstein, Harry. "On the Etiology of Internal Wars." *History and Theory* 4 (1965): 133–63.
Falcón, Romana. "Los origenes populares de la revolución de 1910: El caso de San Luis Potosí." *Historia Mexicana* 29 (1979): 197–240.
Faulk, Odie B., ed. "Projected Mexican Colonies in the Borderlands, 1852." *Journal of Arizona History* 10 (Summer 1969): 115–28.
Fern, H. S. "Britain's Informal Empire in Argentina, 1806–1914." *Past and Present* 4 (November 1953): 60–75.
Flower, B. O. "A Bit of Old Mexico." *Arena* 27 (June 1902): 624–29.
Frank, Andre Gunder. "The Development of Underdevelopment." *Monthly Review* 18 (September 1966): 17–31.
Goldfrank, Walter L. "Theories of Revolution and Revolution without Theory: The Case of Mexico." *Theory and Society* 7 (1979): 135–65.

Selected Bibliography

————. "World System, State Structure, and the Onset of the Mexican Revolution." *Politics and Society* 5 (1975): 417–39.

Goldstone, Jack A. "Theories of Revolution: The Third Generation." *World Politics* 32 (April 1980): 425–53.

González Navarro, Moises. "Social Aspects of the Mexican Revolution." *Journal of World History* 8 (1964): 282–89.

————. "Xenofobia y xenofilia en la Revolución Mexicana." *Historia Mexicana* 18 (April 1969): 569–614.

Graham, Richard. "Political Power and Landownership in Nineteenth-Century Latin America." In Richard Graham and Peter H. Smith, eds., *New Approaches to Latin American History*. Austin: University of Texas Press, 1974.

Hale, Charles A. "The Liberal Impulse: Daniel Cosío Villegas and the *Historia Moderna de México*." *HAHR* 54 (August 1974): 479–98.

————. "The Reconstruction of Nineteenth-Century Politics in Spanish America: A Case for the History of Ideas." *LARR* 8 (Summer 1973): 53–73.

Hall, Martin Hardwick. "Colonel James Reiley's Diplomatic Missions to Chihuahua and Sonora." *NMHR* 31 (July 1956): 232–41.

Hardy, B. Carmon. "Cultural 'Encystment' as a Cause of the Mormon Exodus from Mexico." *Pacific Historical Review* 34 (November 1965): 439–54.

Himmelstein, Jerome L., and Kimmel, Michael S. "Review Essay: States and Revolutions: The Implications and Limits of Skocpol's Structural Model." *American Journal of Sociology* 86 (5): 1145–54.

Hopper, Rex D. "The Revolutionary Process." *Social Forces* 28 (March 1950): 270–79.

Irigoyen, Ulises. "El palacio de Gobierno y el arquitecto Don Pedro Ignacio de Irigoyen." *BSCEH* 4 (October 1942): 186–96.

Iturribarria, Jorge Fernando. "Limantour y la caída de Porfirio Díaz." *Historia Mexicana* 10 (1961): 243–81.

Jackson, Steven, et al. "An Assessment of Empirical Research on *Dependencia*." *LARR* 14 (1979): 7–28.

Jacobs, Ian. "Rancheros of Guerrero: The Figueroa Brothers and the Revolution." In D. A. Brading, ed., *Caudillo and Peasant in the Mexican Revolution*. New York: Cambridge University Press, 1980.

Janowitz, Morris. "Social Stratification and the Comparative Study of Elites." *Social Forces* 35 (October 1956): 81–85.

Joseph, Gilbert M. "The Fragile Revolution: Cacique Politics and the Revolutionary Process in Yucatán." *LARR* 15 (1980): 41–64.

Katz, Friedrich. "Agrarian Changes in Northern Mexico in the Period of Villista Rule, 1913–1915." In James W. Wilkie, et al., eds., *Contemporary Mexico: Papers of the IV International Congress of Mexican History*. Berkeley: University of California Press, 1976.

————. "Labor Conditions on Haciendas in Porfirian Mexico: Some Trends and Tendencies." *HAHR* 54 (February 1974): 1–47.

————. "Pancho Villa: Reform Governor of Chihuahua." In George W. Wolfskill and Douglas W. Richmond, eds., *Essays on the Mexican Revolution: Revisionist Views of the Leaders*. Austin: University of Texas Press, 1979.

————. "Peasants in the Mexican Revolution." In Joseph Spielburg and Scott Whiteford, eds., *Forging Nations: A Comparative View of Rural Ferment and Revolt*. East Lansing: Michigan State University Press, 1976.

————. "El sistema de plantación y la esclavitud: El cultivo de henequén en Yucatán hasta 1910." *Ciencias Políticas y Sociales* 8 (January 1962): 103–36.

Keesing, Donald B. "Structural Change Early in Development: Mexico's Changing Industrial
and Occupational Structure from 1895 to 1950." *Journal of Economic History* 29
(December 1969): 716–39.

Knight, Alan. "Peasant and Caudillo in Revolutionary Mexico, 1910–1917." In D. A.
Brading, ed., *Caudillo and Peasant in the Mexican Revolution*. New York: Cambridge
University Press, 1981.

Langston, W. Stanley. "Centralization Versus Local Autonomy: Coahuilan Politics and the
National Regime." In Thomas Benjamin and William McNellie, eds. *At the Periphery*:
Studies in Regional Mexican History. Albuquerque: University of New Mexico Press,
forthcoming.

Lavis, F. "The Construction of the Chihuahua and Pacific Railroad." *Engineering Record* 55 (2
March 1907): 241–43.

Leal, Juan Felipe. "El estado y el bloque en el poder en México, 1867–1914." *Historia
Mexicana* 23 (1974): 700–721.

León-Portilla, Miguel. "The Norteño Variety of Mexican Culture: An Ethnohistorical
Approach." In Edward M. Spicer and Raymond H. Thompson, eds., *Plural Society in
the Southwest*. Albuquerque: University of New Mexico Press, 1972.

Lobato López, Ernesto. "Contradicción interna del sistema bancario porfirista." *El Trimestre
Económico* 11 (1944–45): 439–70.

Love, Joseph L. "An Approach to Regionalism." In Richard Graham and Peter H. Smith, eds.,
New Approaches to Latin American History. Austin: University of Texas Press, 1974.

McNeely, John H. "The Origins of the Zapata Revolt in Morelos." *HAHR* 46 (May 1966):
153–60.

Marchant, Anyda. "A New Portrait of Mauá the Banker: A Man of Business in Nineteenth-
Century Brazil." *HAHR* 30 (1950): 411–31.

Mathew, W. M. "The Imperialism of Free Trade, 1820–1870." *Economic History Review*, 2d
series, 21 (1968): 568–74.

Meyer, Michael C. "Albert Bacon Fall's Mexican Papers." *NMHR* 40 (April 1965): 165–74.
———. "Perspectives on Mexican Revolutionary Historiography." *NMHR* 44 (April 1969):
167–80.

Meyers, William K. "Politics, Vested Rights, and Economic Growth in Porfirian Mexico: The
Company Tlahualilo in the Comarca Lagunera, 1885–1911." *HAHR* 57 (August 1977):
425–54.

Mignone, A. Frederick. "A Fief for Mexico: Colonel Greene's Empire Ends." *Southwest
Review* 44 (Autumn 1959): 332–39.

Mills, Elizabeth H. "The Mormon Colonies in Chihuahua after the 1912 Exodus." *NMHR* 39
(July 1954): 165–82, and (October 1954): 290–310.

Moore, Mary Lee, and Beane, Delmar L. "The Interior Provinces of New Spain: The Report of
Hugo O'Connor, January 30, 1776." *Arizona and the West* 13 (Autumn 1971): 265–82.

Morner, Magnus. "The Spanish American Hacienda: A Survey of Recent Research and
Debate." *HAHR* 53 (May 1973): 183–216.

Nava, Guadalupe. "Jornales y jornaleros en la minería porfiriana." *Historia Mexicana* 12
(July–September 1962): 53–71.

Niblo, Stephen R., and Perry, Laurens B. "Recent Additions to Nineteenth-Century Mexican
Historiography." *LARR* 13 (1978): 3–45.

Olson, Mancur. "Rapid Growth as a De-stabilizing Force." *Journal of Economic History* 23
(December 1963): 529–52.

Oppenheimer, Robert. "National Capital and National Development: Financing Chile's Central
Valley Railroads." *Business History Review* 56 (Spring 1982): 54–75.

Payne, James L. "The Oligarchy Muddle." *World Politics* 20 (April 1968): 439–53.

Selected Bibliography

Platt, D. C. M. "Dependency in Nineteenth-Century Latin America." *LARR* 15 (1980): 113–30.

Pletcher, David M. "México, campo de inversiones norte americanas, 1867–1880." *Historia Mexicana* 2 (April 1953): 564–74.

Powell, T. G. "Priests and Peasants in Central Mexico: Social Conflict during 'La Reforma.'" *HAHR* 57 (May 1977): 296–313.

Raat, William Dirk. "The Diplomacy of Suppression: *Los Revoltosos*, Mexico, and the United States." *HAHR* 56 (November 1967): 529–50.

Ramsey, Mary B. "Life in Chihuahua." *New England Magazine* 51 (May 1914): 118–31.

Richmond, Douglas W. "Factional Political Strife in Coahuila, 1910–1920." *HAHR* 60 (February 1980): 49–68.

Rosenzweig, Fernando. "El desarrollo económico de México de 1877 a 1911." *El Trimestre Económico* 32 (July 1965): 405–54.

———. "Las exportaciones mexicanas de 1877 a 1911." *El Trimestre Económico* 37 (1960): 537–51.

Safford, Frank. "Bases of Political Alignment in Early Republican Spanish America." In Richard Graham and Peter H. Smith, eds., *New Approaches to Latin American History*. Austin: University of Texas Press, 1974.

Sandels, Robert. "Antecedentes de la Revolución en Chihuahua." *Historia Mexicana* 14 (January 1975): 390–402.

———. "Silvestre Terrazas and the Old Regime in Chihuahua." *Americas* 28 (October 1971): 191–205.

Schryer, Frans J. "A Ranchero Economy in Northwestern Hidalgo, 1880–1920." *HAHR* 59 (August 1979): 418–43.

Scott, James. "Hegemony and Peasantry." *Politics and Society* 7 (1977): 267–96.

Sims, Harold D. "Espejo de caciques: Los Terrazas de Chihuahua." *Historia Mexicana* 18 (March 1969): 379–99.

Skocpol, Theda. "Explaining Revolutions: In Quest of a Social-Structural Approach." In *The Uses of Controversy in Sociology*, ed. Lewis A. Coser and Otto N. Larsen. New York: Free Press, 1976.

Smith, Ralph A. "Apache Plunder Trails Southward, 1831–1840." *NMHR* 37 (January 1962): 20–42.

———. "The Comanche Invasion of Mexico in the Fall of 1845." *West Texas Historical Association Yearbook* 35 (October 1959): 3–28.

———. "The Comanche Sun over Mexico." *West Texas Historical Association Yearbook* 46 (1970): 25–62.

———. "The Fantasy of a Treaty to End Treaties." *Great Plains Journal* 12 (Fall 1972): 26–51.

———. "Indians in American-Mexican Relations before the War of 1846." *HAHR* 48 (February 1963): 34–64.

———. "'Long' Webster and the 'Vile Industry of Selling Scalps.'" *West Texas Historical Association Yearbook* 37 (October 1961): 99–120.

———. "The Mamelukes of West Texas and Mexico." *West Texas Historical Association Yearbook* 39 (October 1963): 65–88.

———. "Mexican and Anglo-Saxon Traffic in Scalps, Slaves, and Livestock, 1835–41." *West Texas Historical Association Yearbook* 36 (October 1960): 98–115.

———. "Poor Mexico, So Far from God and So Close to the Tejanos." *West Texas Historical Association Yearbook* 44 (1968): 78–105.

———. "The Scalp Hunt in Chihuahua in 1849." *NMHR* 40 (April 1965): 117–40.

————. "The Scalphunter in the Borderlands, 1835–1850." *Arizona and the West* 13 (Spring 1964): 5–22.

Sonnichsen, C. L. "Colonel William C. Greene and the Strike at Cananea, Sonora, 1906." *Arizona and the West* 13 (Winter 1971): 343–68.

Stein, Stanley J., and Stein, Barbara H. "Comment: D. C. M. Platt." *LARR* 15 (1980): 131–46.

Thiesen, Gerald. "La Mexicanización de la industria en la época de Porfirio Díaz." *Foro Internacional* 12 (April 1972): 497–507.

Timmons, W. H. "The El Paso Area in the Mexican Period." *Southwestern Historical Quarterly* 84 (July 1980): 1–28.

Twombly, Fred M. "Some Incidents of Life in Mexico." *Proceedings of the New England Railroad Club*, 14 March 1894, pp. 2–49.

Vanderwood, Paul J. "Mexico's Rurales: Image of a Society in Transition." *HAHR* 61 (February 1981): 52–83.

————. "Response to Revolt: The Counter-Guerrilla Strategy of Porfirio Díaz." *HAHR* 56 (November 1976): 551–79.

Vargas Pinera, Luis. "El General Terrazas y su extraordinaria familia." *Excelsior*, no. 8044, 16 April 1939.

Wasserman, Mark. "Foreign Investment in Mexico, 1876–1910: A Case Study of the Role of Regional Elites." *Americas* 36 (July 1979): 3–21.

————. "Oligarquía e intereses extranjeros en Chihuahua durante el Porfiriato." *Historia Mexicana* 12 (January 1973): 279–319.

————. "The Social Origins of the 1910 Revolution in Chihuahua. *LARR* 15 (1980): 15–40.

Waterbury, Ronald. "Non-revolutionary Peasants: Oaxaca Compared to Morelos in the Mexican Revolution." *Comparative Studies in Society and History* 17 (1975): 410–42.

Weyl, Walter E. "Labor Conditions in Mexico." *Bulletin of the Department of Labor* 38 (January 1902): 1–94.

Wolf, Eric R. "Peasant Rebellion and Revolution." In Norman Miller and Roderick Aya, eds., *National Liberation: Revolution in the Third World*. New York: Free Press, 1971.

————. "Review Essay: Why Cultivators Rebel." *American Journal of Sociology* 83 (1977): 742–50.

Woods, Clee. "The World's Greatest Cattleman." *True Magazine* 91 (1944): 38–41, 86.

UNPUBLISHED MANUSCRIPTS AND DISSERTATIONS

Bryan, Anthony T. "Mexican Politics in Transition, 1900–1913: The Role of General Bernardo Reyes." Ph.D. dissertation, University of Nebraska, 1970.

Chávez M., Armando B. "Hombres de la Revolución en Chihuahua." Unpublished manuscript, Chihuahua, n.d.

Estrada, Richard M. "Border Revolution: The Mexican Revolution in the Ciudad Juárez—El Paso Area, 1906–1911. M.A. thesis, University of Texas at El Paso, 1975.

————. "Liderazgo local y regional en la revolución norteña: Chihuahua, la Comarca Lagunera, y Durango, 1910–1913." Unpublished manuscript, El Paso, 1978.

Falla, Walter U. "A Study of Economic Development and Banking in Mexico during the Victorian Age, 1857–1910." M.A. thesis, University of California, Berkeley, 1965.

Haden, Robert T. "The Federalist: Porfirio Díaz and Coahuila, 1884–1886, and Porfirio Díaz and Nuevo León, 1885–1887." Unpublished paper. Cholula, Puebla, 1973.

Selected Bibliography

Hardy, Blaine C. "The Mormon Colonies of Northern Mexico: A History, 1885–1912." Ph.D. dissertation, Wayne State University, 1963.

Knight, Alan. "Nationalism, Xenophobia, and Revolution: The Place of Foreigners and Foreign Interests in Mexico, 1910–1915." Ph.D. dissertation, Oxford University, 1974.

Manahan, R. F. "Mining and Milling Operations of the American Smelting and Refining Company in Mexico, 1899–1948." Mimeograph, 1948.

Meyers, William K. "Interest Group Conflict and Revolutionary Politics: A Social History of La Comarca Lagunera, Mexico, 1888–1911." Ph.D. dissertation, University of Chicago, 1979.

Pletcher, David M. "American Capital and Technology in Northwest Mexico, 1876–1911." Ph.D. dissertation, University of Chicago, 1946.

Roberts, Donald F. "Mining and Modernization: The Mexican Border States during the Porfiriato, 1876–1911." Ph.D. dissertation, University of Pittsburgh, 1974.

Ryan, Howard. "Selected Aspects of American Activities in Mexico, 1876–1910." Ph.D. dissertation, University of Chicago, 1964.

Sandels, Robert L. "Silvestre Terrazas, the Press, and the Origins of the Mexican Revolution in Chihuahua." Ph.D. dissertation, University of Oregon, 1967.

Saragoza, Alex M. "An Elite and a City: Monterrey, Nuevo León, 1890–1910." Paper presented to the American Historical Association, New York, 1979.

———. "Elite Formation in Porfirian Mexico: Origins of the Grupo Monterrey, 1890–1910." Paper presented to the Latin American Studies Association, Bloomington, Indiana, 1980.

———. "The Formation of a Mexican Elite: The Industrialization of Monterrey, Nuevo León, 1880–1920." Ph.D. dissertation, University of California, San Diego, 1978.

Sinkin, Richard N. "Modernization and Reform in Mexico, 1855–1876." Ph.D. dissertation, University of Michigan, 1972.

Voss, Stuart F. "Porfirian Sonora: Economic Collegiality." Paper presented to the Annual Meeting of the American Historical Association, San Francisco, 1978.

———, Balmori, Diana, and Wortman, Miles. "Notable Families: The Origins of Authority in Modern Latin America, 1750–1900." Draft, 1980.

Wasserman, Mark. "Oligarchy and Foreign Enterprise in Porfirian Chihuahua, Mexico, 1876–1911." Ph.D. dissertation, University of Chicago, 1975.

Wells, Allen. "Henequén and Yucatán: An Analysis of Regional Economic Development, 1876–1915." Ph.D. dissertation, State University of New York at Stony Brook, 1979.

Index